PRAISE FOR

A Spicy Touch

FAMI...
NOORI...

> " I love Indian food but its preparation has largely been a mystery to me. Typically I leave that part of it to the professionals. But in this book, Noorbanu Nimji breaks the dishes down into simple, approachable recipes even I can handle. So I see carrot pickle, chana dal and chicken tikka in my near future.

— *John Gilchrist*
**CALGARY FOOD AND
RESTAURANT WRITER**

> " I have collected hundreds of cookbooks over my career and the wealth of knowledge Noorbanu shares in this book should inspire anyone to try every recipe.

— *Chef Andrew Hewson*
CCC

> " When A Spicy Touch first hit the shelves at The Cookbook Co. Cooks over 25 years ago, it was an instant success. Noorbanu's recipes are tried and true and her Kuku Paka recipe is one of my all-time favourites. Dish after dish, this collection of family favourites is sure to delight!

— *Gail Norton*
**CO-OWNER OF
THE COOKBOOK CO. COOKS,
CALGARY, ALBERTA**

> " The brief time I've spent in the kitchen with Noorbanu and Karen generated memories that will last a lifetime. Watching Noorbanu cook was exceptional. Her food creates comfort and intrigue in a perfectly delicious package.

— *Julie Van Rosendaal*
**COOKBOOK AUTHOR AND
CBC RADIO COLUMNIST**

> " It's like Noorbanu and Karen are right here in my kitchen, teaching me to taste and to cook. I've always wanted to understand more about East Indian flavours, and this book has opened the spice box up to me. Thank you.

— *Jennifer Cockrall-King*
**AUTHOR OF
FOOD AND THE CITY AND
*FOOD ARTISANS OF THE OKANAGAN***

A SPICY TOUCH

A SPICY TOUCH

FAMILY FAVOURITES *from*
NOORBANU NIMJI'S KITCHEN

NOORBANU NIMJI AND KAREN ANDERSON

TOUCHWOOD

Together we dedicate this book to home cooks everywhere. Time spent cooking together is about nurturing and sharing. Cooking is a cornerstone to health and a touchstone of familiarity and comfort. We wish you all the joy that our love of cooking has given us.

N.N. and K.A.

I dedicate this book to my son Akbar and my daughters Khadija, Rosie and Nazlin, my sons-in-law Nasir and Hassan. It is also dedicated to my six grandchildren—Tahira, Zaakir, Farah, Soraya, Imram and Khalil. You've all inspired this book. It's filled with your favourite dishes. I hope, in time, these recipes will become the favourites of my great grandchildren as well.

When I wrote my other books, my husband was a constant source of encouragement and inspiration. I'm grateful for the strength these memories provide. I know he would be pleased with the constant love and support I receive from our family and friends.

N.N.

I dedicate this book to my family. To Mom and Dad—Gerri and Reg Robicheau—I'm grateful that you raised me to cook and care about where our food comes from. To my husband and son, Todd and Cole, you mean everything to me. And, I love cooking for you most of all.

K.A.

First edition published in 2015 by A Spicy Touch Publishing Inc. (ISBN 9780969315926)

Second edition published in 2020 by TouchWood Editions Ltd. (ISBN 9781771513333)

The information in this book is true and complete to the best of the authors' knowledge. All recommendations are made without guarantee on the part of the authors or the publisher.

LIBRARY AND ARCHIVES CANADA CATALOGUING IN PUBLICATION

Title: A spicy touch: family favourites from Noorbanu Nimji's kitchen / Noorbanu Nimji and Karen Anderson.
Names: Nimji, Noorbanu, author. | Anderson, Karen (Columnist), author.
Description: Includes index. | Previously published: Calgary. AB : Spicy Touch Publishing (Canada) Inc., 2015.
Identifiers: Canadiana (print) 20190230142 | Canadiana (ebook) 20190238844 | ISBN 9781771513333 (hardcover) | ISBN 9781771513340 (HTML)
Subjects: LCSH: Cooking, Indic. | LCGFT: Cookbooks.
Classification: LCC TX724.5.I4 N54 2020 | DDC 641.5954—dc23

TouchWood Editions gratefully acknowledges that the land on which we live and work is within the traditional territories of the Lkwungen (Esquimalt and Songhees), Malahat, Pacheedaht, Scia'new, T'Sou-ke and W̱SÁNEĆ (Pauquachin, Tsartlip, Tsawout, Tseycum) peoples.

We acknowledge the financial support of the Government of Canada through the Canada Book Fund, and the province of British Columbia through the Book Publishing Tax Credit.

This book was produced using FSC®-certified, acid-free papers, processed chlorine free, and printed with soya-based inks.

Printed in China

24 23 22 21 20   1 2 3 4 5

TECHNICAL CREDITS

EDITOR
Tilly Sanchez-Turri, Calgary, Alberta

INDEXING
Karen Griffiths

PHOTOGRAPHY
Pauli-Ann Carriere, Vancouver, British Columbia

FOOD STYLING
Pauli-Ann Carriere and Karen Anderson

FOOD STYLING CONSULTANT
Julie Van Rosendaal, Calgary, Alberta

PROPS
Karen Anderson, Pauli-Ann Carriere, Julie Van Rosendaal, Inspirati Fine Linens for Everyday, Tracey Barnett and Joanne Unruh

FRONT COVER PHOTOGRAPHY
Pauli-Ann Carriere, Vancouver, British Columbia

PORTRAIT PHOTOGRAPHY
Jeremy Fokkens Photography, Calgary, Alberta

MAKEUP AND HAIR
Teslin Ward Makeup, Calgary, Alberta

DESIGN, LAYOUT, ART DIRECTION
Nina Palmer and Todd Macfie, Platform Design, Calgary, Alberta

TYPOGRAPHY
This book is typeset in Abril, by José Scaglione and Veronika Burian at type-together.com; Titling is set in Domaine Display and other matter in National, both by Kris Sowersby at klim.co.nz

Contents

ACKNOWLEDGEMENTS

Thank you for buying our cookbook.

Thank you to the team of professionals, friends and our wonderful families who helped us bring this book to publication.

To Pauli-Ann Carriere: Thank you for your talent, grace, patience, persistence, humour and intelligence as our photographer and beloved friend.

To Todd Macfie and Nina Palmer of Platform Design: Thank you for your passion for this project and for your love of India's design, typography and food. Your gifts and professionalism as artists, designers and colleagues has been vital.

To Nancy Wise: Thank you for the guidance you've shared to make this book a success.

To Julie Van Rosendaal: Thank you for lending us your talents as a food styling consultant. We appreciate how easy you make it look, how generous you are and how much fun you bring to everything you do.

To Jeremy Fokkens: Thank you for your talents and sweet, gentle ways as our portrait photographer.

To Jennifer Cockrall-King, Lisa Monforton, Kathy Richardier, Janet Tertzakian and Donna McElligott: Thank you for the key bits of editing you lent this project. Your insights were all pivotal in their own way.

To Tahira Karim and Amanpreet Sran: Thank you for proofreading copy with your bright young minds and for your insights into the special considerations needed when cooking for people with allergies.

To Al-Karim Walli: Thank you for your ongoing encouragement, for sharing your knowledge of Ismaili history and for fact checking that truly made a difference to the accuracy of this book.

To Jeremy Draught: Thank you for the tremendous research base you built in *A Spicy Touch: Volume 3*.

To Taryn and all the team at Touchwood Editions: thank you for believing in *A Spicy Touch* and for bringing us into your fold. We look forward to a long and rewarding relationship.

To Tilly Sanchez-Turri: Thank you for your substantive edits, support throughout and insights as a cook, which kept the final copy edits on target. You never lost sight of our goal, to make Indian cooking easier for home cooks everywhere. That the strength of our friendship has only increased after years of recipe testing and teaching cooking classes together, speaks to your patience and generousity. We love you Tilly!

To Wendy Brownie, owner of Inspirati Fine Linens for Everyday, in Calgary: Thank you for loaning us linens from your collection of the world's finest and for your constant enthusiasm and support for this project.

To chef Andrew Hewson: Thank you for helping us find the right cooking terms to describe the process of "blooming" the flavours of Indian cooking.

To Karen's siblings, friends and neighbours: Keith Robicheau, Laurie Rans, Sue Smith, Shawnee Sax, Kim Irving, Susan Gremell, Louise Savoie, Laura Kowalchuck, JoJo Brooks, Naddine Maddell-Morgan, Anne Tingley, Gail Norton, Breanne Larson, Nora Comerford-Seto, Josée Wallace, Sonja Magus and Trudy White-Matthews, thank you for your support, and for lending dishes, doing dishes, and/or eating the dishes we made.

To Karen's husband and son, Todd and Cole: Thank you for being such good company for each other when I'm faced with the solitary task of writing and when I journey to India each year on my quests to understand this complex cuisine at a deeper level. Thank you also for loving Noorbanu as much as I do.

To Noorbanu's daughter Khadija and her husband and son, Nasir and Imran: Thank you for the extensive recipe testing, for cooking beautiful looking food for our photo sessions and for being the next great cooks in the Nimji family.

To Akbar, Nazlin and Rosie: Thank you for your constant kindness, love, advice and support.

Last but not least, to Noorbanu's assistant Marilyn Jerez: Thank you for all your help with prepping, cooking and dishwashing during our continual recipe testing and photography sessions. You've been an incredible support.

Noorbanu Nimji
and Karen Anderson

Calgary, Alberta
November, 2019

The Woman with A Spicy Touch

Noorbanu Nimji is one of the best cooks I've ever met. She is my mentor and a beloved friend.

Noorbanu's knowledge of cooking with spices is innate. Amounts, combinations and flavour memories — she expresses them as intuition as she flows through the preparation of her favourite dishes. Noorbanu's been cooking for her family for more than 60 years. She's taught Indian cooking and written cookbooks for 40 years. She didn't set out to teach and write, but she rose to the challenge when it came.

Noorbanu's story starts in Nairobi, Kenya, where she was born into a Shia Imami Ismaili Muslim family not long after her parents emigrated from Gujarat in India in the 1920s. The Ismailis make up about 12 million of the world's two billion Muslims. They are Shia, part of one branch of Islam, with the Sunni forming the other main group. The Ismaili faith has a long history.

Starting in the early 600s, in the time of The Prophet Mohammed in Medina and Mecca (now modern-day Saudi Arabia), the roots of Ismailism spread east to the Mediterranean, south to Yemen and then further—into North Africa and Persia (now Iran). At the first millennium, it reached Central Asia and finally South Asia, where Ismailis including Noorbanu's ancestors enjoyed several stable centuries in Gujarat, India. In the nineteenth and twentieth centuries, large numbers of these Ismailis moved to East Africa in search of opportunities for future generations.

This history explains how a woman from Nairobi is such a wonderful Indian cook. It also explains that while Noorbanu is Ismaili there is not a singular Ismaili cuisine. The food of the Ismaili people is as diverse as the countries and cultures where they live and practice their faith.

Noorbanu's cooking reflects the dishes of Gujarat and other North Indian regional influences. Life in Kenya added East African dishes to her repertoire. There's also an undeniable influence from Kenya's time under British rule (this also happened in India under the British Raj and explains the love affair with puddings and fruitcakes that you'll find in both countries). The recipes in this book are further influenced by Noorbanu's move to Canada.

The Nimji family left Kenya for Calgary (via England) in 1974 during the expulsion of "non-Africans" from East Africa by then-president of Uganda, Idi Amin. Noorbanu, her family and all of their people, walked away from everything they owned. The Aga Khan, the hereditary Imam (spiritual and temporal leader) of the Ismaili people, sought asylum for East African Ismailis throughout the world. They now live in more than 25 countries.

Soon after her arrival in Calgary, Noorbanu was noticed for the food she shared at community gatherings. It was the first time that so many East African Ismailis were living outside of multi-generational house-holds where recipes were handed down by oral tradition. Favourite ingredients were not available in Canada and cooking mentors were sorely lacking. Noorbanu was asked to teach the displaced youth of her community.

Noorbanu taught for about a decade before a friend looked at her type-written stack of recipes and suggested she publish them in a cookbook. With the help of her family, Noorbanu wrote and published three volumes of *A Spicy Touch* cookbooks in 1986, 1992 and 2007. Although she sold more than a 250,000 copies, Noorbanu's work was not done.

A Spice Apprentice

I met Noorbanu in 1996 when I attended one of her cooking classes. It was fascinating to watch her mastery of Indian cooking, as she easily talked and cooked her way through class. It stuck in my mind.

In 2006, I founded Calgary Food Tours Inc. and got to know Noorbanu's talents more deeply as I became a food columnist for the Canadian Broadcasting Corporation. Noorbanu was my Alberta connection to the story of Great Britain's changing tastes, with its declaration of "curry" as the new national dish. My favourite local Indian cook, Noorbanu, helped me understand the difference between curry (spicy gravy) and masalas (the art of blending spices to create flavourful dishes) and to share the story with a Canadian audience.

Noorbanu and I clicked. Not long after, when she was in search of a writer and recipe tester for a fourth book I offered my services, and Noorbanu hired me on the spot. With Noorbanu's help my own Indian cooking was transformed with afternoons spent quietly folding samosas together, having her by my side teaching me to alter the spicing of a dish and with shopping excursions to source authentic ingredients I'd have never found on my own.

In 2008, I asked Noorbanu if she would teach public classes again — like she had done in her early days in Canada. But, this time with me and to a cross-cultural audience. We designed classes to help others overcome the barriers I had experienced in my early attempts at Indian cooking.

We led our guests directly to the source of ingredients in Calgary. We roasted and ground spices to make everyone their own *masala daba* (spice box). We demonstrated the tricky task of samosa wrapping. Just for fun, we ate at belly-busting Indian buffets and drank a lot of chai. The classes added immensely to our understanding of what you — our fellow home cooks — might like to learn and what would inspire you to buy yet another cookbook.

Another brick was added to the foundation of this book when, from our humble start in Calgary's little India, I was invited to lead cuisine and culture trips to Mother India. I've seen the techniques Noorbanu uses mirrored in the kitchens of great Indian chefs half a world away. Through greater exposure and focused observation, patterns emerge. I am now better able to articulate the underlying principles of this ancient cuisine, thanks to my annual explorations in India. Still, it took something more for us to finish this book.

Let's Rock and Roll

In the Great Alberta Flood of 2013, Noorbanu's inventory of previous editions of *A Spicy Touch* cookbooks were ruined. We joke that it took a lot of water to get us flowing, but we also know every disaster brings a blessing. In this one, losing all those books meant we had to finish what we started so many years ago.

Noorbanu has great energy. In the kitchen, once she has everything ready to go for a recipe she'll often look at me with a sparkle in her eye and say, "Let's rock and roll." She's very happy this book is finally rocking and rolling its way into your kitchen for you and your family to enjoy. Love of family and community is Noorbanu's inspiration.

A Cookbook for Future Generations

This book is a "best of" collection of the Nimji family's favourite recipes. Every recipe has been tested, retested and revised. New recipes have also emerged since that last book was published in 2007.

Noorbanu takes delight in this new millennium's global marketplace. Many ingredients from her ancestral home in India and her birthplace in Africa are more widely available. There is an increased enjoyment of spices now. Noorbanu loves the technological advances and equipment that make classic Indian recipes easier to prepare. All of the recipes in this book are updated to reflect these positive changes in the world.

Another less positive change in the world is that solid home cooking skills are increasingly rare. It's been a few generations since families had a dedicated home cook as the norm. Now, when people do want to cook a nice meal or make dishes of their culture, they find they lack the skills. We hope all the tips we include will help you feel Noorbanu's presence in your kitchen—at your elbow—to teach you as you cook her delicious food.

A Spicy Touch: Family Favourites from Noorbanu Nimji's Kitchen is Noorbanu's first hardcover book and we carefully chose a binding that allows the book to lie flat while you are cooking. The pages are full colour with an easy-to-read font. There are many, many more photos. We've used *The Recipe Writer's Handbook* by Ostmann and Baker (Wiley, 2001) to maximize clarity in our wording and measurements.

The 15 chapters are laid out much like a great Indian feast. There are starters, snacks, soups, salads, chutneys, main dishes, vegetables, rice dishes, breads, desserts, drinks and sweets. There are 225 recipes including 180 gluten-free and 154 vegetarian. Adaptations for allergies are noted throughout.

Experienced Indian cooks (and experienced Ismaili cooks of East African heritage) can dig into these recipes at any point they like. People new to Indian and East African cooking may want to spend more time reading through Chapter One. Here, we help you get ready for success with detailed explanations of the key ingredients and equipment you'd find if you were to tour Noorbanu's spice box, pantry, fridge, freezer and kitchen cupboards. We also explain the pacing and principles in the flavour development of Indian cooking.

Cooking the dishes in this book and enjoying them with your family keeps Noorbanu's legacy of sharing the recipes of her unique culinary heritage alive. Her act of recording these recipes has played a key role in the success of the East African Ismailis people's migration around the globe as her books followed them to wherever they call home. She has successfully ensured this unique culinary knowledge—that might have otherwise been lost—carries on.

For the East African Ismaili people the taste of this food has been a touchstone to comfort them and to help them retain an important part of their culture. For the rest of us, this collection of one family's most beloved recipes can become a delicious cornerstone as humanity builds a more pluralistic world where the best pieces of every culture can be enjoyed.

Karen Anderson

CHAPTER 1

Noorbanu's Kitchen

This book is organized to set you up for success as you make the passage to Indian cooking. The information in this chapter is at the front of the book for a reason.

We want you to know all of the pieces in Indian cooking. Knowledge of the shapes, colours and textures of the spices, ingredients and equipment involved in Noorbanu's recipes will help you fit them together with ease as you cook your way through this book.

Noorbanu is the consummate organizer and a model of efficiency. Cooking from a well-stocked kitchen is second nature to her. Most of us need help getting to her level of functioning.

Let's get started ...

Principles of Indian Cooking

Let's start by introducing you to some of the principles of Indian cooking. Understanding these will help you achieve the results that Noorbanu does, succulent food with depth of flavour. With each recipe in the book, we lay out a similar pattern for you to follow.

We help you make a plan by telling you what ingredients to gather and how to prep them. We set a pace for the cooking to allow for flavours to temper and bloom properly. We guide you to taste the food you are cooking and to adjust the seasoning and spicing to suit your palate. We then share ideas for how to best enjoy the fruits of your labour.

We'll stay with you and guide you all the way. With a bit of time and practice, cooking this food—in this way—will become second nature to you too. Now let's look at the pattern which forms the backbone of the recipes in this book in greater detail.

Make a plan.

Noorbanu approaches every dish with the same organized pattern. She plans what she needs—equipment and ingredients—and thinks about how much she'll make and how long it will take. Next she gathers and preps each ingredient so that everything is in place before she starts to cook. The French call this *mise en place* or *meez*. It not only helps to be this organized before you start cooking an Indian dish; we'd say it's essential.

Set the pace by tempering your spices.

Read through the recipes before you start to cook them. Most of the recipes in this book begin with a process that is a common thread in all Indian cooking, heating spices in oil. This is known as tempering.

When you temper spices in hot oil or ghee it helps them release their own essential oils and with that, the cascade of flavours that will give each dish its essence. Other names for this process are *tardka*, *tarka*, *chaunk* or *vaghar* in North India and *thalithal* in South India. Typical spices that are tempered include black mustard seeds, dried or fresh chillies, curry leaves, cumin, coriander, fennel or fenugreek seeds, ginger, garlic, shallots and asafoetida.

You know when it's time to move onto the next phase of preparation when the seeds of your spices "dance" or pop and splutter in the pan. This usually takes less than a minute (though it varies with cooking temperature) but it's important to wait until "the dance" begins.

Let flavour bloom.

In the next phase of cooking you'll add the other ingredients that form the base of the sauce: onions, tomatoes and wet ingredients. Again, you need to let the ingredients cook until their flavours have been fully extracted and that is usually when you see oil separating from the rest of the sauce.

Indian cooks have traditionally used a great deal of oil in their cooking and though it helps with the flavour extraction process, Noorbanu has cut back on the fat content of her recipes so you won't always see the oil separate as the clue to go forward. We still provide information on how long to let the ingredients cook to extract their full flavour even if you won't be able to see oil separating. It is usually only in the final phase that the meat or vegetable highlight of the dish is added.

Taste, season and spice.

Throughout cooking and especially at the end of the cooking time for each dish, Noorbanu tastes the food she is preparing. This is not unique to Indian cooking but it is something that home cooks forget to do. Sometimes we are more concerned about not missing a

step in a recipe than in teaching our taste buds about our own preferences. It wasn't until I had cooked a lot with Noorbanu that I learned the importance of tasting, tasting again and tasting some more.

The recipes in the book will often give an amount for salt, chillies and key spices and then say—or to taste. It's important that you taste the dish and adjust the amount of seasoning or spicing to your liking as you go, and again, near the end of a dish. A little more salt might bring the flavours together better, a little more chilli powder might zip it up a notch, a little lemon juice might add tanginess and the flavours of some spices can be optional. Practice tasting and adjusting the seasoning and spicing. You'll learn to trust your own palate and the food will taste even better to YOU. Of course, it's also highly likely that you'll love it exactly as the recipe suggests so don't feel you have to change a thing.

Set the table for enjoyment.

In addition to meat, vegetables, rice or whatever she is cooking at the time, Noorbanu and Indian cooks everywhere think about what other elements are needed to balance a meal. Chutneys, breads, salads and pickles are chosen to complement flavours. Indian meals are usually a balance of elements reflected in our taste buds with sweet, sour, salty, bitter, satisfying umami and savoury components.

Noorbanu always sets a pretty table and brings everything she's prepared all at once to serve and enjoy family style. We offer lots of suggestions for other dishes that will contrast and complement each recipe you decide to cook.

Now, let's go scouting through Noorbanu's cupboards. You can tell a lot about a person by what they keep in their cupboards. This is the kitchen of a master cook.

Turmeric

Cumin Seeds

Ground Cumin

Indian
Chilli
Powder

Star Anise,
Cinnamon,
Green Cardamom
Pods,
Whole Cloves,
Black Peppercorns

Black Mustard Seeds

Ground
Coriander

Stock up for Success

It's fundamental: a proper kitchen set up and a fully stocked pantry, fridge and freezer make cooking easier.

Noorbanu's shelves are filled with goodies we can all access. If the quantity of items described here seems a bit overwhelming just remember, Noorbanu has been cooking for her family for over 60 years and she started just like you—one dish at a time.

Let's walk through the ingredients and equipment you're going to need. Let's start with spices.

Spices and Herbs

Spices are the soul of Indian cooking but what are they really? Simply put, they are the seeds, berries, buds, petals, bark and roots of plants used for flavouring, preserving and colouring food. When you've used up all the parts of a plant that are deemed spices, you are left with the green leafy parts and they are known as herbs.

Some plants, like coriander or cilantro are both a spice and an herb.

Use fresh herbs at the end of cooking to brighten the flavours of a dish. If used earlier, they will tire and lose their pungency.

TIPS: Whenever possible it's best to purchase the spices you will use most frequently in these recipes: cardamom, cinnamon, cloves, coriander, cumin, fennel, mustard, pepper, nutmeg, saffron, and star anise in their whole pod, seed or stick form. Whole herbs and spices contain essential oils that are their active ingredients in creating flavour and aroma. All oils oxidize and denature over time, but if kept whole as opposed to ground, the essential oil in spices will last longer. Roasting and grinding your own spices from pods and seeds to make masalas (spice mixtures) helps liberate what oils remain at the time of use. Purchase a spice grinder or have an extra coffee grinder dedicated to the task of spice grinding and roast and grind them, only as you need them.

The Masala Daba

The most important thing I learned in Noorbanu's kitchen is the central role that a masala daba plays in facilitating the preparation of Indian food. *Masala* means spice blend or mixture and *daba* means box. Masala daba is frequently shortened to just "daba" or spice box.

Each Indian cook fills their masala daba with the spices that reflect their region's taste palate. These are the spices most commonly used in that area so it is both practical and logical for the cook to keep them close at hand, especially when each recipe might call for six to ten different spices.

You can find a masala daba at your local Indian grocer or purchase our *A Spicy Touch* masala daba through our **aspicytouch.ca** website. A daba is typically made of stainless steel and will have a tight fitting lid that may or may not be transparent. Look for one with at least seven separate cylinders inside.

Noorbanu keeps whole black peppercorns, whole cloves, whole green cardamom pods, a piece or two of star anise and several pieces of whole Sri Lankan (true) cinnamon bark in the centre of her spice box. Cumin—both as roasted seeds and freshly ground—is in the next two containers. Ground coriander, Indian chilli powder, turmeric and black mustard seeds round out the box.

As you read about the flavour profile of each spice in Noorbanu's masala daba you can begin to imagine the flavours of the recipes in this book. As you cook each recipe and measure the varying amounts of each spice in each dish, you will begin to understand the subtle art of spice blending or mixing which is the definition of masala. Making masalas direct from your very own daba will make Indian cooking a lot easier for you.

Here, we outline the flavour profile, uses, background and/or tips that will enhance your understanding of Indian cooking and spices. The 10 spices in Noorbanu's masala daba are as follows:

Black Pepper

FLAVOUR: *spicy heat*

USES: Grind fresh as needed to season and balance most dishes.

BACKGROUND: Known as "the King of spices", pepper is the world's most traded and consumed spice. It grows as vines that climb tall trees and needs rain to pollinate the flowers that form the fruits that are known as peppercorns. It can be eaten fresh, preserved as green, dried as black or fermented and aged as a white peppercorn.

TIP: Keep the peppercorns whole to contain their flavour.

Cinnamon *(Thajh)*

FLAVOUR: *pungent and intense with fruity notes*

USES: It adds warmth to dishes and rounds out the flavour profile of Garam Masala (page 29).

BACKGROUND: True cinnamon is the dried, aromatic inner bark of the evergreen tropical Asian tree, commonly known as Ceylon or Sri Lankan cinnamon. It is usually sold as cinnamon sticks or ground into a powder. Much of the cinnamon sold in North America is actually from Indonesia and Vietnam from trees known as Cassia. Cassia cinnamons are stronger in flavour and aroma and while we enjoy their dominance in apple pies and cinnamon buns, the true and subtler flavour of Sri Lankan cinnamon is best for Indian (and Mexican) cuisine.

TIP: Noorbanu uses short pieces of the outer bark of true cinnamon for her cooking. It is available at fine spice stores and Indian grocers.

Cloves *(Laving)*

FLAVOUR: *antiseptic, warm and pungent*

USES: In sauces and side dishes, mostly ground up along with other spices, but also used in Biryani where it is normally added whole to enhance presentation and flavour.

BACKGROUND: Cloves are the dried, unopened flower bud of an evergreen tree native to the Moluccas.

Coriander *(Kothmeer; Dhania)*

FLAVOUR: *a warm, nutty, spicy citrus flavour*

USES: The flowers form dried, edible fruit pods as they go to seed which are then used whole or ground to add a hint of citrus flavour to savoury dishes. Hint is the key word here, as too much can be overpowering.

TIPS: Coriander is best purchased as whole seeds and ground as needed. Dry roasting in a pan on the stove or in the oven before grinding enhances flavour. Coriander leaves and seeds are not interchangeable in recipes.

Cumin *(Jeera)*

FLAVOUR: *aromatic, nutty-flavoured seeds that come in three colours: amber, white and black, with amber being the most common*

USES: Season meat sauces, rice, bread, pickles and soups with this almost trademark Indian flavour.

TIP: To release the full flavour profile of cumin, dry roast the seeds in small batches until they are golden. Do this before grinding.

Green Cardamom *(Elaychi)*

FLAVOUR: *bright and minty sweet to start; ending with a cleansing peppery bite*

USES: Cooks treasure cardamom in sweet, savoury and astringent dishes. It enhances puddings, ice cream, cookies, cakes, stews, rice, pickles and chai masalas.

BACKGROUND: Known in India as "the Queen of spices," cardamom is the world's second most expensive spice next to saffron. It grows chiefly in the shaded jungles of South India, in an area known as the Cardamom Hills in the state of Kerala. It looks like a very tall potted palm with long green rhizomatous tendrils sprouting from its base. Orchid-like white flowers grow from the tendrils and yield capsular green fruits about the size of a cranberry. The fruits are dried to pods that deliver an almost anti-septic Eucalyptus or camphor-like aroma and this is most definitely linked to its taste.

TIP: Be frugal with cardamom as a little goes a long way.

NOTE: Black cardamom pods come from a different plant and have a smoky tobacco flavour that will not substitute for the green pods.

Make your own: Ground Cardamom

Though cardamom can be purchased in the pod, seeds or ground, Noorbanu always buys pods and grinds their seeds, as needed. Ground cardamom loses flavour quickly, so grind small batches. To access the seeds, place the pods in a mortar; crush them with a pestle, separate the seeds and process them in a spice grinder. Ten pods should yield 1 teaspoon of ground cardamom depending on the size of the pods.

Indian chilli powder

FLAVOUR: *fruity and spicy*

USES: This adds heat when balancing the flavours of everything from appetizers to savoury dishes and is especially useful in making Vindaloo or spicy chicken wings.

BACKGROUND: In Mexico and the American southwest, chilli powder is a spice made from dried ground ancho chillies with small amounts of cayenne for colour and heat. There might also be cumin, garlic and oregano for added flavour and this TexMex blend is typically used in tacos, fajitas and Chilli Con Carne.

TIP: Use Indian chilli powder for Indian cooking. It's made from hotter chillies, without other spices added. If you can't find it, substitute cayenne powder to taste.

NOTE: We use chilli/chillies in this book in keeping with Canadian/British standards for spelling.

Mustard Seeds *(Rai)*

FLAVOUR: *pungent—usually roasted in hot oil or ghee that causes the seeds to pop and release their characteristic nutty flavour*

USES: Whole seeds typically form the base of aromatic flavour in many dishes as part of the spice tempering process of making a *tarka* or *vaghar*.

Star Anise *(Anasphal)*

FLAVOUR: *liquorice, sweet*

USES: It's distinctive in stewed fruit, desserts, savoury stews, in teas and Chinese five-spice powder.

Turmeric *(Haldhar)*

FLAVOUR: *decidedly fragrant with a musky odour and a pungent, bitter, peppery biting taste reminiscent of ginger*

USES: Flavours and adds colour to dishes and powder and butter, cheese, relishes, pickles and prepared mustard.

BACKGROUND: Turmeric is derived from the powdered tuberous rhizome of a widely cultivated tropical, perennial plant that belongs to the ginger family.

NOTE: Due to its antioxidant, anti-inflammatory properties and its ability to stimulate and increase the immune system response, turmeric's active compound polyphenol curcumin is currently being investigated for its potential role in the treatment of a wide range of medical conditions.

Other Spices

Ajwan (Omum)

FLAVOUR: *like lovage, thyme or caraway, only stronger*

USES: Dry-roast or fry in ghee for vegetable dishes and flat breads. Use very sparingly.

BACKGROUND: These are small brown seeds of a perennial plant commonly known as Bishop's Weed that are native to southern India and also known as *Ajowan, Ajowain* or Indian Thyme. It may be purchased already ground or in seed form.

Asafoetida (Hing)

FLAVOUR: *fetid, garlicky smell yielding an onion or garlic-like taste once cooked*

USES: Small quantities act as a digestive aid in lentil and eggplant dishes and in pickles. It can be found commercially in powdered or lump form.

BACKGROUND: Also known as Devil's Dung, this brownish, bitter, foul-smelling resin-like gum or powder comes from the dried sap extracted from the stems and roots of several species of the plant, which grows mainly in Iran, Afghanistan and Kashmir. In India, it is used especially by the Brahmin caste of the Hindus and by adherents of Jainism, as a substitute for the onions or garlic that they are not permitted to eat.

Cayenne Pepper

FLAVOUR: *hay-like flavour with a bite*

USES: It adds spicy heat.

BACKGROUND: Named for the city of Cayenne in French Guiana, cayenne pepper is an orange-red to dark red condiment consisting of several cultivated varieties of chillies that are dried, pulped and baked into cakes that may then be ground and sifted to make the powder.

Curry Leaves (Mitho Limbo)

FLAVOUR: *pungent in smell, they look much like the leaves of a citrus tree but yield a nutty flavour when cooked*

USES: Typically tempered in oil then cooked with the dish and removed like a bay leaf.

BACKGROUND: These leaves come from subtropical curry trees and are not where the term or flavour known as "curry" comes from. Curry—as the now generic term for a spicy gravy—evolved from the British misspelling of the Dutch word *karee* meaning sauce or gravy.

TIP: Rub these dark green, oval shaped leaves gently with a small amount of warm oil, so that the leaves are lightly coated, and store them in an airtight container in the freezer for a month or more. If they lose their fragrance, they've lost their flavour as well.

Dill *(Suva)*

FLAVOUR: *soft and sweet, sometimes compared to anise*

USES: This spice wakes up the flavour of pickles, salads, vegetables, meats, sauces and soups.

BACKGROUND: India is the primary producer of dill seed for culinary purposes in the world and both the seeds and leaves or oil from each are commercially harvested.

TIPS: Heating or slightly roasting dill seeds will bring out their flavour. The seeds have stronger and more pungent flavour than the leaves.

Fennel *(Variari)*

FLAVOUR: *sweet, minty and liquorice-like*

USES: The oval greenish-brown seeds are dried and used in bread, pickles, liqueurs and meat sauces. Also used as an ingredient in *Paan Masala* (page 33), traditionally served after meals in India to cleanse the breath.

TIPS: Pollen is the most potent form of the plant and though expensive, it is worth the splurge for unforgettable potato salads and fish masalas.

Fenugreek *(Methi)*

FLAVOUR: *grass or peanuts as the herb; burnt sugar as dried seeds*

USES: Provides accent when used sparingly in curry powders and pastes, chutneys and pickles, spice blends and tea.

BACKGROUND: This is a clover-like annual that is both a herb (leaves) and a spice (seeds). The young, aromatic celery-like leaves and sprouts are usually added towards the end of the cooking process. Dried fenugreek leaves are well known from the Kasur region and are frequently called *Kasoori Methi*.

Nutmeg *(Jayfal)*

FLAVOUR: *sharp but sweet*

USES: Almost exclusively added to sweets, nutmeg is also found in small quantities in some spice blends—particularly in Tamil Nadu in the south of India.

BACKGROUND: This evergreen tree native to the East Indies has golden-yellow fruits resembling apricots. As the fruits of the tree mature and lose moisture, the husk splits exposing the shiny brown seed which is commercial nutmeg. This seed is surrounded by a fibrous, lacy aril that separates the seed from the outer husk. When dried and ground, the aril becomes the spice we know as Mace.

Paprika

FLAVOUR: *mild to pungent and hot*

USES: A mild, dark red, powdered seasoning made from sweet red peppers. The seeds are removed and the fruit is dried and ground, adding depth of flavour to stews and sauces.

Saffron (*Kasar*)

FLAVOUR: *hay-like, slightly bitter with similar grassy aroma*

USES: Sparingly used (due to its price) to colour and flavour food.

BACKGROUND: Saffron threads are the stigmas of fall blooming purple flowers grown in Kashmir, Iran and Spain primarily. It is the world's most expensive spice as each crocus provides 3 stigmas only and it takes more than 4,000 flowers to produce 1 ounce. Choose threads (whole stigmas) over powdered saffron. The powder loses its flavour more readily and non-reputable sellers sometimes cut it with other substances of a similar colour, such as marigold, to increase their profit margins.

TIPS: Crush the threads and soak in 1 teaspoon of hot water just before using to amplify the colour extraction. If your saffron is not deep in colour and does not have a noticeable, pungent smell with a hay-like and somewhat bitter flavour, then it is probably past its best.

Noorbanu's Masalas

Masala is a word used throughout India for a spice blend with numerous variations. It can refer to a simple combination of two or three spices or to a complex blend of 10 or more. The most widely used blend is called *garam* (which means warm) masala, the variations of which are countless, depending on the cook and the dish being seasoned.

TIP: The masalas here are Noorbanu's personal recipes. They give the dishes in this book their signature flavours. Each one takes 20 to 40 minutes to roast and cool. Once they are ground and placed in an airtight glass container, they will remain fresh for several weeks if stored in a dark cupboard or up to several months in the refrigerator.

Garam Masala—Basic

Time: 30 minutes
Yield: ½ cup

Most of Noorbanu's recipes call for this masala. It's typically added near the end of cooking to add warmth and round out the flavours of many dishes.

½ cup	cinnamon sticks
2 Tablespoons	green cardamom pods
1 Tablespoon	black peppercorns
1 Tablespoon	cloves
1 teaspoon	grated nutmeg

① Preheat the oven to 300°F.

② Place the cinnamon, cardamom, black peppercorns and cloves on a baking tray and roast in the preheated oven for 10 minutes.

③ Remove the tray of spices from the oven and let them cool to room temperature.

④ Place the roasted spices and the grated nutmeg in the bowl of a spice grinder and process to a fine powder.

⑤ Store away from the light in an airtight glass container.

Garam Masala—Special blend

Time: 30 minutes
Yield: 3 Tablespoons

4	green cardamom pods
3 (½-inch)	sticks cinnamon bark
2 teaspoons	fennel seeds
2	star anise
½ teaspoon	black peppercorns
8	cloves
1 teaspoon	cumin seeds
1 teaspoon	coriander seeds
½ teaspoon	grated nutmeg

① Preheat the oven to 300°F.

② Place the cardamom, cinnamon, fennel, star anise, black peppercorns, cloves, cumin and coriander on a baking tray and roast for 10 minutes in a preheated oven.

③ Remove the tray of spices from the oven and let them cool to room temperature.

④ Place the roasted spices and grated nutmeg in the bowl of a spice grinder and process to a fine powder.

⑤ Store away from the light in an airtight glass container.

Chaat Masala

Time: 20 minutes
Yield: ¼ cup

Chaat masala is the essence of Indian street food with a pungent smell and both sweet and sour tastes on the palate.

TIP: Use it generously in chaat dishes, but sparingly on fresh fruit salads and cooked tandoori meat. Best made fresh in small quantities.

1 teaspoon	cumin seeds
1 teaspoon	black peppercorns
2	whole cloves
1 teaspoon	coriander seeds
1 teaspoon	dried mint leaves
2 Tablespoons	dried mango powder (*amchur*)
1 teaspoon	Indian chilli powder
1 teaspoon	ground ginger
1 teaspoon	salt
1 pinch	asafoetida powder

① Roast the cumin seeds, black peppercorns, cloves and coriander in a broad-based cast iron pan over medium heat—stirring constantly to avoid burning—until the coriander is golden brown and the spices are fragrant (or roast on a baking tray in a 300°F oven for 10 minutes).

② Remove the pan from the heat and add the dried mint leaves, while the spices are still slightly warm and then—once cool—add the mixture to the bowl of a spice grinder and process to a fine powder.

③ Stir in the mango powder, Indian chilli powder, ginger, salt and asafoetida and mix well.

④ Store away from the light in an airtight glass container.

Chai Masala

Time: 30 minutes
Yield: 7 Tablespoons,
enough for 70 cups of tea

¼ cup	cinnamon sticks
1½ teaspoons	cardamom seeds
1 teaspoon	cloves
½ teaspoon	black or white peppercorns, freshly ground
2 Tablespoons	ground ginger
½ teaspoon	ground nutmeg
¼ teaspoon	saffron, optional

① Preheat the oven to 300°F.

② Break the cinnamon sticks into small pieces and roast them along with the cardamom, cloves and peppercorns on a baking sheet in the preheated oven for 10 minutes.

③ Remove the roasted spices from the oven and allow them to cool to room temperature.

④ Place the spices in the bowl of a spice grinder and process to a fine powder.

⑤ Stir in the ginger, nutmeg and saffron and mix well.

⑥ Store away from the light in an airtight glass container.

⑦ Enjoy this in the Chai Masala recipe on page 274.

Kashmiri Masala

Time: 15 minutes
Yield: 2 Tablespoons

This masala is a great way to enrich the flavour and spiciness of any dish. Add 1 teaspoon to start and adjust according to taste.

TIP: This recipe can be tripled or quadrupled.

Wet

1½ teaspoons	Garlic Paste (page 42)
1½ teaspoons	Ginger Paste (page 43)
2 teaspoons	tomato paste
1½ teaspoons	Green Chilli Paste (page 44)

Dry

½ teaspoon	paprika
1 teaspoon	ground cumin
¼ teaspoon	Indian chilli powder
¼ teaspoon	Garam Masala (page 29)
¾ teaspoon	salt
Pinch	saffron

① Combine all of the wet ingredients and stir in the dry ingredients to produce a paste that's a little on the dry side.

② Place in an airtight glass container and store in the fridge.

A Spicy Touch Grilling Masala

Time: 5 minutes
Yield: ½ cup

This recipe was developed by Noorbanu's grandson Imran and Karen when they were on a grilling and tandoori recipe-testing marathon one weekend. Feel free to multiply it during the busy summer months of grilling.

2 Tablespoons	ground Crispy Fried Onions (page 42)
1 teaspoon	ground cumin
1 teaspoon	ground coriander
1½ teaspoons	Garam Masala (page 29)
½ teaspoon	turmeric
2 teaspoons	dry mustard powder
2 teaspoons	Indian chilli powder
½ teaspoon	freshly ground black pepper
½ teaspoon	salt

① Stir all the ingredients together until thoroughly mixed.

② Store away from the light in an airtight glass container.

Paan Masala

Time: 20 minutes
Yield: 4 cups

This is also known as a *Mukhwas* or farewell seeds. A sign of hospitality, the mixture of spices, fruits and sugar combine to create a palate cleanser and are usually served after meals. Noorbanu jokes that when someone gets out the Mukhwas, you know its time to go home. In India, this mixture is frequently offered on a Betel leaf which is folded and eaten whole—spices and leaf. When it is chewed in this way it is called *Paan*.

TIP: *Rangola masala*, rose syrup (be sure to buy a thick viscous one), candy coated fennel and *Dhania Dal* are a few special ingredients that you may only find at an Indian grocer.

1 cup	sweet shredded coconut
1 (7 ounce)	package rangola masala
4 Tablespoons	Dhania Dal, roasted
2 Tablespoons	fennel seeds, roasted
3 Tablespoons	candy coated fennel
2 teaspoons	cardamom seeds
4 Tablespoons	sliced almonds
optional	Rose syrup*

* Wait to add the rose syrup until just a few hours before serving because, once combined, the mixture only stays fresh for a short time. Use 1 Tablespoon of rose syrup to 5 Tablespoons of the Mukhwas mixture to yield 10 servings.

① Put the coconut on a baking tray and place under the broiler of your oven to toast it lightly—watching all the time.

② Turn off the broiler, remove the coconut and set it aside to cool to room temperature.

③ Put the rangola masala, Dhania Dal, fennel seeds, candy coated fennel, cardamom and sliced almonds in a bowl with the coconut and mix well.

④ Store away from the light in an airtight glass container.

MUKHWAS OR FAREWELL SEEDS
SEE PAGE 320

Agar Agar

A vegetarian form of gelatin extracted from algae. It is used in dessert recipes that require gelling and is important in cultures that don't consume the pork products that regular gelatin comes from.

Amchur Powder

This is derived by pulverizing sun-dried, unripe green mangoes into a fine powder. It has a tart, acidic, fruity flavour that adds character to meat, vegetable, and curried dishes as well as fruit *chaats* and is also used as a tenderizer for poultry, game, and fish.

Cashews *(Kajoo)*

These are edible seeds from the evergreen cashew tree, native to Brazil. They have a sweet, buttery flavour. Though they are actually seeds they are used in cooking like nuts. Their high fat content (48 percent) requires that they be stored tightly wrapped in the refrigerator, so they don't turn rancid. Commercial production is now centred in India, which handles 90 percent of the world's trade.

NOTE: Cashews are considered a tree nut for those with such allergies.

Chana Flour *(Besan or gram flour)*

Chana flour is also known as gram flour and should not be confused with Graham Flour which is made of whole wheat. It is a pale yellow flour and a staple in Indian cuisine. It is made from splitting and grinding *chana dal*, that are the split and hulled form of *kala chana* or black chickpeas. Also known as *desi*, they are the earliest type of chickpea. Chana flour is a major source of protein in South India's predominantly vegetarian culture.

TIP: Best results are obtained by sifting chana flour before use to remove any lumps or impurities.

Chickpea Flour

This flour is made from ground (garbanzo) chickpeas and though similar to chana flour it is not the same (see above).

TIP: The flours can be substituted for each other as necessary.

Citric Acid Powder *(limbo na phool)*

An organic, translucent, crystalline (white powder), and relatively strong water-soluble but non-toxic acid. It occurs in relatively large quantities in citrus fruits as well as in other fruits and vegetables and is a natural preservative. In cooking, it is used to produce a sour, acidic or tart taste and to complement fruit flavours in drinks, jams and jellies, candy, sherbets, water ices and wine.

TIP: It can be added to recipes as a substitute wherever fresh lemon juice is called for.

Coconut *(Nariyal)*

The large, brown hard-shelled seed of the coconut palm containing white flesh and a partially fluid-filled central cavity. Grated fresh coconut flesh can be tightly covered and refrigerated for up to four days or frozen for up to six months. Commercially available coconut comes in cans or plastic bags, either sweetened or unsweetened, shredded or flaked and dried, moist or frozen.

Coconut milk and coconut cream are common ingredients in this book because coconuts were part of Noorbanu's Kenyan cooking heritage.

TIPS: Be careful not to confuse sweetened cream of coconut, used mainly for desserts and mixed drinks, with unsweetened coconut milk or cream. Use the unsweetened kind for the savoury dishes in this book. Avoid buying "lite" or "light" cans of coconut as the water that decreases the fat content also decreases the flavour.

Dal *(daal, dhal and dhall)*

See photos on next page

Dal is a Hindi word for about 60 varieties of dried legumes simply cooked in water and seasoned with a variety of spices, tomatoes and onions. This is the chief source of protein for the third of India's population who are vegetarian. Though this all sounds simple, legumes can be confusing when you are shopping for them.

Overall they are beans, peas and lentils that grow in pods that are specifically grown for their dried seeds versus fresh seedpods. Where it gets tricky, is that each type of dal can come in four different forms.

They can be whole with the skin intact, whole without the skin, split with the skin on, and split with the skin off. Even though all four forms come from one source, they taste and look remarkably different and—here's the kicker—they have four different names!

To help you in your efforts to "give peas a chance" we've identified the most common legumes in Noorbanu's recipes with corresponding photos.

Chana
Whole black chickpeas or *kala chana*

Chana Dal
These are split *kala chana*. They have a sweet nutty flavour and are ground to make chana flour, also known as *gram* flour or *besan*.

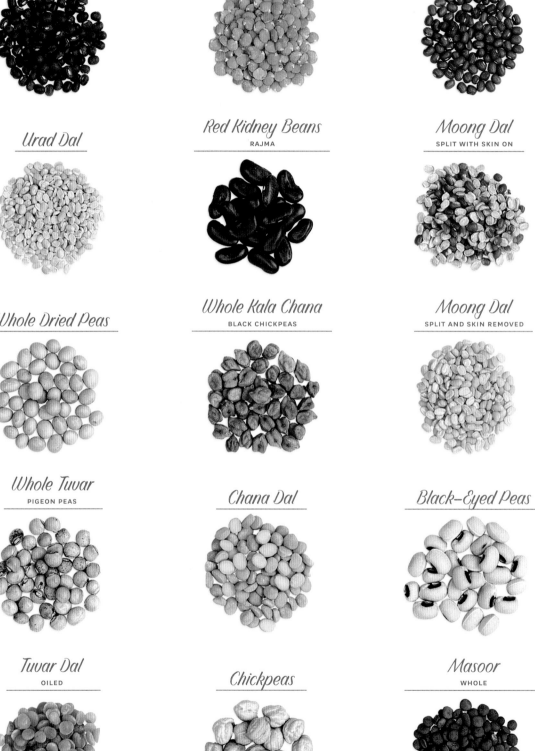

Whole Urad

Masoor Dal

Moong Beans

Urad Dal

Red Kidney Beans
RAJMA

Moong Dal
SPLIT WITH SKIN ON

Whole Dried Peas

Whole Kala Chana
BLACK CHICKPEAS

Moong Dal
SPLIT AND SKIN REMOVED

Whole Tuvar
PIGEON PEAS

Chana Dal

Black-Eyed Peas

Tuvar Dal
OILED

Chickpeas

Masoor
WHOLE

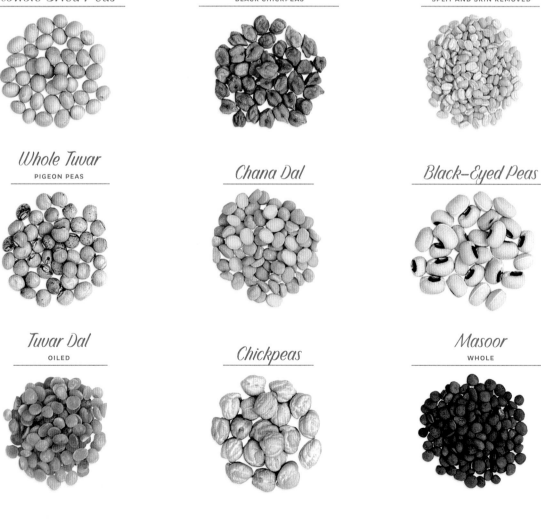

See photos to the left
←

Chickpeas
Whole garbanzo beans

Moong beans
Whole green lentils

Moong Dal
Split and skinned moong beans

Masur/Masoor
Red/orange lentils

Tuvar Dal *(tur, toor, arhar)*
These have tan skins or jackets when whole but are usually sold skinned, oiled and split, which reveals their yellow interior. Rinse the oil off before using. Enjoy them for their mild nutty flavour.

Urad
Black gram/lentils—These whole beans have black skins covering a creamy white interior. The skins have a nutty flavour.

Urad Dal
These split and skinned lentils are a little bland and frequently ground to use as a thickening agent in South Indian cooking.

Rajma
Red kidney beans

Whole Tuvar/Pigeon Peas
These are the source of *tuvar dal* as split and skinned yellow lentils.

Dhania Dal
Split, roasted coriander seeds are called *Dhania Dal* and are eaten as a snack and used in various masalas, like *Paan Masala* (page 33).

Graham Flour
Not to be confused with *Gram* flour, Graham flour is a type of whole wheat flour that is made by grinding the whole grain (bran, germ and endosperm) wheat kernel in two separate stages. The endosperm is ground to produce fine white flour and the bran and germ are ground coarsely. The two components are then recombined creating coarse-textured flour that bakes and keeps quite well. This flour is named after Sylvester Graham (1794–1851) an American Presbyterian minister and early advocate of dietary reform.

Gram Flour
See Chana Flour.

Gum Arabic *(Gund)*
This is a natural fluid exuded by various African trees of the genus Acacia. It is colourless, tasteless and odourless and is used in commercial food preparation to thicken, emulsify and stabilize foods including candy, ice cream and sweet syrups. It's also known as Acacia or Xantham gum.

Gur
See Jaggery.

Jaggery
This is an unrefined semi-solid form of sugarcane. It comes in several forms. The solid, cake-like block is the most common. It has a sweet, winey fragrance and taste that lends a distinct flavour.

NOTE: Sugar made from date palms is Gur but many people use Gur and jaggery interchangeably.

TIPS: If it's difficult to grate, break the jaggery into small pieces and melt it by boiling it in milk. If you cannot find jaggery you can substitute demerara sugar instead. Demerara is a partly refined, golden brown sugar. It's not coloured with molasses like other brown sugars.

Olive Oil
Cardiovascular disease is common in people of South Asian descent so Noorbanu started using olive oil more in *A Spicy Touch: Volume III—A fusion of East African and Indian Cuisine*. Olive oil is part of a Mediterranean diet that has been shown, in clinical trials, to reduce the risk of Cardiovascular disease. If you are concerned about heart health, feel free to use olive oil for the recipes in this book. We often do when the traditional taste of the finished dish is not affected.

Pistachios *(Pista)*
These edible, oily, green or yellow kernels are the fruit of a tree by the same name. They have a pleasing, mild, resinous flavour and are used extensively in savoury foods as well as for their yellowish green colouring in confections and *kulfi*.

Poppy Seed *(Khaskhas)*
Also called *Maw*, they are derived from the opium poppy and yet are not themselves narcotic. Small in size (it would take 900,000 seeds to equal 1 pound), they can be bluish-grey, beige or brown in colour and have a crunchy texture and nutty flavour.

Rice (*Chokha*)

There are more than 7,000 varieties of rice. It is an annual herbaceous cereal grass grown extensively in warm weather climates. Rice varieties have standard classifications—long, medium and short grain—based on the ratio of length to width and not absolute length. Basmati rice is a long-grained variety and is widely used in Indian cooking because the long firm separate grains that form as the rice is cooked are perfect for *pilaus* (pilafs) and *biryanis*. Cooking also brings out the fragrance of the rice that is said to improve with aging.

BACKGROUND: Pakistan and the Dehra Dun region of North of India are reputed as the best basmati growing regions. When buying basmati, ask for a brand from those regions and one that has been aged for several years before being milled and brought to market.

TIPS ON STORING: Rice can be stored in an airtight container in a cool, dark place almost indefinitely. The aging and storage in burlap bags does cause some dust to settle on the rice so it's important to rinse the rice four or five times with cold water before cooking with it.

TIPS ON CLEANING: To clean it, place the rice in a bowl and fill the bowl with cold tap water—rubbing the kernels together with your hands as the bowl fills. Strain the rice and repeat the process, rubbing the rice under cold running water until the drained water is no longer cloudy. Once the water runs clear, fill the bowl with water to cover the rice by at least two inches and let the rice soak for 10 to 20 minutes. Do not rub the rice after soaking as you might break the softened grains.

TIPS ON COOKING RICE: Karen likes to joke that the world is divided into people with rice cookers and those without them. She's had a rice cooker since 1994, but Noorbanu could never imagine the need for one. Here are Noorbanu's tips for cooking rice on the stove-top in a good heavy-bottomed pan.

FOR THE WATER TO RICE RATIO: If cooking more than 2 cups of rice, you can reduce the amount of water from the usual 2:1 ratio of water as in the following examples: to cook 3 cups of rice use 5 cups of water; 4 cups of rice use 7 cups of water and so on. In some recipes in this book, Noorbanu uses even less water: 1½ cups of water to 1 cup of rice.

FOR COOKING: See Fluffy Basmati Rice (page 249).

Sev

These are vermicelli noodles made from chana or wheat flour as opposed to the usual rice flour ones used in Asian cooking. They are fried in oil and seasoned with salt for use as a topping in *chaat*. Buy the long, thin, toasted *sev* that often comes from Pakistan. It may also be referred to as *Nylon Sev* because in Nairobi, when the nylon fabric was introduced, it was believed to be the best material and was gradually added to the names of favourite (high quality) foods.

Sunflower Oil

This is Noorbanu's cooking oil of choice for frying because of its high smoke point and neutral taste. She also uses it in some baking because of its neutral flavour.

NOTE: In North Indian food, mustard and canola oils are commonly used but you won't find them in Noorbanu's kitchen as she does not enjoy their flavour in her recipes.

TIP: When frying sweet dishes use fresh oil or oil previously used only for frying sweet dishes.

Tamarind *(Ambli)*

This is the fruit of the Asian evergreen tree sometimes known as an Indian Date. The pods contain small seeds embedded in an edible, sour-sweet pulp that, when dried, becomes extremely sour. Tamarind pulp concentrate is used as a popular souring agent in Indian cuisine, in much the same way that lemon juice is used in the west. It is used to season chutneys, curry dishes and pickled fish. It is also used to make sweet syrup flavouring for soft drinks. It can be purchased in jars of concentrated pulp with seeds, as canned paste or as whole pods that have been dried and pressed into blocks, or ground into powder.

Make your own: Tamarind Paste

Simmer a block of pressed tamarind in 2 cups of water for about 30 minutes, breaking it up with a wooden spoon. Let it cool then strain it into a bowl through a fine sieve. Store in the refrigerator in a clean, tightly sealed container for 8 weeks or in the freezer for up to 1 year.

Tukmaria *(takmaria, sabja, subja or falooda, faludo)*

These are the seeds of several varieties of the herb basil. When soaked, they become gelatinous and are used in Asian drinks and desserts.

Yellow and Red Food Colouring

These are available in powdered form at Indian grocers and are commonly used in baking. To obtain an orange colour, mix a few drops of yellow and red colouring together.

The Refrigerator

Chillies *(Marchu, Mirchi)*

Also known as hot peppers, chillies range in length from a quarter inch to over 12 inches and in diameter from as thin as a pencil to others which are round and globular. There are more than 200 varieties ranging in colour from yellow to green to red and black. As a general rule, the smaller the chilli, the hotter it will be because proportionally, a small chilli contains more seeds and veins. This is where capsaicin—the substance that gives chillies their fiery nature—is found. Milder, larger varieties of chillies are called bell peppers. The heat of chillies is measured in Scoville Heat Units (SHU) with bell peppers ranking 0 SHU, jalapeños 3,000 to 6,000 SHU, habañeros 300,000 SHU and Ghost chillies 1,000,000 SHU. Chillies are used to make a variety of products including paste, powder, dried flakes, Tabasco™ sauce, cayenne and paprika.

TIPS: Wear gloves or wash your hands thoroughly after handling chillies and avoid touching your eyes and sensitive mucous membranes. Residual oils containing capsaicin can cause great discomfort in these sensitive places. Fresh chillies will keep for several days in the produce drawer of a refrigerator. Noorbanu typically uses jalapeños, Serranos or long green chillies. When frying or cooking whole chillies in oil for a recipe, make a slit along the length of both sides. Otherwise, the hot oil tends to cause them to pop (explode is more like it).

Coriander leaves

Also known as Cilantro, these are used whole or chopped to flavour and garnish salads, *Dal* and curries.

TIP: Purchase fresh looking leaves with an even, dark colour and no sign of wilting and use promptly. Either wash and dry them and store between layers of paper towel in an airtight container in the refrigerator or chop the roots off and stand them in a glass of water with a plastic bag to cover the delicate leaves.

Crispy Fried Onions

Onions are the second most used vegetable in the world after tomatoes. Noorbanu uses yellow onions because they've been the most common onion available in Canada. In India, red onions are used almost exclusively. Feel free to substitute red onions or shallots for the recipe below.

TIP: Because it takes a while to make your own, we've included this picture of a good store-bought brand of crispy fried onions. We like this one because it has no additives or preservatives. Keeping these on hand will greatly reduce the amount of time needed to make the recipes that call for them.

Make your own:
Crispy Fried Onions

Time: 30 minutes
Yield: 6 cups

The crispy texture and caramelized flavour of the onions achieved by frying them is important to the taste and texture of many dishes and they are absolutely essential to the flavour of most biryanis.

4 lbs	onions (about 18 cups)
2 teaspoons	salt
6 cups	sunflower oil

① Cut the onions in ½ and then slice them thinly crosswise.

② Sprinkle with salt and set aside for 10 minutes.

③ Heat the sunflower oil in a large heavy-bottomed pan.

④ Squeeze the water out of the onions by pressing them between paper towels and fry them in small batches on medium-high heat until they start changing colour.

⑤ Lower the heat and continue frying until they are golden brown.

⑥ Remove the onions with a slotted spoon and spread them over a paper towel-lined baking tray. The onions will darken and become crispier as they cool (as long as they are spread out).

⑦ Store in an airtight container in the refrigerator for 2 to 3 months.

Garlic *(Lasan)*

A hardy, perennial Asiatic plant from the lily family and a cousin to leeks, chives, onions and shallots, the garlic bulb breaks up into separable cloves, each encased in its own parchment-like membrane.

TIPS: Garlic is best used fresh, but can be stored in an open container, away from other foods, in a cool, dark place for up to eight weeks. Crushing, chopping, or pressing garlic will release more of its essential oils and produce a sharper, more assertive flavour than slicing alone or leaving cloves whole.

Make your own: Garlic Paste

Time: 15 minutes
Yield: 2 cups

Garlic can be finicky to peel. Noorbanu breaks the bulbs into separate cloves and puts them in the freezer for about an hour to increase the ease of peeling them.

1 lb	fresh garlic
½ cup	lemon juice *or* white vinegar *or* water

① Cut off the root end off and peel each clove.

② Put the garlic into a food processor or spice grinder with just enough lemon juice or vinegar or water to make a fine paste.

③ Add water if more fluid is required.

④ Store in an airtight container in the refrigerator for 8 to 10 days or in the freezer for up to a year.

Ghee

This is clarified, semi-fluid butter used in Indian cooking and sold in most grocery stores.

Make your own: Ghee

Time: 30 minutes
Yield: 1 cup

Clarifying butter removes the water content and milk solids giving it a higher smoke point (about 375°F) and a nutty, caramel-like flavour and aroma.

TIPS: A larger batch is the same amount of work and you can freeze small portions for up to 1 year. At room temperature ghee will be semi-solid. If time is short and you have no ghee on hand and no time to make it, you can prevent regular butter from burning by adding a small amount of vegetable oil to it.

1 lb	unsalted butter

① Put the butter in a saucepan and slowly melt it so that the milk solids (which sink to the bottom of the pan) separate from the golden liquid on the surface.

② Simmer until all of the moisture evaporates and the milk solids begin to brown.

③ Strain through a sieve, store in a glass bottle and refrigerate for up to 6 months.

Ghisoda

Also known as a Ridge Gourd, it belongs to a group of tropical, Old World gourds or vines, grown chiefly for their ornamental fruits. Picked young, before maturity, the fruit can be cooked and eaten as a vegetable. It's called *Si Gua* in China and in Asian markets.

Ginger *(Adhu)*

A perennial plant from tropical and subtropical Asia, it's grown for its pungent, aromatic rhizome, which is sold fresh, dried, powdered, cooked, candied, preserved or pickled. The flavour is peppery and slightly sweet and the aroma is pungent and spicy. Ginger is best used fresh and appears in a variety of forms: as a paste, chopped, grated or slivered.

Make your own: Ginger Paste

Time: 10 minutes
Yield: 2 cups

TIP: Slice the ginger in thin slices before putting it in the food processor. This will prevent its fibres from forming undesirable long "hairs" in the paste.

1 lb	peeled young fresh ginger root
½ cup	lemon juice *or* white vinegar *or* water

① Rinse the ginger to remove any dirt in the crevices.

② Cut off all of the scars and hard parts and peel the outer skin.

③ Slice thinly and place in the bowl of a food processor or spice grinder with the water, vinegar or lemon juice and process to a fine paste.

④ Add water if more fluid is required.

⑤ Store in an airtight glass container in the fridge for 8 to 10 days or in the freezer for up to 1 year.

Green Chilli Paste

Noorbanu buys lots of green chillies in season when they are at their best price and then prepares this ready to use paste.

TIP: *Sambal Oelek* —a commercially prepared red chilli paste—works as a substitute.

Make your own:
Green Chilli Paste

Time: 10 minutes
Yield: 1 cup

Vary the chillies you choose until you find the ones with the right SHU (see chillies above) for your palate. Karen likes jalapeños, Noorbanu likes those mixed with Serranos, or long green or red chillies.

TIP: If you find the chillies you've chosen too hot, you can add sweet banana pepper chillies or any other variety of chillies that are not as hot to reduce the heat to a level more acceptable to your palate.

½ lb	fresh chillies
½ cup	lemon juice *or* white vinegar *or* water

① Wash the chillies, remove the stems and put them into a food processor with the lemon juice or vinegar or water.

② Blend the mixture to a fine paste.

③ Use just enough liquid to make a fine paste. If more fluid is required, simply add more water.

④ Store in an airtight glass container in the refrigerator or freezer.

Guvar

Cluster beans is the other name for this important legume crop which, though delicious on its own and in vegetable curries, is the chief source of guar gum—an important natural suspension agent in many processed foods.

Karela

This Bitter Melon is the fruit of a vine that originated in India but spread to China in the 14th Century. Look for this Indian version which has more wrinkles and is pointed at both ends. The flesh is bitter but it ends up tasting quite delicious when cooked in curries.

Mango *(Karee)*

The edible fruit of a tropical evergreen tree, mangoes have smooth green rinds that turn yellow with red highlights when the fruit is ripe. The flesh is sweet, juicy and yellow-orange in colour and surrounds a large, single fibrous seed or stone. Mangoes are in season from May through September and though imported fruit can be found in stores, sporadically, at other times of year. They are also available canned and in a variety of other processed states, including nectar, purée, or as pulp. Dried mango is available in chunks and strips. Green, unripe mangoes are also used to make the Indian seasoning *amchur.* India currently produces 75 percent of the world's commercial crop of mangoes.

TIP: Ripe mangoes can be stored in a plastic bag in the refrigerator for up to 5 days, and under-ripe fruit can be ripened in a paper bag at room temperature.

Meats

Noorbanu usually takes meat out of its packaging, places it in a colander and rinses any visible blood off under a little cold running water before use.

Paneer *(panir or paner)*

This is one of the few types of cheese indigenous to the Indian subcontinent. It is an unaged, acid-set (usually with lemon juice), unsalted, non-melting cheese which does not include rennet and is consequently completely vegetarian and a primary source of protein for Buddhists who adhere to a vegetarian diet. Paneer is used in curries because it doesn't melt at normal cooking temperatures.

Make your own: Paneer
Time: 30 minutes
Yield: 12 ounces

The buttermilk in this recipe adds a tangy depth to the flavour. Of all the recipes in this book, this one has saved Karen more time than any other. Despite living in a large city with lots of Indian markets, she used to drive over an hour round trip to source paneer. Now, she makes this recipe in about 30 minutes flat. Since she prefers using local organic milk, she also has control over the quality of the ingredients as an added bonus.

TIP: Pressing the cheese for 30 minutes will yield a softer, fluffier cheese; several hours will yield a very firm cheese.

2 litres	whole milk (3.5%)
1 litre	buttermilk
Cheesecloth and a sieve or fine-meshed strainer	

① Bring the 2 litres of whole milk to a slow boil in a heavy-bottomed pan on medium-high heat (this might take 20 minutes) stirring continuously so the sugars in the milk don't burn and stick to the bottom of the pan.

② Add the buttermilk once the whole milk is frothy and large bubbles are boiling up.

③ Stir continuously for another few minutes and watch as the milk separates into curds and liquid (whey).

④ Stop when there is no further formation of curds and strain the mix through a cheesecloth-lined sieve.

⑤ Gather the cheesecloth tightly around the curds and set a heavy object on them.

⑥ Place the strainer over a large bowl in the fridge until the cheese is set to the firmness you desire.

Saragavo

Commonly known as "Drumsticks," these long pods come from a tree native to the Himalayan region of Northwest India. They are fast-growing and have been widely cultivated in Africa as a food source. They taste a bit like beans or asparagus. The outer threads must be peeled off before cooking.

Sugar Syrup (*Chasni*)

Also called simple syrup, different consistencies of sugar syrup are required for different desserts. Sugar syrup is a solution of sugar and water that is cooked over a low heat until clear, and then boiled for a minute or so.

Make your own: Sugar Syrup

The syrup can be made in various densities depending on the ratio of sugar to water:

THIN SYRUP
1:3 parts sugar to water

MEDIUM SYRUP
1:2 parts sugar to water

THICK SYRUP
1:1 parts sugar to water

NOTE: In some of the recipes in Chapter 15, you need the sugar (or jaggery) and water solution to get to a "hard crack" stage before going to the next step. We describe that process in those recipes and also give the probable temperature to check for this on a candy thermometer.

Yogurt

Noorbanu likes to make her own yogurt so that she can control both the fat content of the milk and the final consistency. You can make very low fat yogurt by dissolving 1 cup of skim milk powder in 4 cups of skim milk. The addition of the powder gives the yogurt a thicker consistency.

Make your own: Yogurt

Time: 30 minutes
Yield: 3 cups

Yogurt is easy to make. Once it sits overnight you can enjoy it in a variety of ways and without all the plastic containers that come with commercially prepared brands.

TIP: Yogourmet™ starter is available at most health food stores or you can use 2 Tablespoons of organic yogurt as your starter instead. Once you've got your own yogurt going simply save 2 Tablespoons from each current batch to start the next batch.

4 cups	milk, 1 or 2%
1 package	Yogourmet ™

① Bring the milk to a boil and let it cool until slightly warm to touch.

② Add the Yogourmet ™ and stir well.

③ Pour the mixture into 2 or 3 small glass bowls, cover and leave in a warm place overnight to set.

   TIP: Noorbanu puts hers in a cold oven with the light on and finds it's the perfect temperature for yogurt.

④ Refrigerate before serving.

The Freezer

We both feel a freezer helps us practice the important food principle of frugality.

Freezer management tips:

Keep an eye on grocery prices and buy garlic, ginger and green chillies in season when they are most affordable and then use the recipes in this chapter to make large batches of garlic, ginger and green chilli pastes ahead.

Stock up on frozen vegetables: mixed vegetables, corn, pigeon peas, spinach and green peas as they are generally inexpensive, versatile and add nutrition to many recipes.

Keep small batches of *Naan* and *Rotli* on hand.

Buy large packages of meat when they are on sale, divide them into the portions your favourite recipes call for and thaw as needed.

Taking the above principle a little further, Karen buys a quarter beef directly from a local rancher each year (oh the joys of living in Alberta). The cost is greatly reduced and she knows exactly how the animal was raised, slaughtered and processed.

Karen also buys a share in a Community Supported Fishery (**skipperotto.com**) and orders and takes delivery of frozen product as needed.

Homemade Beef or Chicken Stock

It costs pennies, is easy to make and does not have the added salt or chemicals of some commercial brands.

Cassava *(Mhogo in Kishwahili)*

Also known as *Manioc* or *Yuca*, cassava is a shrubby, perennial tropical plant with large tuberous, starchy roots that range from six to twelve inches in length and two to three inches in diameter. The roots are peeled and boiled as a vegetable like potatoes. Cassava starch is also the source of tapioca. It can be stored fresh, unpeeled for up to four days but in Canada, we mostly buy it in frozen one pound bags.

TIP: Cassava must be boiled to make it safe to eat as it contains low levels of cyanide.

Make Your Own:
Curry in a Hurry Sauce Base

Time: 20 minutes
Yield: 1 recipe portion or multiplied as you like up to 6 times.

Use 1 portion the day you make this and keep any multiples in the freezer. When you need to prepare something quickly, thaw it in a saucepan on the stove and add in previously cooked meat, paneer or vegetables of your choice.

For one Recipe Portion:

2 Tablespoons	sunflower or olive oil
¼ teaspoon	Garam Masala (page 29) Leave out if you are using this for vegetable curry
½ cup	canned crushed tomatoes
2 teaspoons	Garlic Paste (page 42)
2 teaspoons	Ginger Paste (page 43)
½ teaspoon	turmeric
¼ teaspoon	Indian chilli powder
2 teaspoons	ground cumin
½ teaspoon	ground coriander
¼ teaspoon	paprika
1 teaspoon	tomato paste
2 Tablespoons	Crispy Fried Onions (page 42)
¼ cup	water

① Mix all of the ingredients together and either freeze for later use or set aside and begin preparation of the meat, paneer or vegetables.

For Meat:

② Heat 2 Tablespoons of olive oil and cook 1 pound of meat (chicken, lamb or beef) on medium-high heat until browned on all sides.

③ Add 1 portion of the sauce recipe per pound of meat and cook until the oil separates.

④ Add a little hot water as needed to make gravy and top with fresh cilantro leaves before serving.

For Paneer or Vegetables:

⑤ Omit the Garam Masala and Crispy Fried Onion when making the sauce but otherwise follow the steps above.

⑥ Enjoy with Basmati Rice (page 249).

Spring Roll Wrappers

In a true cross-cultural fusion, Noorbanu discovered that using spring roll wrappers instead of traditional samosa dough resulted in a light and crunchy outer coating that we all LOVE. The brand Noorbanu prefers—TYJ Spring Roll Wrappers™—is found in the freezer section of most Asian Markets.

Equipment

Pots and pans

- Heavy-bottomed pots
- Frying pans with close-fitting lids
- Non-stick (Teflon) frying pans—both an 8- and 10-inch pan with lids.
- Pressure Cooker
- Wok—also called a *karai* or *kadhai* in India and Pakistan. The *kadhai* in India are beautiful deep conical heavy-bottomed vessels made of copper or cast iron.

For the Oven

- Baking trays—a selection is necessary for sorting and roasting seeds, lentils and nuts as well as broiling kebab and baking sweets
- Cake tins—at least 2 round ones of the same size
- Casserole dish with a close-fitting lid, great for *biryanis*
- Clay pizza stone—good for making naan bread or for indirect cooking on the grill

Small appliances

- Deep-fryer—this is a luxury. You can use oil in a deep wok but it's nice to have a deep-fryer where you can set the temperature and be sure of its consistency during cooking.
- Digital kitchen scale—choose one that provides weight in ounces and grams. We've tried to give you measurements in teaspoons, Tablespoons and cups but there are just some recipes (baking and sweets) where you need the finely tuned measurement of an electronic scale.
- Electric blender
- Electric kettle—preferably with automatic shut-off.
- Electric mixer
- Food processor or mill
- Ice cream maker
- Microwave oven
- Rice cooker—half of you will have one; half of you will not. It's the way of the world.
- Spice grinder—once you really get into Indian cooking, you'll want to dedicate a special coffee or spice grinder just for this task. Until then, try grinding bread crumbs or rice in between spices to get rid of strong flavours.
- Toaster oven—great for roasting small batches of nuts or cooking for a few people.

Utensils

- Bamboo or metal skewers
- Box grater
- Candy thermometer
- Citrus juice press
- Kitchen scissors and/or shears
- Mandolin, a slicing apparatus
- Measuring cups and spoons
- Micro-plane grater
- Rolling pin
- Sharp knives
- Sifter
- Slotted spoon
- Storage containers—lots—plus airtight, screw top glass jars suitable for cupboards and fridge or freezer storage
- Strainer, sieve and/or colander
- Vegetable peeler
- Wooden spoons
- Zester

Miscellaneous

- Aluminum Foil
- Paper Towel
- Parchment paper
- Wax paper

NOTE: Chopping and slicing are knife skills terms used frequently throughout the book. The term "finely cut" is distinct and is used with tender herbs and occasionally onions, when a lighter touch is needed so that the juices and/or oils are not released.

Now You Are Ready to Cook with *A Spicy Touch*

If you have questions, comments or ideas for us please contact us.

EMAIL info@aspicytouch.com
FACEBOOK /aspicytouch
TWITTER @aspicytouch
INSTAGRAM @aspicytouch

Cooking is social and you are our community of wonderful fellow home cooks. We hope you'll enjoy this collection of family favourites and find your own family's favourites as you enjoy this food together.

CHAPTER 2

Soups and Salads

AVOCADO, MANGO
AND ALMOND SALAD,
(RECIPE, PAGE 56)

Turmeric-infused Chicken Soup

NOORBANU'S CURE FOR THE COMMON COLD

TIME	YIELD	GLUTEN-FREE
a little prep and then a few hours to simmer	6–8 servings	

Along with turmeric's well-documented health benefits this soup adds the heavenly scent of cinnamon and cloves, the kick of a little freshly ground black pepper and the accent of ginger and garlic. While we can't guarantee it will cure your cold, we do think it will lift the blues that come with having one.

TIPS: Buy a three-pound chicken and cut it into pieces or use bone-in chicken pieces to achieve the most flavourful soup. Noorbanu always washes the chicken pieces with a little vinegar before cooking them.

You can add a little more turmeric at the end of the cooking time if you'd like to amplify the soup's golden hue.

2–3 lbs	chicken, cut in pieces and prepared as noted above
9 cups	water
½ teaspoon	whole black peppercorns
5 small pieces	cinnamon bark
6	whole cloves
1 teaspoon	Ginger Paste (page 43)
1 teaspoon	Garlic Paste (page 42)
1 teaspoon	turmeric
½ cup	finely chopped onion (1 medium)
1–2 teaspoons	chicken bouillon powder or 1 cube (omit for gluten-free)
¾ teaspoon	salt, or to taste
¼ teaspoon	freshly ground black pepper, or to taste

① Put all of the ingredients in a soup pot and bring to a boil over medium-high heat.

② Reduce the heat to medium and simmer partially covered for 1 to 2 hours or until the chicken is falling off the bones.

③ Remove the chicken from the soup, let it cool enough so you can work with it, and then remove the meat from the bones.

④ Discard the bones and store the meat in the refrigerator until needed.

⑤ Place the soup pot in the fridge for a few hours so that any fat rises to the top and hardens.

⑥ Remove the hardened fat with a spoon and strain the broth to remove the whole spices.

⑦ Reheat the broth after returning the reserved meat to the pot.

⑧ Taste the soup and adjust the seasoning of salt and pepper to your liking.

⑨ Enjoy by the steaming hot bowl full. It's delicious—whether you have a cold or not.

Variation:

CHICKEN WITH BASMATI RICE SOUP

Karen likes to add a ½ cup of cleaned and soaked basmati rice and 2 cups of diced vegetables (carrots, onion, celery and zucchini) to this soup when reheating it to give it even more flavour and nutrition. A sprinkle of fresh parsley or coriander leaves brightens the flavour and presentation before serving.

Lentil and Vegetable Soup

TIME	YIELD	GLUTEN-FREE
45 minutes plus 1 hour soaking time	2–3 servings *This recipe multiplies well.*	*& VEGETARIAN*

Remember to soak the lentils for an hour and you'll be surprised how quickly you can have a homemade soup in your bowl. Vary the vegetables as your tastes and the seasons change or use frozen vegetables to make this soup even quicker to prepare.

¼ cup	lentils (*masoor dal*)
1½ cups	finely chopped mixed vegetables (peas, celery, onion, beans, carrots, cauliflower, cabbage, kale, potatoes)
3 cups	chicken or vegetable broth
1 Tablespoon	rolled oats
½ teaspoon	salt, or to taste
1 teaspoon	freshly ground black pepper, or to taste

① Soak the *masoor dal* for at least 1 hour in enough water so they are covered by 2 inches.

② Rinse the *masoor dal* in a colander under cold running water and drain.

③ Put the *masoor dal*, mixed vegetables, broth and rolled oats into a soup pot and bring to a boil on medium-high heat.

④ Lower the heat to medium-low and simmer until the vegetables are tender and the broth is reduced to your desired consistency (about 30 to 45 minutes).

⑤ Taste the soup and adjust the seasoning of salt and pepper to your liking.

⑥ Enjoy hot as a hearty snack, or lunch.

Moong Bean Soup

TIME
90 minutes plus
overnight soaking time

YIELD
6–8 servings

*GLUTEN-FREE
& VEGETARIAN*

This is a very nutritious soup that is easy to make. All you need to do, is remember to put your beans to soak before you go to bed the night before you'd like to make it. After soaking, wash the beans, chop the vegetables and then put everything in a pot with the water and forget about it while it simmers away.

1 cup	Moong beans
8 cups	chicken or vegetable broth
½ cup	finely chopped onion (1 small)
1 stalk	finely chopped celery
½ cup	finely chopped carrot
½ cup	chopped tomato (1 small)
¼ cup	finely chopped red bell pepper
¼ cup	finely chopped green bell pepper
½ teaspoon	Garlic Paste (page 42)
Salt, to taste	
¼ teaspoon	freshly ground black pepper, or to taste

① Strain the soaked Moong beans through a colander, change the water several times and use your hands to rub any skins off and remove any dirt or small beans that did not swell.

② Add the beans to a soup pot with the broth, onion, celery, carrot, tomato, bell peppers and Garlic Paste and bring to a boil on medium-high heat.

③ Lower the heat and simmer for about 1 hour.

④ Enjoy seasoned with the salt and pepper to your liking.

Avocado, Mango and Almond Salad

TIME
15 minutes

YIELD
4 servings

*GLUTEN-FREE
& VEGETARIAN*

The sweetness of mango and oranges, the crunchiness of bell peppers, and the smooth and satisfying flavour of avocado make this a favourite during mango season.

For the Salad:

½ cup	slivered almonds
2 cups	mixed salad greens
1	peeled and sliced mango (ripe but firm)
1	red bell pepper, chopped in small sticks (julienned)
1	green bell pepper, chopped in small sticks (julienned)
2	oranges—cut the peel off with a paring knife and then cut between the segment walls to release the flesh
2	ripe avocados
2 teaspoons	lemon juice
½ cup	finely chopped green onions

For the Dressing:

¼ cup	orange juice
1 teaspoon	olive or avocado oil
½ teaspoon	Garlic Paste (page 42)
2 teaspoons	brown sugar or honey
½ teaspoon	ground cumin
¼ teaspoon	freshly ground black pepper, or to taste
½ teaspoon	salt, or to taste

① Preheat the oven to 350°F and toast the almonds on a baking tray for a few minutes—until they are a very light, golden colour. Remove them from the oven and set aside to cool.

② Spread the salad greens on a large shallow bowl or platter and arrange the mangoes, bell peppers, and orange segments over them.

③ Halve the avocados, remove the pits and slice the flesh into lengthwise pieces. Coat the pieces with lemon juice (to prevent browning) and arrange on top of the salad.

④ Sprinkle the green onions on top.

⑤ Put the salad dressing ingredients in a jar, shake well and drizzle over the salad.

⑥ Enjoy garnished with the toasted almonds.

AVOCADO, MANGO
AND ALMOND SALAD,
SEE PAGE 50

Bean Salad with a Spicy Touch

NOORBANU LENDS HER SPICY TOUCH TO THIS CLASSIC SALAD

TIME	YIELD	GLUTEN-FREE
30 minutes	4–5 servings	*& VEGETARIAN*

TIP: You can make this a day ahead and the flavours will be even more pronounced. If you don't have your own Ambli Ni Chutney (page 104) on hand, you can substitute a commercially prepared tamarind sauce.

1	(19 ounce/540 mL) can mixed beans
½ cup	finely chopped red onion
½ cup	finely chopped red bell pepper
½ cup	finely chopped green bell pepper
½ cup	finely chopped yellow bell pepper
½ cup	finely chopped celery
1 teaspoon	Garlic Paste (page 42)
1 teaspoon	Sambal Oelek, or to taste
1 Tablespoon	finely cut coriander leaves
2 teaspoons	olive oil
1 teaspoon	mustard seeds
1 teaspoon	cumin seeds
5 chopped	fresh curry leaves
½ cup	Ambli Ni Chutney (page 104)
3 Tablespoons	fresh lemon or lime juice
¼ teaspoon	salt, or to taste
¼ teaspoon	freshly ground pepper, or to taste

① Empty the can of beans into a colander and rinse under cold running water, then drain well.

② Place the beans, red onion, bell peppers, celery, Garlic Paste, Sambal Oelek and coriander leaves in a salad bowl.

③ Heat the olive oil in a small saucepan, add the mustard seeds, cumin seeds and curry leaves, cover with a lid and listen for when the seeds start to splutter and pop—about 1 minute.

④ Remove from heat and pour over the salad.

⑤ Add the Ambli Ni Chutney and lemon or lime juice and toss.

⑥ Season with salt and pepper, taste and adjust to your liking.

⑦ Enjoy straight away or chill and take to a picnic or outdoor barbecue.

Cabbage Salad with a Kick

TIME	YIELD	*GLUTEN-FREE*
40 minutes	6 servings	*& VEGETARIAN*

This salad is an excellent partner for summer's suppers from the grill.

½	green cabbage, roughly chopped
½	red cabbage, roughly chopped
5	carrots, diced in a food processor
1	red pepper, chopped in small sticks (julienned)
1 bunch	green onions, sliced on diagonal
1½ cups	mayonnaise
½ cup	plain Greek yogurt
½ cup	sweet chilli sauce
1 Tablespoon	sesame oil
¼ cup	rice wine vinegar
1 finely	diced jalapeño, or to taste
¼ cup	finely cut coriander leaves
Salt and pepper, to taste.	

① Place the cabbage, carrots, peppers, and green onions in a large bowl.

② Mix the mayonnaise, yogurt, chilli sauce, sesame oil, vinegar, jalapeño and coriander leaves together and then add the mixture to the vegetables and stir until thoroughly coated.

③ Season the salad with salt and pepper to taste.

④ Enjoy with your favourite grilled food.

Kachumber

TIME
10–15 minutes

YIELD
4 servings as a side
*This recipe
multiplies well.*

*GLUTEN-FREE
& VEGETARIAN*

This simple combination of mixed vegetables is part relish, part *salsa* and part spicy salad.

½ cup	carrots (1 carrot)
½ cup	onion (1 small)
1 cup	tomato (1 medium)
¼	green bell pepper
1½ teaspoon	finely cut coriander leaves
1	finely chopped chilli, red or green, or to taste
1 Tablespoon	vinegar or lemon juice
¼ teaspoon	salt, or to taste

① Cut the carrot, onion, tomato, and bell pepper into quarters and slice thinly. Make sure all the vegetables are cut to the same consistency.

② Put the vegetables in a bowl and add the coriander, chilli, vinegar or lemon juice and toss to mix well.

③ Add the salt, taste the salad and adjust the seasoning to your liking.

④ Enjoy as a side with many dishes and always with *biryani.*

Shaved Fennel and Cumin Salad

TIME	YIELD	*GLUTEN-FREE & VEGETARIAN*
30 minutes	4 servings	

This salad features bright citrus and subtle fennel flavours with a little tropical avocado to give it staying power. We love to pile Jeera Prawns (page 165) on top and serve it for lunch or as a light supper.

2	small fennel bulbs
3	blood oranges (may substitute navel oranges or grapefruit)

For the Dressing:

make 1/2 dressing qty.

1 finely diced	shallot
1 teaspoon	honey
2 Tablespoons	lime juice
¼ cup	mayonnaise
¼ cup	olive oil
1 teaspoon	ground cumin
¼ teaspoon	Indian chilli powder
Salt and pepper, to taste	

For the Presentation:

2	avocados
Juice and zest of 1 lime	
Salt and pepper, to taste	

① Remove the outer layer of the fennel bulb and chop off the tops, reserving the fronds.

② Slice the fennel bulbs as thinly as possible, place them in a large bowl and set aside.

TIP: Use a mandolin if you have one.

③ Remove the top and bottom of the oranges with a paring knife and then slice the peel—including the inner pith—away in strips from the sides of the orange. Cut the orange into horizontal slices.

④ Prepare the dressing by whisking the shallot, honey, lime juice, mayonnaise, olive oil, cumin and chilli powder in a bowl.

⑤ Taste the dressing and season it with salt and pepper to your liking.

⑥ Toss the dressing with the fennel.

⑦ Place the oranges on a platter in a circle and then stack the fennel in the middle of the oranges.

⑧ Halve and slice the avocados and then place them on the fennel.

⑨ Drizzle with the fresh lime juice and sprinkle with the zest.

⑩ Sprinkle with a little more salt and freshly ground pepper.

TIP: Maldon Salt or Fleur de Sel are finishing salts that work beautifully here.

LEFT: **WADA,** RECIPE, PAGE 91
RIGHT: **BHAJIAS,** RECIPE, PAGE 67

CHAPTER 3

Snacks and Starters

Batata Wada

SPICY MASHED POTATO FRITTERS

TIME	YIELD	GLUTEN-FREE
40–50 minutes	10 fritters	& VEGETARIAN

Whoever said not to "fritter away" your time, never tried these spice infused mouthfuls of goodness.

TIP: Use dry, white potatoes and get the spice mix ready while they are boiling.

ALLERGY NOTE: If allergic to legumes, use corn flour instead of chana flour.

1 lb	peeled, boiled and mashed white potatoes (about 3 medium)
4 cups	sunflower oil for frying
1 Tablespoon	sunflower oil
½ teaspoon	cumin seeds
½ teaspoon	mustard seeds
½	finely chopped chilli (preferably Serrano)
2	whole cloves
4–5	fresh curry leaves (optional)
½ cup	frozen peas
1 Tablespoon	water
¼ teaspoon	turmeric, (optional)
½ teaspoon	ground cumin
½ teaspoon	Garlic Paste (page 42)
½ teaspoon	Ginger Paste (page 43)
½ teaspoon	Green Chilli Paste (page 44), or to taste
½ teaspoon	salt, or to taste
1 Tablespoon	lemon juice
¼ cup	finely cut coriander leaves
3 Tablespoons	chana flour
¼ teaspoon	salt, or to taste
Water to make a paste	

① Prepare the potatoes and set aside.

② Heat the 4 cups of the sunflower oil in a wok or deep-fryer set to 350°F.

   TIP: If you don't have a thermometer, it is ready when a drop of water sizzles immediately when splashed in the oil.

③ Heat the 1 Tablespoon of oil in a saucepan at medium heat, add the cumin and mustard seeds, chopped chilli, cloves, and curry leaves and cover and cook until the seeds pop.

④ Stir in the peas, water, turmeric, cumin, garlic, ginger and chilli pastes and salt and cook until the peas are tender, the water is absorbed and the mixture is dry, approximately 10 minutes.

⑤ Remove the cloves and curry leaves.

⑥ Add the pea mixture to the mashed potatoes with the lemon juice and coriander leaves and using your hands, make 10 (golf ball size) fritters and set them aside.

⑦ Prepare a paste for coating the potato fritters by whisking the chana flour and salt with enough water to make a medium consistency paste (like cake batter).

⑧ Dip and roll each fritter (one at a time) into the paste until it is coated and immediately deep-fry until golden brown.

⑨ Place the potato fritters on a paper towel-lined baking tray to drain.

⑩ Enjoy with Ambli Ni Chutney (page 104) or Apple and Mint Chutney (page 105).

Bher

A CRUNCHY CHICKPEA, POTATO AND MANGO SNACK

TIME	YIELD	*VEGETARIAN*
30 minutes	4–6 serving	

Sweet, sour, salty, crunchy and savoury— this is a favourite teatime snack for Noorbanu's family.

TIP: You can find *Sev* at Indian Grocers

ALLERGY NOTE: For legume allergies, substitute corn instead of chickpeas and cassava chips and sunflower seeds instead of *Sev* and roasted peanuts.

2 ½ cups	potato (3 large), boiled, cooled and cut in 1-inch cubes
2 Tablespoons	oil
4-8 chopped	curry leaves
½ teaspoon	mustard seeds
¼ teaspoon	cumin seeds
½ teaspoon	salt, or to taste
1 teaspoon	Green Chilli Paste (page 44)
1 Tablespoon	lemon juice
3 Tablespoons	finely cut coriander leaves, divided
1	(19 ounce/540 mL) can chickpeas
1 cup	thin fried Sev (available at Indian Grocers and in the ethnic foods section at some large supermarkets)
½ cup	potato chips
½ cup	roasted peanuts
1 chopped	fresh raw mango
1 cup	finely chopped onions

① Heat the oil in a saucepan on medium heat, add the curry leaves, mustard seeds, cumin seeds and cook until the seeds pop and splutter.

② Add the salt, chilli paste, lemon juice, and 1 Tablespoon of the coriander leaves with the cubed potatoes and chickpeas and cook stirring for 2 to 3 minutes.

③ Layer the chickpea potato mixture with the *Sev*, crushed chips, peanuts and chopped mango on a platter—or several individual serving plates.

④ Garnish with the finely chopped onion and remaining coriander leaves.

⑤ Enjoy individual servings drizzled with Yogurt (page 46) and Ambli Ni Chutney (page 104).

Bhajia

MIXED VEGETABLES PAKORAS

TIME	YIELD	GLUTEN-FREE & VEGETARIAN
30 minutes	40 tasty little snacks	

These (always gluten-free) treats are easy to make when unexpected guests arrive. This recipe calls for potato, spinach and onion, but Japanese eggplant, bell peppers, or diced zucchini may be added or substituted.

TIPS: Sifting the chana flour will produce a smoother batter. Noorbanu usually cooks these outside when the weather is good so the deep-frying odours don't linger inside her home.

ALLERGY NOTE: For legume allergies, substitute an equal amount of corn flour for the chana flour.

2 cups	chana flour, sifted into a bowl
¾ cup	water
1 Tablespoon	finely cut coriander leaves
¼ teaspoon	turmeric
1 teaspoon	ground cumin
1 teaspoon	Garlic Paste (page 42)
1 teaspoon	Ginger Paste (page 43)
1 teaspoon	Green Chilli Paste (page 44) or Sambal Oelek
1 teaspoon	coarsely ground black pepper
1 teaspoon	salt
½ teaspoon	ajwan (omum) seeds, optional
1	onion, divided in 2 lengthwise and thinly sliced
2	potatoes quartered and thinly sliced
1½ cups	finely chopped spinach
5 whole	hot chillies—jalapeño or Serranos—cut a slit in their sides
¾ teaspoon	baking powder

Oil for deep-frying

① Whisk the chana flour and water to form a thick pancake-like batter.

② Stir in the coriander leaves, turmeric, cumin, garlic, ginger and chilli pastes, black pepper, salt and *ajwan* (if desired) and set aside for a few minutes.

③ Stir in the onion slices, potatoes, spinach and whole hot chillies—adjusting the moisture with a few additional drops of water so the mixture still has the consistency of a thick cake batter.

③ Stir in the baking powder just before you are ready to start frying.

④ Heat the oil in a wok or deep-fryer set to 375°F.

TIP: If you don't have a thermometer, it is ready when a drop of water sizzles immediately when splashed in the oil.

⑤ Add 1 Tablespoon of the hot deep-fryer oil to the *bhajias* batter and mix thoroughly but gently just before frying the mixture by the dropped Tablespoon.

⑥ Fry 8 to 10 bhajias at a time and cook until golden brown. Drain on a paper towel-lined baking tray.

⑦ Enjoy hot with Tomato Chutney (page 115) and Ambli Ni Chutney (page 104).

LEFT SIDE OF PLATE: BHAJIA, SEE PAGE 67
RIGHT SIDE OF PLATE: WADA, SEE PAGE 91

Cassava Oven Fries

TIME	YIELD	GLUTEN-FREE
30 minutes	3–4 serving	& VEGETARIAN

Fried cassava (*mhogo*) is a snack Noorbanu enjoys a lot. When she lived in East Africa it was served everywhere from restaurants to roadside stalls. This healthier baked version receives her classic spicy touch.

1	(1 lb or 400 gram) package frozen cassava
Water for boiling	
1 teaspoon	salt, divided
½ teaspoon	Indian chilli powder
½ teaspoon	citric acid powder
2 teaspoons	oil

① Preheat the oven to 425°F.

② Cut the cassava into 1-inch wide strips, remove any fibrous "strings" and boil in water with the first addition (½ teaspoon) of salt until cooked but still firm. Drain and set aside to cool.

③ Put the cooled cassava in a bowl and toss with the oil, Indian chilli powder, remaining salt and citric acid.

④ Bake in a single layer on an oiled baking sheet in the preheated oven until golden brown—about 25 minutes.

⑤ Enjoy as a snack with Ambli Ni Chutney (page 104), or with other spicy chutneys of your choice.

Chana Bateta

PEAS AND POTATO

TIME	YIELD	GLUTEN-FREE
1 hour	10–12 serving	*& VEGETARIAN*

This recipe is easy and inexpensive to make. It's also vegetarian and packed with nutrition—but it's taste alone that has made it a family favourite for a light lunch or teatime treat.

ALLERGY NOTE: For legume allergies, substitute corn flour for the chana flour and corn niblets for the chickpeas.

1 Tablespoon	oil
1 Tablespoon	chana flour
½ teaspoon	Green Chilli Paste (page 44)
2 Tablespoons	finely cut coriander leaves, divided
2 lbs	potatoes cut in ½ inch cubes (about 6–8 medium)
1 teaspoon	salt
¼ teaspoon	turmeric
2 teaspoons	ground cumin
2 ½ cups	water
1	(19 ounce/540 mL) can chickpeas, rinsed and drained
¾ cup	Ambli Ni Chutney (page 104)
½ cup	chopped raw green mango

① Heat the oil in a saucepan.

② Stir in the chana flour and cook on medium heat until a light golden colour.

③ Stir in the chilli paste and half the coriander leaves and cook for 1 minute.

④ Add the potatoes, salt, turmeric, cumin; cook and stir for 1 minute more.

⑤ Add 2 ½ cups water and simmer covered until the potatoes are cooked—about 10 to 15 minutes.

⑥ Stir in the chickpeas, Ambli Ni Chutney and mango and cook for 5 minutes more adding water as necessary to end up with gravy that is approximately 2 inches above the vegetables.

⑦ Garnish with the rest of the coriander leaves.

⑧ Enjoy topped with Ambli Ni Chutney (page 104) and Chevdo (page 70), Wada (page 91) and/or potato chips.

NOTE: If you prefer thicker gravy, blend some of the mixture in a food processor and return it to the pot.

Chevdo

Your new favourite snack mix

TIME	YIELD	*GLUTEN-FREE*
1 hour	3 pounds	*& VEGETARIAN*

This recipe makes enough of this tasty snack to share with friends and family.

TIPS: *Pawa* are rice flakes available at Indian grocers. Frying the *pawa* and preparing the *vahgar* (whole spices fried in the oil), can create a pungent odour so Noorbanu always waits for a fine weather day when she can open up all the windows and doors to ventilate her kitchen. Rice Crispies can be used instead of *pawa*, though the taste won't be the same.

For the Snack Mix:

Oil for deep-frying

1 ¾ cups	thick pawa (or Rice Crispies)
¼ cup	golden raisins
1 cup	Hickory Sticks
½ cup	fried chana dal (available at Indian grocers)
½ cup	roasted almonds
½ cup	roasted cashews
1 cup	roasted peanuts, small in size, with skins on (Spanish peanuts)
2 teaspoons	Indian chilli powder
1 teaspoon	turmeric
2 teaspoons	salt, or to taste
½ cup	sugar
¼ teaspoon	citric acid powder

For the Vaghar:

2 Tablespoons	sunflower oil
1 ½ teaspoons	mustard seeds
1 teaspoon	coriander seeds
4	whole cloves
14	chopped small curry leaves
1 Tablespoon	sesame seeds
4–5	whole dried chillies
1 Tablespoon	coriander leaves

For the Snack Mix:

① Heat a wok that's half full of oil on medium-high until a drop of water splutters and disappears immediately.

② Puff the *pawa* by adding a handful to a sieve and then lowering it into the oil for a few seconds.

③ Shake the sieve gently to remove any excess oil and then empty the *pawa* into a paper towel-lined colander to drain.

④ Continue frying these small batches until all the *pawa* is puffed.

⑤ Put the *pawa* into a container large enough to hold all the ingredients.

⑥ Put the raisins in a sieve and lower into the oil until they puff up. Drain and add to the *pawa*.

⑦ Add the Hickory Sticks, fried dal, almonds, cashews, and peanuts and gently toss the mixture.

⑧ Make a well in the mixture and add the chilli powder, turmeric, salt, sugar and citric acid and cover the container.

For the Vaghar:

① Heat the oil in a saucepan on medium-high.

② Add the mustard seeds, coriander seeds, cloves, curry leaves, sesame seeds, and dried chillies and cook covered until the seeds start to pop. Leave for a few seconds (ensuring spices do not burn), add the coriander leaves and then quickly pour the mixture into the well you made in the snack mixture.

③ Cover the mixture for 5 minutes then toss to thoroughly coat all the ingredients.

④ Enjoy with your favourite cold drink. It also goes with Chana Bateta (page 69) or Bher (page 65)

Variation:

ALLERGY-FREE CHEVDO: Noorbanu's granddaughter Tahira is allergic to nuts and legumes. She makes a delicious version of this recipe by omitting the chana and nuts and adding extra raisins, *pawa*, Rice Crispies, cassava chips, potato chips and sunflower seeds.

Coconut Prawns

TIME	YIELD
45 minutes	4–6 servings

These have a spicy little bite that you don't expect in a coconut prawns.

1–1½ litres	sunflower oil
1 lb	raw, shelled and deveined large prawns (25 – 30 per pound)
½ teaspoon	salt
2 Tablespoons	all-purpose flour
2 Tablespoons	cornstarch
1	beaten egg
½ teaspoon	salt
½ teaspoon	pepper
½ teaspoon	Indian chilli powder
½ cup	unsweetened dried shredded coconut
½ cup	Panko* bread crumbs

① Pour the sunflower oil into a deep-fryer and set the temperature to 375°F.

② Rinse the prawns, pat them dry with paper towels, then make a slit running along the back side until the flesh spreads like butterfly wings—making sure not to cut the whole way through.

③ Sprinkle the prawns with the salt and let them sit for 30 minutes then pat them dry with paper towel.

④ Combine the flour, cornstarch, egg, salt, pepper and chilli powder in a bowl and whisk in water as needed to make a thick pancake-like batter. Set aside.

⑤ Mix the coconut and *Panko* in another bowl. Set aside.

⑥ Dip each prawn in the batter making sure to open the butterflied section, then move it to the coconut crumb mixture to roll and coat it.

⑦ Lower the prawns (immediately) into the oil and deep-fry until golden brown.

⑧ Enjoy with a sweet-chili sauce, mango chutney or Ambli Ni Chutney (page 104)

* *Panko* are coarse bread crumbs available at Japanese markets, specialty stores and most large grocers.

Dhebra

MILLET PAKORAS

TIME	YIELD	*VEGETARIAN*
30 minutes	10 servings	

These are a nice breakfast treat and a truly unique taste.

Sunflower oil for deep-frying

1 cup	millet flour
¼ cup	whole wheat flour (can substitute chana flour)
2 Tablespoons	oil
1 teaspoon	Garlic Paste (page 42)
1 teaspoon	Ginger Paste (page 43)
½ teaspoon	Green Chilli Paste (page 44), or to taste
½ teaspoon	salt, or to taste
¼ teaspoon	turmeric
1 teaspoon	sesame seeds
1 ½ teaspoons	chopped fenugreek leaves fresh, dried or frozen—optional
1 ½ teaspoons	finely cut coriander leaves
1 Tablespoon	Yogurt (page 46)
Water	

① Heat the oil in a wok to 375 °F.

② Sift the millet and whole wheat flour together; add the oil and mix.

③ Stir in the garlic, ginger and chilli pastes, salt, turmeric, sesame seeds, fenugreek leaves, coriander leaves and yogurt and knead into pliable dough with water.

④ Divide the dough into 10 equal balls and flatten each into thin 2 ½ inch round patties.

⑤ Deep-fry the *pakoras* until golden brown on both sides.

⑥ Enjoy with Yogurt (page 46) and Apple and Coriander Chutney (page 108).

Dhokra

SAVOURY SEMOLINA CAKE

TIME	PLUS	YIELD	*VEGETARIAN*
45 minutes	overnight resting of the batter	2 (9-inch) cake pans	

You need to start this recipe the night before you want to make it. Noorbanu has an old double-decker stainless steel steamer so she can make two of these cakes at one time. If you don't have such a thing, divide the dough into two separate bowls and use half of the baking powder in bowl one as you steam the first cake pan. Then, right before steaming the second batch, add the rest of the baking powder.

2½ cups	semolina (*sooji*)
1¾ cup	Yogurt (page 46)
1¾ cups	water
6 Tablespoons	oil
½ teaspoon	Garlic Paste (page 42)
½ teaspoon	Ginger Paste (page 43)
½ teaspoon	Green Chilli Paste (page 44)
½ teaspoon	Sambal Oelek
1 teaspoon	sugar
1 teaspoon	citric acid powder
1 ½ teaspoons	salt
½ teaspoon	ground cumin
3 Tablespoons	baking powder
1 Tablespoon	finely cut coriander leaves
2 Pinches of	finely crumbled Kasoori Methi (dried fenugreek leaves)
Pinch of	chilli powder

① Combine the semolina, yogurt and water in a large bowl and leave overnight on the counter.

② Stir in the oil, garlic, ginger and chilli pastes, Sambal Oelek, sugar, citric acid, salt and cumin the next day just prior to when you want to steam the cakes.

③ Bring the water in your steamer to a full boil.

④ Add the baking powder to your batter and pour it—evenly divided—into 2 (9-inch round × 2-inch deep) cake pans that have been sprayed with cooking spray.

⑤ Place the cake pans into the steamer and sprinkle chopped corriander leaves, Kasoori Methi, and sprinkle a pinch of chilli powder on the cakes then cover and steam on medium heat for 15 to 20 minutes.

⑥ Remove the lid and cook uncovered another 5 minutes to let the top of the cakes dry out.

⑦ Take the cake pans out of the steamer but leave the cake in the pan to cool.

⑧ Transfer to a serving plate and cut the cake into wedges or diamond shape pieces by first making horizontal cuts at 3-inch intervals across the pan and then turning to make equal distance cuts at a diagonal.

⑨ Enjoy with Dhokra Chutney (page 78).

Dhokri

SAVOURY CURRIED CHANA FLOUR CAKE

TIME	PLUS	YIELD	*VEGETARIAN*
45 minutes	overnight resting of the batter	18 - 24 servings, cut as desired	

There are many versions of these light and fluffy steamed cakes. Some *Dhokri* have a little rice flour. Noorbanu's daughter Khadija likes this recipe with *chana flour* because it delivers such a nice texture. The Dhokri Chutney (page 78) is made to eat with this dish and round out the flavours.

TIP: Check to see that you have the equipment outlined below before you start.

ALLERGY NOTE: For legume allergies, use rice or semolina flour instead of chana flour.

For the Cake:

1 cup plus 2 Tablespoons chana flour

1 Tablespoon	semolina (*sooji*)
¾ cup	Yogurt (page 46)
¾ cup	water
1 teaspoon	citric acid powder
¾ teaspoon	salt
½ teaspoon	Ginger Paste (page 43)
½ teaspoon	Green Chilli Paste (page 44) or Sambal Oelek
4 Tablespoons	sunflower oil (we tried but found olive oil too heavy for this)
2 teaspoons	sugar
½ teaspoon	ground cumin
Dash	turmeric
2 teaspoons	baking powder
½ teaspoon	baking soda

For the Vaghar:

1 Tablespoon	oil
¼ teaspoon	mustard seeds
¼ teaspoon	cumin seeds
4	fresh curry leaves
3	hot chillies—jalapeño or Serranos, slit or cut into pieces
1 Tablespoon	finely cut coriander leaves
1 Tablespoon	unsweetened shredded coconut

For the Cake:

① Sift the chana flour and semolina into a bowl, stir in the yogurt and water and let sit on the counter overnight.

② Grease a (9-inch round × 2-inch deep) cake pan and find a stove-top pan with a lid that the cake pan fits into while sitting in a 1-inch water bath. Bring the water to boil in the pan.

③ Add the citric acid, salt, ginger and chilli paste or Sambal Oelek, sunflower oil, sugar, cumin, turmeric and coriander leaves to the chana flour mixture and stir to form a smooth cake-like batter.

④ Stir in the baking powder and baking soda just before cooking.

⑤ Pour the batter into the cake pan and place into the water bath pan, cover and steam on medium heat for 15 to 20 minutes.

⑥ Remove the pan from the bath, leave the Dhokri in the cake pan and cool.

⑦ Transfer to a plate, cut the cake into diamond shape pieces by first making horizontal cuts at 1½ to 2-inch intervals across the pan and then turning to make equal distance cuts on the diagonal.

For the Vaghar:

① Heat the oil in a small saucepan on medium heat and add the mustard and cumin seeds, the curry leaves and hot chillies.

② Pour this vaghar over the cut squares to infuse with the aroma and flavour.

③ Lift the squares from the pan and arrange on a platter then sprinkle with the fresh coriander leaves and coconut.

④ Enjoy with Dhokri Chutney (page 78).

Dhokra Chutney

TIME	YIELD	GLUTEN-FREE
5 minutes	½ cup	& VEGETARIAN

This easy chutney is the perfect pairing Dhokra—a savoury steamed cake made of semolina (*sooji*). They go together so well in fact, it's hard to imagine one without the other.

4 Tablespoons	canned crushed tomato
¼ teaspoon	garlic
2 Tablespoons	Sambal Oelek
½ teaspoon	salt
¼ teaspoon	ground cumin
¼ teaspoon	Indian chilli powder
1 teaspoon	sunflower oil
¼ teaspoon	sugar

① Stir all of the ingredients together in a bowl until smooth.

② Enjoy with Dhokra (page 75) or Dhokri (page 76).

Dhokri Chutney

TIME	YIELD	GLUTEN-FREE
5 minutes	½ cup	& VEGETARIAN

This chutney is especially for Dhokri.

1 teaspoon	Indian chilli powder
1 teaspoon	paprika
¼ teaspoon	Garlic Paste (Page 42)
½ teaspoon	lemon juice
½ teaspoon	salt
1 Tablespoon	tomato paste
¼ teaspoon	ground cumin
¼ teaspoon	dried parsley
1½ Tablespoons	sunflower oil

① Stir all of the ingredients together in a bowl until smooth.

② Enjoy with Dhokri (page 76).

Khari Puri

DEEP-FRIED SPICED BREAD

TIME	YIELD	*VEGETARIAN*
30 minutes	12 portions	

This is a spicier snack time version of traditional Puri (page 236).

ALLERGY NOTE: For legume allergies, substitute corn flour for the *chana flour*.

Sunflower oil for frying

1 cup	all-purpose flour
1 Tablespoon	chana flour
½ teaspoon	salt
¼ teaspoon	coarsely ground black pepper
¼ teaspoon	ajwan (*omum*)
3 Tablespoons	warm vegetable oil
½ cup	cold water

① Heat the oil to 350°F in a wok or deep-fryer.

② Mix the all-purpose and chana flour, salt, black pepper, *ajwan* and oil and form into pliable dough with just enough cold water as required.

③ Knead the dough on a lightly floured surface for 2 minutes.

④ Divide the dough into 12 equal balls and roll each into a 5-inch circle on a lightly floured surface.

⑤ Make several small slits in each *puri* with a knife.

⑥ Deep-fry on both sides until golden brown and crispy.

⑦ Drain on paper towels.

⑧ Enjoy as a snack.

Masala Spiced Omelette

TIME	YIELD	GLUTEN-FREE
10 minutes	1 servings	& VEGETARIAN

Omelettes are one of the most versatile meals in a cook's repertoire. You can enjoy this one for breakfast, brunch or for a light lunch or supper with a refreshing salad (See Chapter 2).

3	eggs
¼ teaspoon	Garlic Paste (page 42)
½ teaspoon	chopped chillies, jalapeño or Serrano
3 Tablespoons	chopped green or red onions
1 Tablespoon	chopped tomato
⅛ teaspoon	turmeric
½ teaspoon	ground cumin
¼ teaspoon	salt, or to taste
¼ teaspoon	freshly ground black pepper
¼ teaspoon	Indian chilli powder
1 Tablespoon	oil or butter

① Break the eggs into a deep bowl and beat until fluffy.

② Stir in the garlic, chillies, onions, tomato, turmeric, cumin, salt, pepper and chilli powder and mix well.

③ Heat a nonstick frying pan and add the oil or butter. Pour in the egg mixture and cook until golden brown on the bottom.

④ Turn over and cook the other side.

⑤ Enjoy with Rotli (page 268) or Parotha (page 269), toast and the chutney of your choice.

Meat and Potato Patties

TIME
60 minutes

YIELD
20 appetizer portions

Samosa filling is used to stuff these potato patties. Karen thinks they are the quintessential fritter.

2 litres	sunflower oil for deep-frying
1	samosa filling recipe of your choice: Beef (page 95), or Chicken (page 96)
4 lbs	peeled, boiled and mashed potatoes (6–8 medium)
½ teaspoon	salt
½ teaspoon	Green Chilli Paste (page 44)
1 teaspoon	ground cumin
2 cups	bread crumbs
4	eggs

① Prepare the meat mixture and potatoes.

② Combine the mashed potatoes, salt, chilli paste and ground cumin and divide this mixture into 20 even portions.

③ Take a potato portion in the palm of your hand and flatten it to a ½ inch thick circle then place a spoonful of the meat mixture in the centre and gather the potato around it to form a small ball—flatten slightly.

④ Put the bread crumbs in 1 bowl and lightly beat the 4 eggs in another.

⑤ Heat the sunflower oil in a wok (about a third full) to 375°F or until a drop of water disappears immediately upon hitting the hot oil.

⑥ Roll the fritters in the bread crumbs, coat in the beaten eggs and then gently slide them directly into the wok of oil.

⑦ Deep-fry the fritters a few at a time.

⑧ Remove them with a slotted spoon to a paper towel-lined baking tray when they are golden brown.

⑨ Enjoy as a special appetizer or with a green salad for lunch.

Ondhvo

A QUICK AND SAVOURY
VEGETABLE CAKE

TIME	YIELD	*VEGETARIAN*
90 minutes	8 servings	

When we came to this recipe in our review of the ones that would make the book, Noorbanu smiled and said—*Oh, this is very tasty and we must include it.* High praise indeed. Besides, this way you can have your cake and eat your vegetables too.

For the Cake:

2 cups	semolina (*sooji*)
¾ cup	gram flour
1 ¼ cups	Yogurt (page 46)
1 ¼ cups	water
1 ¼ cups	sunflower oil, divided
1 Tablespoon	sugar
1 ¼ teaspoon	citric acid or lemon juice
1 ¼	salt
1 teaspoon	ground cumin
¼ teaspoon	turmeric
1 teaspoon	Garlic Paste (page 42)
1 teaspoon	Ginger Paste (page 43)
1 teaspoon	Green Chilli Paste (paste 44)
1 ¼ cup	frozen peas and carrots
2 cups	finely shredded cabbage (½ lb approximately)
¾ cup	chopped green onion
2 teaspoons	sesame seeds
2 teaspoons	mustard seeds
1 Tablespoon	finely cut fresh curry leaves
1 ¼ teaspoons	baking powder

For the Topping:

1 Tablespoon	finely sliced jalapeño (halved and seeds removed)
1 teaspoon	sesame seeds
1 teaspoon	mustard seeds
12 -15	whole fresh curry leaves

For the Cake:

① Preheat the oven to 350°F.

② Mix the semolina, gram flour, yogurt, water and the first addition (¾ cup) of the oil in a large bowl.

③ Stir in the sugar, citric acid, salt, cumin, turmeric, garlic, ginger and chilli pastes.

④ Stir in the mixed vegetables, cabbage and green onion and set aside.

⑤ Heat the remaining ½ cup of oil in a small saucepan on medium heat, add the sesame seeds, mustard seeds and cut curry leaves and cook until the seeds pop and splutter—about 30 seconds.

⑥ Let this cool slightly and then stir it into the vegetable mixture.

⑦ Stir in the baking powder.

⑧ Pour the mixture into a 9-inch round cake pan that's been coated with cooking spray.

For the Topping:

① Decorate with the topping of jalapeño slices, mustard and sesame seeds and curry leaves.

② Bake at 350°F for about 60 minutes or until golden and a wooden toothpick comes out clean when inserted in the centre.

③ Enjoy with Ambli Ni Chutney (page 104) or Vegetable Sambhar (page 114).

Paapdi Chaat

A CRUNCHY CHICKPEA AND POTATO SNACK

TIME	YIELD	*VEGETARIAN*
30 minutes	4–6 servings	

Chaat is a word used across India and Pakistan to refer to small servings of savoury snacks, typically served roadside from small carts or stalls. The ingredients for *Paapdi Chaat* are very popular on Indian buffets in Calgary but it wasn't until Karen saw Noorbanu combine these ingredients in this way that she realized why the chickpea and potato mixture was always displayed beside the bowls of *paapdi* and certain chutneys. The dish was lost without the translation a mentor provides until that point, but has been correctly combined and devoured ever since.

ALLERGY NOTE: For legume allergies, substitute corn niblets for the chickpeas. For nut allergies, substitute sunflower seeds for the peanuts.

1 lb	potatoes, cut into half-inch cubes, boiled, drained and cooled
1	(19 ounce/540mL) can of chickpeas, rinsed and drained
1 teaspoon	ground cumin
½ teaspoon	Indian chilli powder
½ teaspoon	salt
1½ cups	paapdi—fried tortillas pieces (recipe follows)
½ cup	sev (available at Indian Grocers and in the ethnic foods section at some large supermarkets)
¼ cup	chopped green onion
2 Tablespoons	finely cut coriander leaves
¼ cup	cashews or peanuts, roasted

① Place the potatoes in one bowl and chickpeas in another.

② Mix the ground cumin, Indian chilli powder, and salt and sprinkle half over the cooked potatoes and half over the chickpeas.

③ Layer in a serving bowl—the chickpeas first, followed by potatoes and then the broken tortillas. Top with *sev*.

④ Sprinkle with the green onions, coriander leaves and nuts.

⑤ Enjoy by placing a scoop of the *chaat* on a plate and drizzling the top with a combination of Apple and Mint Chutney (page 105), Ambli Ni Chutney (page 104), Yogurt (page 46) and hot sauce of your choice.

VARIATION: Moong beans, soaked overnight and cooked, can be used instead of chickpeas.

Paapdi

FRIED TORTILLA PIECES

TIME	YIELD	
30 minutes	1 lb	*VEGETARIAN*

Once fried, this snack is called *Paapdi* and is the key ingredient in *Paapdi Chaat*. Although not typically East Indian, tortillas are a readily available and delicious substitute for the samosa pastry commonly used for *paapdi* in India. The salt mixture imparts a sweet and sour taste.

Sunflower oil for frying

1 lb	package tortillas
1 teaspoon	salt
1 teaspoon	Indian chilli powder
½ teaspoon	citric acid powder
¼ cup	sugar

① Heat the oil in a wok or deep-fryer to 375°F.

② Cut the tortillas into 2-inch by 1-inch strips.

③ Mix the salt, chilli powder, citric acid powder and sugar in a small bowl.

④ Fry small batches of tortillas in oil in a wok on medium heat until golden brown and crisp.

⑤ Transfer to a paper towel-lined tray to drain and then sprinkle with salt mixture, to taste.

⑥ Store in an airtight container.

⑦ Enjoy as part of the *Paapdi Chaat* recipe on the previous page or on their own as a delicious alternative to potato chips.

Reshmi Bhajia

SPICY PANCAKE FRITTERS

TIME	YIELD	
30 minutes	8 servings	*GLUTEN-FREE & VEGETARIAN*

Fritters are always worth the effort.

1½ cups	chana flour
1 cup	water (approximately)
3 Tablespoons	chopped onion
3 Tablespoons	grated potato
1½ Tablespoons	finely cut coriander leaves
1½ Tablespoons	finely cut fresh fenugreek leaves (substitute spinach if unavailable)
½ teaspoon	freshly ground black pepper
1½ teaspoon	salt
1 teaspoon	Garlic Paste (page 42)
1 teaspoon	Ginger Paste (page 43)
½ teaspoon	Green Chilli Paste (page 44), or to taste
¼ teaspoon	turmeric
1 teaspoon	ground cumin
1 beaten	egg
1 Tablespoon	warm sunflower oil
Additional sunflower oil for frying	

① Sift the *chana flour* into a bowl and stir in the water to form a cake-like batter.

② Add the onions, grated potatoes, coriander leaves, fenugreek leaves, black pepper, salt, garlic, ginger and chilli pastes, turmeric, cumin, egg and warm oil to the batter and mix well.

TIP: You want the batter to pour easily so add a little more water if necessary.

③ Heat 1 Tablespoon of sunflower oil in a frying pan on medium-high heat and pour a ½ cup of the batter on 1 side of the pan and with a spoon quickly spread the mixture evenly to form a 5 inch circle. Depending on the size of your frying pan, you may fry 2 or 3 portions at once.

④ Fry the pancakes until golden brown on each side, adding more oil as needed.

⑤ Place them on a paper towel-lined baking tray to remove any excess oil.

⑥ Serve hot with Coriander Chutney (page 108), Coconut Chutney (page 107) or Ambli Ni Chutney (page 104).

Siro

A SWEET APPETIZER

TIME	YIELD	*VEGETARIAN*
60 minutes	10–12 servings	

Noorbanu's granddaughter Tahira enjoys this warm soothing snack to get rid of a chill after being outside in our long Canadian winters.

TIP: Be sure to use a saucepan that you can cover with a lid and place in the oven when you make this dish.

ALLERGY NOTE: For nut allergies see the variation below.

2 ½ cups	whole milk (3.5%)
¾ cup	sugar
⅛ teaspoon	yellow food colour powder or saffron threads
¾ cup	butter
1 cup	semolina (*sooji*)
½ cup	boiling water
¼ teaspoon	saffron
¼ teaspoon	nutmeg, grated
½ teaspoon	ground green cardamom seeds (about 8 pods)
½ cup	evaporated milk
1 teaspoon	finely slivered almonds
1 teaspoon	finely slivered pistachios
½ teaspoon	white poppy seeds

① Preheat the oven to 250°F.

② Put the milk, sugar and food colouring in a medium saucepan and bring to a boil on medium-high heat.

③ Melt the butter on medium heat in another saucepan and add the semolina—cooking and stirring until golden brown.

④ Remove the semolina mixture from the heat and slowly add the boiling water stirring until thick and smooth.

⑤ Return this mixture to medium heat and slowly add the milk mixture, stirring well.

⑥ Lower the heat to minimum and add the saffron, nutmeg and cardamom.

⑦ Cook until almost dry and then add the ½ cup of evaporated milk, cover the saucepan with a lid and bake at 250°F for 20 minutes.

⑧ Remove the mixture from the pan to a plate.

⑨ Decorate with the almonds, pistachios and white poppy seeds.

⑩ Enjoy hot with pappadums or Bhajias (page 67).

SIRO WITH GOLDEN RAISINS (NUT ALLERGY VARIATION): Noorbanu cooks golden raisins in butter until they are plump and adds them as a topping instead of the nuts for her granddaughter who is allergic to nuts.

Superchatako

FINGER-LICKING SPICY FRIES

TIME	YIELD	GLUTEN-FREE
30 minutes	4–6 servings	& VEGETARIAN

Besides being fun to say, this word translates to finger-licking and that is exactly how good this dish tastes.

TIP: Canned *patra* is sliced taro root. It is available at Indian grocers or in the international aisle at large supermarket chains.

¾ lb	frozen French fries
1	(14 ounce/398 mL) can patra, halved vertically and sliced

For the Topping:

½ Tablespoon	sunflower oil
½ teaspoon	mustard seeds
5 fresh curry	leaves (*Limdho*)
½ teaspoon	cumin seeds
Dash	ajwan (*omum*)
¼ teaspoon	turmeric
1 teaspoon	ground cumin
½ teaspoon	Indian chilli powder
2 teaspoons	salt
1 Tablespoon	lemon juice
1 Tablespoon	finely cut coriander leaves

① Preheat the oven to 400°F.

② Bake the French fries on a baking tray for 20 minutes.

③ Slice the *patra* and prepare the topping in the last 5 minutes of baking time.

④ Heat the sunflower oil in a large saucepan on medium heat and add the mustard seeds, curry leaves, cumin seeds and *ajwan* and cook covered until the seeds pop and splutter—about 1 minute.

⑤ Add the fries.

⑥ Stir in the turmeric, ground cumin, chilli powder, sugar, salt and lemon juice.

⑦ Add the *patra*, toss to coat and simmer on low until the *patra* are heated through.

⑧ Transfer to a platter and top with the coriander leaves.

⑨ Enjoy with Yogurt (page 46) and Ambli Ni Chutney (page 104).

Super Tasty Vegetable Kebabs

TIME	YIELD	GLUTEN-FREE
30 minutes	22 kebabs	& VEGETARIAN

The name of this recipe says it all.

1½ cups	cooked rice
1 cup	peeled and cubed potatoes
1 cup	frozen peas, thawed
1 cup	cauliflower florets
½ cup	frozen spinach, thawed and chopped
¼ cup	chopped green onion
½ cup	sifted chana flour
½ teaspoon	salt
¼ teaspoon	turmeric
½ teaspoon	ground cumin
½ teaspoon	Garlic Paste (page 42)
½ teaspoon	Ginger Paste (page 43)
1½ teaspoon	Green Chilli Paste (page 44)
2 Tablespoons	finely cut coriander leaves
2 Tablespoons	finely cut fresh mint leaves (optional)
Sunflower oil for frying	

① Put the rice in the bowl of a food processor and process for 4 pulses.

② Add the potatoes, peas, cauliflower and spinach and process for 1 minute or until everything is finely chopped.

③ Transfer the mixture to a large bowl and add the chopped onion, *chana flour*, salt, turmeric, ground cumin, garlic, ginger and chilli pastes, coriander leaves and mint (if using).

④ Combine the ingredients by hand until thoroughly mixed.

⑤ Take about 1 Tablespoon of the mixture and shape it into a ball and place on a baking tray. Repeat—the mixture should make about 22 kebabs.

⑥ Heat the sunflower oil into a wok or deep-fryer to 375°F.

⑦ Put a few balls at a time into the oil being careful not to overcrowd them or turn them until they've had a chance to set and cook slightly.

⑧ Fry until they are golden brown and cooked through.

⑨ Remove with a slotted spoon and drain on a paper towel-lined baking sheet.

TIP: If you are using a deep-fryer, then perhaps 10 to 15 kebabs can be fried together, depending on the size of the fryer.

⑩ Enjoy hot with your choice of chutney, as *hors d'oeuvres*, or as a snack.

Wada

BLACK-EYED BEAN DUMPLINGS

TIME	PLUS	YIELD	*GLUTEN-FREE & VEGETARIAN*
60 minutes	soaking overnight time for the beans	24 dumplings	

Remember to put the beans to soak overnight and the recipe will come together quickly the next day. Whole black-eyed beans can be used in this recipe but the split version make it easier to remove the husk.

1½ cups	split black-eyed beans, soaked overnight
1 small	boiled potato
1 small	onion, chopped in chunks
½ teaspoon	ground cumin
½ teaspoon	Garlic Paste (page 42)
½ teaspoon	Ginger Paste (page 43)
½ teaspoon	Green Chilli Paste (page 44)
½ teaspoon	salt
1 Tablespoon	finely cut coriander leaves
Sunflower oil for deep-frying	

① Rinse the beans and remove the husks by rubbing them between your hands and washing them in several changes of water. Drain.

② Place the beans, potato and onion in the bowl of a food processor and pulse to make a thick smooth mixture (add a little bit of water if necessary) then transfer to a mixing bowl.

③ Stir in the cumin, ginger, garlic and chilli pastes, salt and coriander leaves and mix until well blended (the dough should be quite stiff).

④ Heat the oil in a wok or deep-fryer to 375°F.

⑤ Coat a soup spoon with the hot oil then using the same spoon take a spoonful of the mixture and slide it carefully into the cooking oil. Repeat and cook a few at a time. Alternatively, you can make 24 golf ball-sized balls and flatten them into patties before slipping them into the deep-fryer.

⑥ Fry until golden brown on both sides.

⑦ Enjoy as a light lunch or snack with Coconut Chutney (page 107) and Ambli Ni Chutney (page 104).

VARIATION: Use half black-eyed beans and half split *moong dal*.

CHAPTER 4

Samosas

Samosas are an all-time favourite Indian snack and Noorbanu's recipe is famous for its taste and texture. Each bite starts with an assertive crunch—derived from the inventive use of spring roll wrappers instead of traditional samosa dough—and finishes with the well-balanced spicing that is the trademark of a great Indian cook.

Samosas

BEEF, CHICKEN OR VEGETABLE

TIME	PLUS	YIELD
a few hours	thawing time for the wrappers	36 samosas

To help you learn the intricacies of samosa wrapping we've included step-by-step photos.

TIPS:

- Stock up on spring roll wrappers and keep them in your freezer to pull out and thaw in the fridge overnight when you want to make a batch.

- Make your meat filling a day ahead—you'll be glad you broke up the work involved in this recipe.

- Use a very sharp knife to finely cut the onions. Avoid any blunt chopping strokes that press on the onion and cause them to release their water.

- Keep all of the pastry—after cutting and separating it—covered in between damp kitchen cloths. Otherwise, it will dry out too quickly to work with.

- Gather a friend to help.

- Reward yourselves by frying up a few of these delectable treats before you tuck the batch into the freezer for future use.

- Always fry from frozen; don't thaw first.

To Make the Beef Filling:

2¼ lbs	lean ground beef
4 Tablespoons	water
1 teaspoon	salt
1 teaspoon	Garlic Paste (page 42)
1 teaspoon	Ginger Paste (page 43)
1 teaspoon	Green Chilli Paste (page 44) or Sambal Oelek
2 Tablespoons	lemon juice
½ teaspoon	turmeric
1 teaspoon	ground cumin
1 teaspoon	Indian chilli powder
2 cups	finely cut yellow onion
1 cup	finely cut green onion (cut in ½ lengthwise first)
½ cup	finely cut coriander leaves
1 teaspoon	Garam Masala (page 29)
Salt to taste	
1 (or more)	seeded and finely cut jalapeño (optional)

① Put the ground beef in a colander and remove any visible blood from the exterior of the meat by rinsing it briefly under cold running water. (Removing visible blood helps achieve a fine crumbled texture and a more enjoyable samosa filling.)

② Heat a large wok on medium heat and add the ground beef with the 4 Tablespoons of water.

③ Stir continuously, breaking up the meat, until evenly browned and finely crumbled.

④ Drain the meat (if any oil accumulates) and return to the pan with the salt, ginger, garlic and chilli pastes, lemon juice, turmeric, cumin, and Indian chilli powder. Stir until the meat is coated and dry.

TIP: It is very important to get the meat dry, as any moisture will make the wrappers too soggy to work with.

⑤ Cool the mixture completely and add the yellow and green onions, coriander leaves and Garam Masala.

TIP: It is important to wait until the meat mix is cool so that it does not pull the water out of the onion and coriander.

⑥ Adjust the salt and, if desired, add the optional jalapeño. Keep in mind that the pastry wrappers tone down the overall spiciness of the meat mixture.

To Make the Chicken Filling:

1 Tablespoon	olive oil
2 teaspoons	Garlic Paste (page 42)
2 teaspoons	Ginger Paste (page 43)
2 teaspoons	Green Chilli Paste (page 44), or to taste
2 teaspoons	ground cumin
1 teaspoon	turmeric
1 teaspoon	Indian chilli powder
1½ teaspoons	salt or to taste
2 Tablespoons	lemon juice
2¼ lbs	finely chopped cooked chicken (about 5 cups)
2 teaspoons	Garam Masala (page 29)
2	finely chopped jalapeños
2 cups	finely cut green onion
1 cup	finely cut yellow onion
2 Tablespoons	finely cut fresh coriander leaves

① Heat the olive oil in a large fry pan and add the garlic, ginger, and chilli pastes, ground cumin, turmeric, Indian chilli powder, salt, and lemon juice and cook for 1 to 2 minutes.

② Stir in the chicken and mix thoroughly.

③ Remove the pan from heat, add the Garam Masala and spread the mixture on a baking tray to cool.

④ When this chicken mixture has cooled, add the jalapeños, green and yellow onions and coriander leaves, mix and set aside.

To Make the Vegetable Filling:

1 Tablespoon	sunflower oil
¼ teaspoon	ajwan (*omum*)
½ teaspoon	mustard seeds
4	cloves
3 – 4	chopped fresh curry leaves
2 ½ cups	diced potatoes (or frozen hash browns)
1 ¼ cups	frozen mixed vegetables
⅔ cup	frozen corn
1 teaspoon	salt
½ teaspoon	Garlic Paste (page 42)
½ teaspoon	Ginger Paste (page 43)
½ teaspoon	Green Chilli Paste (page 44) or Sambal Oelek to taste
1 teaspoon	ground cumin
¼ teaspoon	turmeric
1 cup	finely chopped yellow onion
2 Tablespoons	lemon juice
2 Tablespoons	finely cut coriander leaves
½ teaspoon	Garam Masala (page 29)
2 finely	chopped jalapeños (optional)

① Heat the oil in a wok on medium heat, add the *ajwan*, mustard seeds, cloves, and curry leaves and cook covered until the mustard seeds start popping—about 1 minute.

② Stir in the *ajwan* followed by the potatoes, mixed vegetables, corn, salt, garlic, ginger and chilli pastes, cumin, and turmeric.

③ Cook covered at low heat until the vegetables are tender.

④ Stir in the onion and lemon juice and cook until completely dry.

⑤ Remove from heat and set aside to cool.

⑥ Add the coriander leaves, Garam Masala and jalapeños (if using), discard the cloves and set aside.

For the Paste and Pastry:

2 Tablespoons	all-purpose flour
3 Tablespoons	water
1	package (30 sheets, 10 × 10-inch) frozen spring roll wrappers

TIP: We like the TYJ Spring Roll Wrappers™ that are available at many Asian grocers.

Make a paste by combining the flour and water in a small bowl and stirring briskly until it becomes smooth, thick and glue-like.

Samosa Folding Instructions

CUT AND FOLD AS PER PHOTOS AND INSTRUCTIONS

START HERE

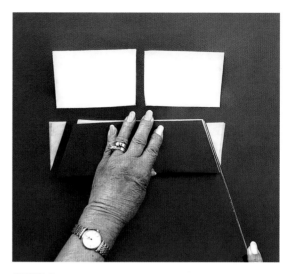

STEP 2

Separate 18 pieces and cut them in half to yield 36 short pieces. Put all of the long pieces into 1 pile and cut the ends at a steep angle.

STEP 1

Thaw the pastry in the refrigerator overnight or at room temperature for a few hours (never in a microwave).

Cut into 3 equal pieces.

TIP: You can download a Samosa cutting template (like the one above) from **aspicytouch.ca**

STEP 3

Pull all of the long and short pieces apart carefully and then collate the long ones in groups of 2.

Store the wrappers in 2 separate damp kitchen cloths. Otherwise, they become too dry to work with.

STEP 4

Place 1 short piece in the centre of 1 set of 2 long pieces (top), then fold the top right end down until it forms a diamond shape on the wrapper underneath as shown.

TIP: The short piece adds strength without adding bulk to the folds.

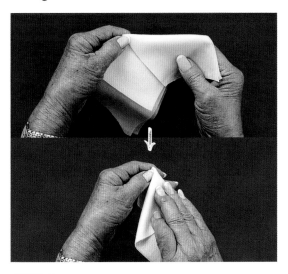

STEP 5

Pinch the top of the diamond shape to hold it in place while picking up the rest of the diamond—as a unit. Fold it up, to the left and onto the wrapper lying underneath.

STEP 6

Pick the folded conical wrapper up in your non-dominant hand. Hold the back of the pocket against your palm. Use your thumb in front to hold the flaps open.

TIP: At this point, you should look inside the cone to make sure the corner fold was tight and there is no hole in the bottom. If you can see through, you'll need to refold it until it is tight. This is important because it will prevent leakage of filling during the frying process.

Fill the pocket with about 2 Tablespoons of the filling mixture of your choice.

STEP 7

Apply paste to the lower inner flap.

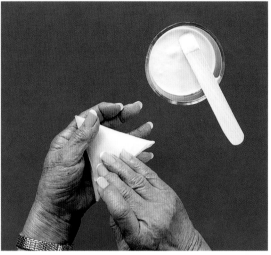

STEP 9

Pull both the outer flaps onto the body of the samosa triangle—making sure the last corner is also tightly closed.

STEP 8

Pull the lower inner flap down snugly onto the samosa, making sure the corner it creates is also tightly closed and then apply paste to the remaining outer flap.

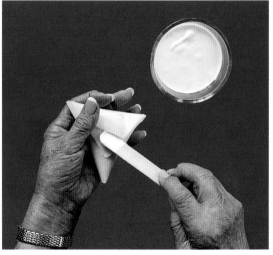

STEP 10

Separate the 2 outer flaps and apply more paste between them.

Pull the last flap down tightly. You should have a full, but not bulging triangle with 3 tightly sealed corners.

TIP: Stack the filled samosas in rows on a baking tray—they don't need to be covered at this point. If not eating immediately, pack them into plastic containers (so they won't get crushed in your freezer) with wax paper between the layers. They freeze well for up to 2 months but ours usually get eaten long before that. When you are ready to eat them deep-fry directly from frozen (do not thaw them first).

For Deep-Frying the Samosas:

Sunflower oil for frying

Heat the oil in a wok or deep-fryer to 375°F and deep-fry about 10 samosas at a time until golden brown—turning as they fry. Drain on a paper towel-lined baking tray.

Enjoy as a snack or starter with your favourite chutneys. We like Ambli Ni Chutney (page 104), Coriander Chutney (page 108), hot sauce or a squeeze of fresh lemon.

Chutneys and such

Ambli Ni Chutney

TAMARIND CHUTNEY

TIME	YIELD	
1 hour	6 cups	*GLUTEN-FREE & VEGETARIAN*

We eat this chutney with all our favourite snacks—Paapdi Chaat (page 85), Samosas (Chapter 4), and/or Bhajia (page 67). Noorbanu's granddaughter says it's the Indian equivalent of ketchup.

TIP: We also find this chutney indispensible as an ingredient to add depth of flavour—a sweet and sour element—to many savoury dishes. Though 6 cups might seem like a lot, you can freeze it in 1 cup containers for up to a year. Thaw it as you need it. It will last fresh in the refrigerator for up to 2 weeks.

1 (14 ounce)	block tamarind pulp
6 cups	water (to start plus a bit more as needed)
½ cup	sugar (use jaggery or demerara sugar)
2 Tablespoons	white vinegar
1 teaspoon	Indian chilli powder, or to taste
1 teaspoon	salt

① Place the tamarind pulp and water in a saucepan on medium heat and simmer for 30 minutes breaking the block up with a wooden spoon. Alternatively, you can soak the tamarind in hot water overnight.

② Let the mixture cool, then mash the pulp with a potato masher and strain it through a sieve to remove the tamarind fibres and pods.

③ Put the fibres and pods back into the original saucepan, add a bit more hot water, mix thoroughly and press through the sieve again.

④ Pour the strained liquid back into the saucepan, add the sugar, boil on high heat until it is fully dissolved in the mixture and then continue boiling for a few minutes.

⑤ Stir in the vinegar, chilli and salt, let cool and then pour into storage containers.

⑥ Enjoy with your favourite snacks or store for future use as noted above.

Apple and Mint Chutney

TIME	YIELD	*GLUTEN-FREE & VEGETARIAN*
10 minutes	1 cup	

We love to make this bright fresh chutney for cooking classes. People are always delightfully surprised at how fast and easy it is to make.

1 or 2	whole chillies, jalapeño or Serrano
½ teaspoon	salt
1	peeled, cored and chopped tart apple (Granny Smith apples work well)
1 Tablespoon	lemon juice
½ cup	fresh mint leaves
2 cups	fresh coriander leaves
1 teaspoon	sugar
1 teaspoon	sunflower oil

① Place all the ingredients in the bowl of a mini-chopper or food processor and process to a fine paste.

② Enjoy with samosas or any grilled meat.

Variation:

APPLE MINT AND YOGURT CHUTNEY:
Mix 1 to 2 teaspoons of this chutney with a cup of yogurt to make a milder, creamy green chutney.

TIP: Without the yogurt, this chutney will last for 10 to 12 days in the refrigerator and can be frozen for up to a year.

Carrot Pickle

TIME	YIELD	
75–90 minutes including marinating time	1–1 ½ cups	*GLUTEN-FREE & VEGETARIAN*

Ease of preparation combined with delicious results make the bit of chopping in this recipe worth it.

TIP: You can find coarsely ground mustard seeds at Indian Grocers.

1 cup	carrots (2 medium)
4 fresh	chillies, jalapeño or Serrano
½ cup	red or green bell pepper (½ a large)
½ teaspoon	salt
¼ - ½ teaspoon	Indian chilli powder
¼ teaspoon	turmeric
1 teaspoon	coarsely ground mustard seeds
2 Tablespoons	white vinegar

① Peel the carrots and cut them into thin 2-inch long (match stick) strips.

TIP: A mandolin slicer with a julienne setting is a great time saver for this job.

② Cut the chillies and bell pepper into similar strips.

③ Combine the carrots, chillies and peppers in a large bowl, stir in the salt, chilli powder, turmeric, mustard seeds and vinegar and let stand for 1 hour.

④ Enjoy with any curry dish, *biryani*, *pilau* or Parotha (page 269).

Variation:

CARROT TOMATO CORIANDER PICKLE
Delete the mustard and white vinegar and add—instead—2 teaspoons of tomato paste, 1-2 Tablespoons olive oil, ¼ teaspoon citric acid powder and 1 Tablespoon of finely chopped coriander leaves. Enjoy as above.

Coconut Chutney

TIME	YIELD	
20 minutes	2 cups	*GLUTEN-FREE & VEGETARIAN*

In South India's beautiful state of Kerala—which translates to "land of coconuts"—you eat a little bit of this chutney with the traditional breakfast of *sambhar* (lentil soup) and *idli* (steamed rice breads), as part of a thali (traditional Ayurvedic lunch) and with grilled fish for dinner. We've both had the pleasure of enjoying a day filled with coconut and fresh fish in "the backwaters" of this place known as God's own country. A little taste of this chutney takes us right back there.

1 cup	coconut milk
1 cup	fine, desiccated unsweetened coconut
1 teaspoon	sugar
½ teaspoon	salt
½ cup	fresh coriander leaves
1 Serrano	chilli
1 Tablespoon	lemon juice

① Heat the coconut milk in a saucepan on medium heat until warm, remove it from heat and add the coconut, sugar and salt. Let stand for 15 minutes.

② Put the coriander leaves, chilli and lemon juice in a mini chopper/electric grinder and process to a smooth paste.

③ Add the coconut mixture and blend for another 2 minutes.

④ Enjoy with Boti Kabab (page 176), Cassava Oven Fries (page 68) or fresh fish.

TIP: This chutney will last for 10 to 12 days in the refrigerator and can be frozen for up to 3 months.

Variation:

CORIANDER AND COCONUT CHUTNEY
Add 1 Tablespoon of Coriander Chutney (Page 108) to this recipe for a little extra colour and zip.

Cucumber Raita

TIME	YIELD	
15–20 minutes	2 cups	*GLUTEN-FREE & VEGETARIAN*

TIP: This raita will keep in the refrigerator for 8 to 10 days and makes a great vegetable dip.

1 cup	peeled and grated Long English cucumber
Salt, to taste	
1 cup	Yogurt (page 46)
¼ teaspoon	ground cumin
¼ teaspoon	freshly ground black pepper
½ teaspoon	chopped chilli, jalapeño or Serrano, or to taste
1 Tablespoon	finely cut fresh mint leaves
1 Tablespoon	finely cut coriander leaves

① Squeeze any water from the cucumber after grating it and place it in a bowl.

② Stir in the yogurt, cumin, pepper, chilli, mint and mix well.

③ Garnish with the coriander leaves.

④ Enjoy with Parotha (page 269), Rotli (page 268) or spicy grilled meats.

Variation:

FRESH VEGETABLE RAITA
Substitute cauliflower, celery, carrots, broccoli, onion or radish for the cucumber and follow the recipe above.

Coriander Chutney

TIME	YIELD	
5 minutes	¾ cup	*GLUTEN-FREE & VEGETARIAN*

Bright is the flavour of this favourite chutney. Use the highly edible stems of your coriander along with the leaves.

1 bunch	washed and sorted coriander leaves with bottom tips cut off
1 – 2	roughly chopped jalapeño or Serrano chillies
Salt, to taste	
2 teaspoons	lemon juice

① Place all the ingredients in the bowl of a mini chopper or food processor and process to a smooth paste.

② Store in the refrigerator.

③ Enjoy with samosas, snacks and barbecued foods.

Variation:

MINT CHUTNEY
Substitute ½ the bunch of coriander with ½ a bunch of mint leaves.

Eggplant Raita

TIME	YIELD	GLUTEN-FREE
60 minutes	3 ½ cups	& VEGETARIAN

Raita is like the Indian equivalent of salsa. They are best made and served fresh.

1 large	eggplant
1–2 teaspoons	olive oil
2 Tablespoons	chopped green onion
½ teaspoon	Green Chilli Paste (page 44)
½ teaspoon	ground cumin
1 Tablespoon	finely chopped fresh tomato
¼ teaspoon	salt, or to taste
2 cups	Yogurt (page 46)

① Preheat the oven to 350°F.

② Brush the eggplant with olive oil and bake on a parchment paper lined baking tray for 45 to 50 minutes.

③ Remove the eggplant from the oven and cool it by placing it in a bowl of iced tap water.

④ Cut the eggplant in ½ lengthwise, use a spoon to scrape the seeds away and then scrape the flesh into a bowl and mash with a fork.

⑤ Stir in the onion, chilli paste, cumin, tomato, salt and yogurt.

⑥ Enjoy with Rotli (page 268).

Instant Tomato Chutneys

TIME	YIELD	GLUTEN-FREE
15 minutes	¾ cup	& VEGETARIAN

Why eat plain ketchup when you can add *A Spicy Touch*?

½ cup	ketchup and 2 Tablespoons water

Or

1 cup	blended fresh tomato (1 medium)

Plus

2 Tablespoons	lemon juice
½ teaspoon	Indian chilli powder, or to taste
¼ teaspoon	salt

Or

½ cup	ketchup
1–2	Tablespoons Sriracha hot sauce
¼ teaspoon	salt

① Whisk all the ingredients into a smooth paste in a bowl.

② Enjoy with Cassava Oven Fries (page 68) or a Masala Spiced Omelette (page 80).

Cucumber Raita

Lime Pickle

Carrot Pickle

Tomato Chutney

Apple Mint

Ambli Ni Chutney

Lemon Chutney

Vegetable Sambhar

Coriander Chutney

Marcha No Sambhar

Coconut Chutney

Sweet Dried Fruit Pickle

Lemon Chutney

TIME	PLUS	YIELD	GLUTEN-FREE
20–35 minutes	2 to 3 days standing time	2 lbs	& VEGETARIAN

In an everything-old-is-new-again way, fermented pickles like this are being rediscovered by a whole new generation. This is an easy one to make.

1 lb	lemons
1½ teaspoons	turmeric
1½ teaspoons	salt
3 cups	sugar
1 teaspoon	Indian chilli powder, or to taste

① Quarter each lemon, remove the seeds and slice each quarter into thin slices, OR chop in a food processor.

② Sprinkle the lemon slices with turmeric and salt and set aside—at room temperature—for 2 to 3 days in a covered glass or stainless steel bowl.

③ Place the lemon mixture in a saucepan on medium-high heat, add the sugar and bring to a boil.

④ Boil the mixture until the juices and sugar thicken to syrup consistency.

TIP: To be sure it's done, insert a candy thermometer and wait until the temperture reaches 170° F.

⑤ Add the chilli powder and remove the mixture from the heat.

⑥ Let cool and then transfer and store in clean glass jars. Keep refrigerated.

⑦ Enjoy with fish and chicken dishes.

Marcha No Sambhar

SAUTÉED SPICY HOT PEPPERS

TIME	YIELD	*GLUTEN-FREE*
10 minutes	2 cups	*& VEGETARIAN*

This recipe is especially for people who like things with a little extra zip. Noorbanu is one of you, so you're in good company.

TIP: Use gloves to avoid exposure to the capsaicin, which is a naturally occurring substance found in hot chillies that can greatly irritate human skin and mucous membranes.

2 ½ ounce	long thin hot chillies (about 30) Noorbanu likes Serrano chillies too
2 Tablespoons	sunflower oil
½ teaspoon	mustard seeds
½ teaspoon	cumin seeds
¼ teaspoon	turmeric
½ teaspoon	salt, or to taste
1 teaspoon	ground cumin
1 Tablespoon	ground coriander
1 Tablespoon	lemon juice

① Slit the chillies lengthwise (halfway down).

② Heat the oil on medium-low heat, add the mustard and cumin seeds, cover and cook until the seeds pop and splutter.

③ Add the chillies and cook, stirring for a few minutes.

④ Add the turmeric, salt, cumin, coriander and lemon juice. Stir for 1 to 2 minutes.

⑤ Enjoy this as a complement to any main dish.

Sweet Dried Fruit Pickle

TIME	PLUS	YIELD	GLUTEN-FREE
30–60 minutes active time	some stirring during the 48-hour standing period	approximately 4 ½ lbs	& VEGETARIAN

Karen loves this chutney on a piece of Naan (page 266) that's been stuffed with left-over leg of lamb and slathered with Cucumber Raita (page 108). She thinks it's the best sandwich ever.

TIP: Look for *Kharek* (dried dates) at Indian grocers. Do not use regular dates, as they will ferment a pickle that's not meant to be fermented.

½ lb	dried dates (*Kharek*)
½ lb	dried apples, cut bite-size
½ lb	dried apricots, cut bite-size
½ lb	dried pears, cut bite-size
2 ounce	dried red chillies
4 Tablespoons	split mustard seeds
2 Tablespoons	split fenugreek seeds
2 teaspoons	salt
2 teaspoons	Indian chilli powder
2 teaspoons	turmeric
½ cup	lemon juice
4 cloves	chopped garlic
8 1" pieces	cinnamon bark
8	whole cloves
8	whole black peppercorns
1 cup	warm sunflower oil
4 ½ cups	sugar
3 cups	water

On the first day:

① Soak the dates in hot water for 2 hours then remove the pits and cut into bite-size pieces.

② Combine the dates, dried apples, apricots and pears, chillies, mustard seeds, fenugreek seeds, salt, chilli powder, turmeric, lemon juice, garlic, cinnamon, cloves, peppercorns and warm oil in a large bowl.

③ Mix well and let stand overnight.

On the second day:

① Combine the sugar and water in a saucepan, cook and stir on low heat until just sticky, or 170° F on a candy thermometer.

② Add this hot syrup to the fruit mixture, mix well and cover.

③ Let stand for 24 hours more, stirring several times.

On the third day:

① Transfer the pickle mixture into clean glass jars and store in the refrigerator.

② Enjoy with any main dish, Bhajia (page 67), Meat Cutlets (page 129), or with Rotli (page 268).

Vegetable Sambhar

MARINATED VEGETABLES

TIME	YIELD	GLUTEN-FREE
40 minutes	4 cups	& VEGETARIAN

Have the ingredients cut, measured and ready to go for this fast-paced recipe with multiple additions.

TIPS: A slicing mandolin with julienne setting for cutting the long thin strips of vegetables in this recipe is a great time saver. You can replace ½ the Serrano chillies with green bell pepper slices to decrease the spiciness of the pickle.

1–2 Tablespoons	sunflower oil
1 teaspoon	mustard seeds
1 teaspoon	cumin seeds
10–12	fresh curry leaves (*Limdho*)
10–12	halved Serrano chillies
1 cup	carrots (2 medium) cut in thin 2-inch strips
6 cups	shredded cabbage (1 medium cabbage)
1 cup	peeled green mango, cut in thin 2-inch strips
¼ cup	water
2 teaspoons	ground cumin
1 teaspoon	Garlic Paste (page 42)
½ teaspoon	turmeric
½ teaspoon	paprika
1 teaspoon	salt
½ teaspoon	Indian chilli powder
2 Tablespoons	lemon juice, or to taste
1 Tablespoon	sugar
2 Tablespoons	Ambli Ni Chutney (page 104)

① Heat the oil and add the mustard and cumin seeds, curry leaves and chillies cooking until the seeds start to pop and splutter.

② Add the carrots and cook for 4 minutes before adding the cabbage, mango and water.

③ Cook this mixture on low heat until all the water is absorbed—approximately 10 to 15 minutes.

④ Stir in the cumin, garlic, turmeric, paprika, salt and chilli powder and continue to cook until the carrots are tender.

⑤ Stir in the lemon juice, sugar, Ambli Ni Chutney and continue cooking until the liquid is absorbed again.

⑥ Transfer to clean glass containers and keep in the fridge until ready to serve.

⑦ Enjoy with any curry dish.

Tomato Chutney

	TIME	YIELD	GLUTEN-FREE
	5 minutes	½ cup	& VEGETARIAN

1 teaspoon	Indian chilli powder
1¼ teaspoons	Garlic Paste (page 42)
¼ teaspoon	citric acid powder or lemon juice
½ teaspoon	salt
1 Tablespoon	tomato paste
1¼ teaspoons	ground cumin
½ teaspoon	dried parsley
1½ Tablespoons	olive oil

① Combine all ingredients except the oil and mix thoroughly.

② Add the oil and mix until well blended.

③ Enjoy with Dhokri (page 76) or any other snack.

Beef and Lamb

MAIN DISHES

KOFTA CURRY
(RECIPE, PAGE 124)

Beef Nihari

A TRADITIONAL BEEF STEW BREAKFAST DISH

TIME	PLUS	YIELD
30 minutes	5–6 hours of stewing time	4 servings

Nihari was traditionally eaten as a hardy breakfast before a day of manual labour. There are many versions but ultimately it's the quality of the meat and the cooking time that delivers a rich, spicy, tender stew. Though some cooks substitute chicken, no true fan will ever accept it being made with anything other than beef. Karen likes to make it in a slow cooker and triples the recipe because it tastes great leftover and freezes well.

1½ lb	beef, sirloin tip
4 Tablespoons	butter
3 Tablespoons	canned crushed tomatoes
1 Tablespoon	Yogurt (page 46)
1 teaspoon	Garlic Paste (page 42)
2 teaspoons	Ginger Paste (page 43)
½ teaspoon	Green Chilli Paste (page 44)
1 teaspoon	ground cumin
½ teaspoon	turmeric
1 teaspoon	paprika
2 Tablespoons	Crispy Fried Onions (page 42), ground
1	(13½ ounce/370 mL) can beef broth
1 teaspoon	salt, or to taste
5 cups	hot water
1½ Tablespoons	whole wheat flour
¼ cup	water
1 teaspoon	Garam Masala, Special Blend (Page 30)
2 Tablespoons	finely cut coriander leaves

For the Garnish:

¼ cup	chopped chillies, Jalapeño or Serrano
½ cup	chopped green bell peppers
½ cup	slivered fresh ginger
½ cup	Crispy Fried Onions (page 42)

① Preheat the oven to 325°F

② Cut the beef into large chunks.

③ Melt the butter on medium heat in a pot that is oven safe.

④ Cook the beef in the butter in small batches. Leave space between the pieces to allow for browning. If it's too close, it will end up boiling in its own juices instead of searing them in.

⑤ Add the crushed tomatoes and cook for 2 minutes.

⑥ Add the yogurt and cook for another 2 minutes.

⑦ Stir in the garlic, ginger and chilli pastes, ground cumin, turmeric, paprika, and fried onions and cook until the oil starts to separate.

⑧ Add the beef broth, salt and hot water and place the pot in the preheated oven (or transfer to a slow cooker on low heat) for 5 to 6 hours—until the meat is tender and falls apart easily.

⑨ Remove the meat with a slotted spoon to a bowl and set aside.

⑩ Bring the meat broth to a boil on the stove.

⑪ Mix the flour and water to form a smooth paste in a small and then gradually stir this mixture into the broth, stirring continuously until thick gravy forms—about 5 to 10 minutes.

⑫ Return the meat to the pot and add the Garam Masala and coriander leaves just before serving.

⑬ Enjoy with Naan (page 266) and invite your guests to enjoy their serving with a range of accompaniments, including: green chillies, green peppers, ginger and fried onions.

Bharazi Khavo

BEEF AND PIGEON PEAS WITH RICE

TIME	YIELD	GLUTEN-FREE
2 hours, including cooking the rice	6–8 servings	

Use of canned pigeon peas and a rice cooker make this recipe easier than it sounds at first and the results will make it your new comfort food—East African style.

ALLERGY NOTE: For legume allergies, eliminate the pigeon peas.

For the Beef and Pigeon Peas:

1 lb	stewing beef or a sirloin grilling steak cut into ¾-inch cubes
1 teaspoon	Ginger Paste (page 43)
1 teaspoon	salt, divided
1 cup	water
2 Tablespoons	olive oil
½ cup finely	chopped onions
½ cup finely	chopped fresh tomatoes
1½ teaspoons	Garlic Paste (page 42)
¼ cup	Yogurt (page 46)
1½ teaspoon	ground cumin
½ teaspoon	paprika
1	(19 ounce/540 mL) can pigeon peas, drained
2	chillies, slit—preferably Serrano
½ cup	red bell pepper, cut into ¼-inch lengthwise slices
1 cup	milk
2 Tablespoons	coconut cream powder
1 Tablespoon	lemon juice
½ teaspoon	Garam Masala (page 29)
1 Tablespoon	finely cut coriander leaves

For the Rice:

1½ cups	basmati rice
2 teaspoons	olive oil
¼ cup	chopped onion
½ teaspoon	Garlic Paste (page 42)
1¼ teaspoon	salt
¼ teaspoon	turmeric
3 cups	water
½ Tablespoon	coconut cream powder

For the Beef and Pigeon Peas:

1. Place the beef, Ginger Paste, salt, and water in a pot and simmer on low, until the meat is tender—about 1½ hours. There should be only a ½ cup of beef stock remaining. If there is more, continue simmering to reduce the volume.

   TIP: A pressure cooker will reduce the cooking time to about 30 minutes total.

2. Heat the olive oil in another saucepan on medium heat, add the onions and cook until a light golden colour.

3. Stir in the tomatoes, Garlic Paste, yogurt, salt, cumin and paprika and cook for 3 to 4 minutes or until the tomatoes are heated through.

4. Stir in the beef, pigeon peas, chillies and red bell peppers.

5. Mix the milk and coconut cream powder together and add this to the beef and pigeon peas, stirring as you go.

6. Continue cooking until the stew thickens.

7. Add the lemon juice, Garam Masala and coriander leaves just before serving.

For the Rice:

1. Wash and soak the rice for 10 minutes.

2. Heat the olive oil in a pot or the bowl of a rice cooker, stir in the onion and cook until transparent.

3. Stir in the Garlic Paste, salt and turmeric, and cook for one minute.

4. Add the water and coconut cream powder, and let the mixture boil for 2 to 3 minutes.

5. Add the rice and cook for 5 minutes (or close the rice cooker lid and let it do its thing).

6. Lower the heat to minimum and simmer until the rice is cooked and all the water has been absorbed.

7. Simmer until the rice is dry.

8. Top the rice with the beef and *bharazi* for presentation on a platter.

9. Enjoy with Carrot Pickle (page 106) and Kachumber (page 59).

Karai Gosht

WOK COOKED DRY LAMB CURRY

TIME	YIELD	GLUTEN-FREE
2 hours	2 to 3 servings, recipe can be multiplied as needed	

Karai is an Indian word for wok. Woks are found in various forms throughout Asia and the antique ones around India are made of copper or cast iron. Cooking in them actually adds necessary elements to the people's diet. Karen says if she had to choose just one pot from her kitchen it would be her wok because you can fry, sauté, steam, braise or boil all in this one vessel.

1 lb	lamb, cubed and washed under cold water
2 teaspoons	Ginger Paste (page 43)
1 cup	water
1 Tablespoon	butter
1 Tablespoon	olive oil
3 Tablespoons	chopped onions
¾ teaspoon	salt, or to taste
1 ½ teaspoons	ground cumin
2 teaspoons	Garlic Paste (page 42)
1 cup canned	crushed tomatoes
1 chopped	chilli (jalapeño or Serrano)
¼- ½ teaspoon	Garam Masala (page 29)
1 Tablespoon	finely cut coriander leaves

① Place the washed meat, ginger and water in a saucepan and cook on medium heat until tender—about 90 minutes—adding more water if needed.

TIP: Wait to start the rest of the recipe until the meat is tender in the first step.

② Heat the butter and oil in a wok on medium heat, add the onions and cook until golden brown.

③ Use a slotted spoon to transfer the cooked meat to the wok with the onions, stir and cook a few minutes.

④ Reserve the meat broth from their original pan.

⑤ Stir in the salt, cumin, Garlic Paste, tomatoes, and chilli and cook until the oil separates.

⑥ Add the reserved meat broth as needed to develop thick gravy for the meat.

⑦ Finish the dish by adding the Garam Masala and coriander leaves just before serving.

⑧ Enjoy with Rotli (page 268) or Naan (page 266).

Khima Matar

GROUND BEEF AND PEAS CURRY

TIME	YIELD	
30–35 minutes	4–6 servings	*GLUTEN-FREE*

Noorbanu's granddaughter Tahira describes this as Ismaili comfort food.

ALLERGY NOTE: For legume allergies substitute spinach or another green vegetable for the peas.

2 Tablespoons	olive oil
1 cup	onion, chopped
1 cup	tomato (2 medium), blended in a food processor
2 teaspoons	tomato paste
2 Tablespoons	water
1 teaspoon	Garlic Paste (page 42)
1 teaspoon	Ginger Paste (page 43)
½ teaspoon	Sambal Oelek
½ teaspoon	Indian chilli powder, or to taste
½ teaspoon	turmeric
1 teaspoon	ground cumin
1 lb	lean ground beef, rinsed under cold water
2 cups OR 1 ½ cups	peas French-cut beans
1 cup	water
½ teaspoon	Garam Masala (page 29)
2 Tablespoons	lemon juice
1 Tablespoon	finely cut coriander leaves

① Heat the oil in a wok on medium heat, add the onion and cook until it starts changing colour to golden brown.

② Stir in the tomatoes, tomato paste, water, garlic and ginger pastes, Sambal Oelek, chilli powder, turmeric and cumin and cook for 2 minutes.

③ Add the meat to the pan and cook for 10 minutes on low-medium heat.

④ Add the peas or beans and cup of water, cooking until the vegetables are tender.

⑤ Stir in the Garam Masala, lemon juice and coriander leaves.

⑥ Enjoy hot with Rotli (page 268), Naan (page 266), or Fluffy Basmati Rice (page 249).

Kofta Curry

MEATBALL CURRY

TIME	YIELD
55 minutes	3–4 servings

Everyone loves meatballs and these spice-filled delicacies disappeared quickly during our photo shoot for the book. They are as delicious as they look.

For the Meatballs:

1 lb	lean ground beef
½ teaspoon	Garlic Paste (page 42)
½ teaspoon	Ginger Paste (page 43)
½ teaspoon	Green Chilli Paste (page 44)
½ teaspoon	salt, or to taste
½ teaspoon	ground cumin
1 Tablespoon	finely cut coriander leaves
¼ teaspoon	Garam Masala (page 29)
1 slice	bread, soaked then squeezed
1 Tablespoon	onion, grated (optional)

For the Sauce:

2 Tablespoons	olive oil
½ cup	chopped onion
½ cup	canned crushed tomato
½ teaspoon	Garlic Paste (page 42)
½ teaspoon	Ginger Paste (page 43)
½ teaspoon	Sambal Oelek
½ teaspoon	ground cumin
¼ teaspoon	turmeric
½ teaspoon	ground coriander
½ teaspoon	salt, or to taste
1 Tablespoon	Yogurt (page 46)
1 cup	water
1 Tablespoon finely cut coriander leaves	

① Combine the ground beef, garlic, ginger and chilli pastes, salt, cumin, coriander leaves, Garam Masala, bread and onion until mixed thoroughly and then shape into balls the size of a walnut (about 24). Place in the refrigerator until needed.

② Heat the oil in a saucepan on medium heat, add the onion and cook until golden brown.

③ Stir in the tomato, garlic and ginger pastes, Sambal Oelek, cumin, turmeric, coriander, salt and yogurt and cook for 3 to 4 minutes.

④ Add the water and bring to a boil.

⑤ Gently add the meatballs and cook, without stirring for about 10 to 15 minutes.

⑥ Lower the heat and simmer for another 10 minutes.

⑦ Enjoy hot garnished with coriander leaves and accompanied by Parotha (page 269), Rotli (page 268), or rice, pickles, salads and Yogurt (page 46).

KOFTA CURRY
SEE PAGE 116

Lamb Masala

LAMB COOKED WITH A SUBTLE SPICE BLEND

TIME	YIELD	GLUTEN-FREE
2 hours	4–5 servings	

This is an easy dish for lamb lovers.

2 lbs	boneless, lean lamb
½ cup	water
½ cup	vinegar
2 Tablespoons	olive oil
1 cup	chopped onion
2 teaspoons	Garlic Paste (page 42)
2 teaspoons	Ginger Paste (page 43)
½ teaspoon	Green Chilli Paste (page 44)
1 cup	finely chopped tomatoes
2 teaspoons	tomato paste
½ teaspoon	turmeric
2 teaspoons	coarsely ground cumin
½ teaspoon	Garam Masala (page 29)
2 Tablespoons	finely cut coriander leaves

① Cut the lamb into 1-inch cubes removing fat and silver skin as you go.

TIP: You can have your butcher do this for you but it will be more expensive. Look for a deboned leg or shoulder and cut it up yourself to save money.

② Marinate the lamb in a bowl with the water and vinegar for 20 minutes then drain and set it aside.

③ Heat the olive oil in a heavy-bottomed pan on medium-high; add the onion and cook and stir until it becomes soft and translucent.

④ Reduce the heat to medium-low and continue cooking until the onion turns golden brown.

⑤ Stir in the garlic, ginger, and chilli pastes and cook until fragrant—about 1 minute.

⑥ Stir in the tomatoes and cook for 5 minutes.

⑦ Stir in the lamb and cook covered in a preheated oven at 350°F for 90 minutes or until the meat is fork tender.

TIP: Check about every half hour while in the oven and add water if required.

⑧ Return the dish to the stove-top on medium heat once tender and add the tomato paste, turmeric and cumin and cook until the oil separates. This indicates that the curry is ready.

⑨ Garnish with the Garam Masala and coriander leaves.

⑩ Enjoy with Rotli (page 268), Naan (page 266), or Parotha, (page 269).

Lamb Rogan Josh

SLOW COOKED SPICY LAMB CURRY

PREP TIME	PLUS	COOKING TIME	YIELD	GLUTEN-FREE
55 minutes	at least 2 hours marinating time	2 hours	4–5 servings	

After a little prep, pop this in the oven and forget about it for a few hours. The slow cooking will deliver a deep reddish brown richly satisfying meal. *Rogan Josh* (translates to *cooked in oil with heat*) was originally a Persian dish adopted by the Kashmiri and now found the world over. The colour originates from liberal use of *Kashmiri chillies* and this version is in keeping with the elaborate spicing that's also characteristic. The finish with fresh coriander and mint is essential so don't skip it.

1½ lbs	lamb, cut into 1-inch cubes

For the Marinade:

1½ teaspoons	Garlic Paste (page 42)
1½ teaspoons	Ginger Paste (page 43)
½ teaspoon	Sambal Oelek
1½ Tablespoons	white vinegar
1 cup	Yogurt (page 46)

For the Sauce:

2 Tablespoons	olive oil
2 cups	finely chopped onion
2 teaspoons	ground cumin
1½ teaspoons	ground coriander
2 Tablespoons	tomato paste
½–1 teaspoon	Indian chilli powder, or to taste
¼ teaspoon	turmeric
1 teaspoon	Garam Masala (page 29)
¾ teaspoon	salt
2 Tablespoons	finely cut coriander leaves
1 Tablespoon	finely cut fresh mint leaves

1. Mix the lamb with garlic, ginger, and Sambal Oelek, vinegar and yogurt in a bowl and set it aside to marinate for 2 hours or overnight in the refrigerator.

2. Heat the olive oil in a heavy-bottomed ovenproof pan on medium-high heat, add the onion and cook and stir until the onions soften and turn translucent.

3. Reduce the heat to medium and cook until golden brown.

4. Stir in the marinated lamb and cook for 5 minutes.

5. Stir in the ground cumin and coriander, tomato paste, ground chilli, turmeric, and place in an oven preheated to 325°F for 1–2 hours or until meat is tender.

   TIP: Check the fluid level regularly and add water as required. The cooking time depends on the quality of the meat.

6. Stir in the Garam Masala, salt, chopped coriander and mint leaves just before serving. The gravy should be fairly thick.

7. Enjoy hot with Rotli (page 268) or Naan (page 266).

Mayai Mani

GROUND BEEF AND EGG CASSEROLE

TIME	YIELD	GLUTEN-FREE
40 minutes	4 servings	

This may not be your mother's meatloaf but it sure might be the Ismaili equivalent.

1 lb	lean ground beef
3 Tablespoons	olive oil
1 cup	chopped tomato (2 medium)
1 Tablespoon	water
1 teaspoon	tomato paste
½ teaspoon	Garlic Paste (page 42)
½ teaspoon	Ginger Paste (page 43)
¼ teaspoon	Green Chilli Paste (page 44), or to taste
¼ teaspoon	turmeric
½ teaspoon	ground cumin
1 Tablespoon	Crispy Fried Onions (page 42)
½ teaspoon	salt
¼ teaspoon	Garam Masala (page 29)
2 Tablespoons	lemon juice
1 Tablespoon	finely cut coriander leaves
1 beaten	egg
3	eggs

1. Preheat the oven to 350°F.
2. Heat a fry pan and cook the ground beef stirring and breaking up any lumps until it is brown and dry, then strain it in a colander.
3. Add oil to the same pan and heat it on medium heat before adding the tomato, water, tomato paste, garlic, ginger, chilli paste, turmeric, cumin, fried onion and salt, cook stirring until the tomato is soft—about 2 to 3 minutes.
4. Stir the meat back into this mixture and simmer for 10 minutes.
5. Stir in Garam Masala, lemon juice and coriander.
6. Spread half of the beaten egg in a shallow baking dish.
7. Pour the meat mixture into the pan and coat the top with the other half of the beaten egg.
8. Make three holes in the meat and break an egg into each.
9. Sprinkle the coriander on top, place in the preheated oven and bake for 15 minutes or until the eggs set.
10. Enjoy hot with bread, Naan (page 266) or Rotli (page 268).

Meat Cutlets

TIME	YIELD
30 minutes	6 patties

With lean ground meat and the zip of Indian spices and fresh chillies, these patties really are a lean and mean addition to your plate or burger rotation. They are definitely a Nimji family favourite.

2 slices	whole wheat bread
1 ¼ lbs	ground beef or lamb
½ teaspoon	ground cumin
½ teaspoon	Garlic Paste (page 42)
½ teaspoon	Ginger Paste (page 43)
½ teaspoon	Green Chilli Paste (page 44)
½ teaspoon	salt
¼ teaspoon	Garam Masala (page 29)
1 Tablespoon	finely cut coriander leaves
1 cup	bread crumbs
2	beaten eggs
½ –1 cup	sunflower oil

① Soak the bread in warm water for 1 minute and then squeeze the water out using your hands.

② Mix the moist bread, meat, cumin, garlic, ginger and chilli pastes, salt, Garam Masala and coriander leaves in a bowl and then divide into 6 balls.

③ Flatten the balls into ½-inch thick patties.

TIP: The patties will contract as they cook but they need to be this thin to cook through properly from the start.

④ Coat the patties on both sides with the bread crumbs.

⑤ Heat the oil in a fry pan—it should be about 1-inch deep.

⑥ Dip the patties in the eggs and shallow fry until golden brown on both sides.

TIP: Noorbanu likes to use an electric skillet on her balcony to keep the oil splatter and odour out of her home.

⑦ Enjoy with potatoes, salad, lemon wedges and Coconut Chutney (page 107) or between a bun with a bit of lettuce and a splash of Cucumber Raita (page 108).

Meat Curry with Fresh Fenugreek Leaves

TIME	YIELD	*GLUTEN-FREE*
1 hour and 45 minutes	2–3 servings, multiply as desired	

After the initial browning of the meat, it is left to slowly braise in the sauce for almost 2 hours. The result is beautifully tender meat accented with the flavour of fresh fenugreek (*methi*). You'll find the fresh leaves at Indian produce markets. Be adventurous—it's fun to source your nearest Indian Grocer.

3 Tablespoons	olive oil
½ cup OR 2 Tablespoons	chopped onion (1 medium) Crispy Fried Onions (page 42)
1½ lb	steak, cut in 1-inch cubes (use sirloin tip or another tender cut)
1½ teaspoons	Garlic Paste (page 42)
1½ teaspoons	Ginger Paste (page 43)
¼ - 1 teaspoon	Green Chilli Paste (page 44), or to taste
1 cup	canned crushed tomatoes
½ teaspoon	salt, or to taste
1 teaspoon	ground cumin
½ teaspoon	ground coriander
½ teaspoon	Indian chilli powder, or to taste
¼ teaspoon	ground turmeric
1 cup	chopped fresh fenugreek leaves
¼ teaspoon	Garam Masala (page 29)
1 Tablespoon	finely cut coriander leaves

① Heat the oil in a wok on medium heat and fry the onions until they are light brown.

② Stir in the meat, garlic, ginger and chilli pastes and fry until the meat is brown on all sides.

③ Stir in the tomato, salt, cumin, coriander, chilli powder and turmeric and cook covered until the meat is tender. Add water as needed but keep the gravy thick in consistency.

④ Add the fenugreek (*methi*) leaves and Garam Masala and cook until the fenugreek leaves wilt.

⑤ Garnish with the coriander leaves just before serving.

⑥ Enjoy with Rotli (page 268) or Naan (page 266).

FRESH FENUGREEK (*METHI*)

Muthia

MEAT AND VEGETABLES
IN COCONUT CREAM WITH DUMPLINGS

TIME	YIELD	GLUTEN-FREE
shop, prep and settle in for a few hours until this feast is ready	8–10 servings	

Muthias are delicious little dumplings and this dish is the favourite of Noorbanu's daughter Rosie, who has a very special memory of her Mother making it for her birthday when she was a little girl. In Africa, Noorbanu had to make coconut milk from scratch and collect the myriad of ingredients needed fresh from the market. Noorbanu admits this is a hard recipe because so many of the ingredients need individual preparation but, she also says the result is a very beautiful and unique dish. She would encourage you to smile, be happy and give it a try.

For the Muthia Dumplings:

2 cups	millet flour
½ cup	medium unsweetened shredded coconut
½ teaspoon	salt
½ teaspoon	ground cumin
¼ teaspoon	turmeric
½ teaspoon	Garlic Paste (page 42)
½ teaspoon	Green Chilli Paste (page 44)
1 Tablespoon	oil
½ cup	canned coconut cream (save rest of can for stew)
1 Tablespoon	finely cut coriander leaves
1 Tablespoon	finely cut fresh fenugreek (*methi*) leaves

For the Stew:

2 lbs	lamb or beef, cut in cubes
½ teaspoon	Ginger Paste (page 43)
Salt, to taste	
1½ cups	water
1 cup	oil
2 cups OR	chopped onion (2 large)
¼ cup	Crispy Fried Onions (page 42)
½ cup	chopped fresh Fenugreek (*methi*) leaves
2 cups	chopped tomatoes (2 medium)
2 teaspoons	tomato paste
1½ teaspoons	Garlic Paste (page 42)
1½ teaspoons	Ginger Paste (page 43)
½ teaspoon	Green Chilli Paste (page 44) or Sambal Oelek
¾ teaspoon	ground cumin
1 teaspoon	salt, or to taste

½ teaspoon	turmeric
2–3	Japanese eggplant cut in 3 × 1-inch pieces
2	(12 ounce/300 gm) packages of frozen chopped spinach
1 lb	frozen green peas
4–5	Saragavo (drumsticks) cut in 3–4 inch lengths and pre-boiled
½ lb	guvar (cluster beans) pre-boiled
1	(19 ounce/540 mL) can dry pigeon peas
½ cup	chana dal, soaked and cooked
2 medium	potatoes, quartered and pre-boiled
1	(14 ounce/398 mL) can coconut cream plus leftovers from dumplings
4 Tablespoons	lemon juice
½ cup	finely cut coriander leaves
1 teaspoon	Garam Masala (page 29)
1 cup	whipping cream

For the Muthia Dumplings:

① Mix all the ingredients and use a little water if necessary to bind into firm dough.

② Place a spoonful of the dough in your hand and squeeze gently to form a slender oval dumpling about ½-inch × 2-inches.

③ Repeat until all the dough is used.

④ Set the dumplings aside until called for in the stew.

For the Stew:

① Place the meat, ginger, salt and water in a pressure cooker and process for 20 minutes OR simmer covered until the meat is tender.

TIP: Wait until the meat is done before starting the rest of the recipe—but go ahead and do all the prep of the individual ingredients.

② Heat the oil in a large pot, add the onions and cook until golden brown.

③ Stir in the fenugreek leaves and cook until they wilt—about 1 minute.

④ Stir in the tomato, tomato paste, garlic, ginger and chilli pastes, cumin, salt and turmeric and cook for about 3 minutes.

⑤ Stir in the eggplant, spinach, frozen peas and the cooked meat (reserving the stock) and cook to combine the flavours and soften the vegetables—5 to 7 minutes.

⑥ Stir in the Saragavo (drumsticks), guvar (cluster beans), the pigeon peas, chana dal, potatoes and cook for another 10 minutes.

⑦ Stir in the meat stock and enough water to make 6 cups of fluid total, then add the coconut cream and bring to a boil.

⑧ Set the dumplings on top and cook covered on low heat for 10 minutes. Do not stir until the dumplings are cooked.

⑨ Stir in the lemon juice, coriander leaves, Garam Masala and whipping cream and place in a preheated 250°F oven for 20 minutes.

⑩ Enjoy hot with tossed salad or Kachumber (page 59).

Naryal Vaaro Mhogo

CASSAVA IN COCONUT CREAM

TIME	YIELD	GLUTEN-
1 hour	6–7 servings	*FREE*

A typical East African dish featuring the versatility of cassava. Widely grown in Africa, it's estimated that *cassava* feeds one-fifth of the world's population.

1 lb	cubed beef OR chicken breasts
2 cups	water
1 teaspoon	Ginger Paste (page 43)
½ teaspoon	salt
1	(1 lb or 400 gm) package frozen cassava (*mhogo*)
2 ½ cups	water
1 teaspoon	salt, divided
1 teaspoon	Garlic Paste (page 42)
½ teaspoon	Green Chilli Paste (page 44)
⅛ teaspoon	turmeric (optional)
1 teaspoon	ground cumin
1	(14 ounce/398 mL) can coconut cream
1 Tablespoon	lemon juice
1–2 Tablespoons	finely cut coriander leaves

① Put the beef, 2 cups of water, ginger and salt in a pot on medium heat and simmer until tender about 30 to 90 minutes depending on the type and quality of meat used.

TIP: A pressure cooker shortens the cooking time. Note: if using chicken, simply heat 2 teaspoons of olive oil in a pan and cook the cubed chicken with the ginger and salt on medium heat until brown on all sides.

② Cut the *cassava* into cubes, removing the thick fibrous string from the middle and cook on medium heat in the 2 ½ cups water and ½ teaspoon salt until tender.

③ Stir in the garlic and chilli pastes, turmeric, cumin, coconut cream, lemon juice and coriander leaves as well as the meat and its broth.

④ Add water if necessary to cover the *cassava* and meat and continue cooking for a further 5 to 7 minutes to meld all the flavours.

⑤ Enjoy along with the vibrant tastes of Coriander Chutney (page 108) and Coconut Chutney (page 107).

Spiced Meat and Macaroni in Coconut Cream

TIME
30 minutes

YIELD
4 servings,
multiply as desired

This is comfort food straight out of Noorbanu's life in Africa. It's like North American "Mac'n cheese" without the dairy and with a little kick of spice to keep it exciting. Noorbanu once multiplied this recipe to serve 80 people at a community gathering and it still tasted great.

1 lb	chicken, lamb or beef, cut in 1-inch cubes
½ teaspoon	Garlic Paste (page 42)
½ teaspoon	Ginger Paste (page 43)
½ teaspoon	salt
¼ cup	butter
1 cup	chopped onion
1 cup	chopped fresh tomato
½ teaspoon	ground coriander
1 teaspoon	ground cumin
½ teaspoon	Indian chilli powder
¼ cup	water, if needed
½ lb	macaroni
1 teaspoon	salt
5 cups	water
1	(14 ounce/398 mL) can coconut cream
1 small	diced jalapeño
1 Tablespoon	lemon juice
1 Tablespoon	finely cut coriander leaves

① Marinate the meat in a bowl with salt and the garlic and ginger pastes for 30 minutes.

② Melt the butter in a large skillet on medium heat, add the onion and cook until golden brown – about 10 minutes.

③ Stir in the marinated meat, tomatoes, coriander, cumin, and chilli powder and continue to cook, adding water—as little as possible—to keep the meat from sticking.

TIP: You can make the recipe ahead to this point, refrigerate it for up to 24 hours and then reheat it when you are ready to complete the steps that follow.

④ Cook the macaroni with remaining 1 teaspoon salt in 5 cups of water while the meat is simmering.

⑤ Preheat the oven to 250°F.

⑥ Pour the coconut cream in a third saucepan and add the jalapeño, lemon juice and coriander leaves and bring to a boil.

⑦ Arrange the meat in a casserole dish, top with macaroni, pour the coconut cream over top and bake in the preheated oven for 10 minutes.

⑧ Enjoy with a crisp green salad.

BUTTER CHICKEN
(RECIPE, PAGE 138)

Butter Chicken

MARINATE	TIME	YIELD	GLUTEN-FREE
3–4 hours or overnight	60 minutes	4 servings	

TIP: Karen usually doubles or triples this recipe hoping for leftovers as she thinks it tastes even better the next day.

This is one of Noorbanu's most succulent recipes. It's origins lie in 1950s New Delhi. Noorbanu learned to make it when she came to Canada. As the story goes, the owner of the *Moti Mahal* restaurant complained there was always leftover tandoori chicken at the end of each day. To please his boss (and to save his job) the very practical chef took those char-flavoured bits of chicken and served them up in a butter and cream tomato sauce the next day. Noorbanu's version is accented with the flavour of *Kasoori Methi*—dried fenugreek leaves.

1½ lb	chicken breast, boneless and skinless

For the Marinade:

3 Tablespoons	Yogurt (page 46)
1½ teaspoons	Garlic Paste (page 42)
1½ teaspoons	Ginger Paste (page 43)
2 teaspoons	tomato paste
½ teaspoon	Green Chilli Paste (page 44)
½ teaspoon	paprika
1 teaspoon	ground cumin
¼ teaspoon	Indian chilli powder
¼ teaspoon	Garam Masala (page 29)
Pinch	saffron
¾ teaspoon	salt

BUTTER CHICKEN
SEE PAGE 136

For the Sauce:

¼ cup	roughly chopped onion
2	2-inch pieces red bell pepper
2	2-inch pieces green bell pepper
¾ cup	water, divided ¼ cup then remainder as needed
¼ cup	butter
1 cup	crushed tomato
2 teaspoons	fenugreek (*methi*) leaves
1¼ cups	whipping cream (Substitute ½ cup half-and-half cream to reduce fat)

1. Cut the chicken into bite-size pieces.

2. Combine all of the marinade ingredients in a large glass bowl and stir in the chicken pieces. Cover and marinate 3 to 4 hours or overnight in the refrigerator.

3. Place the onion, red and green bell peppers and ¼ cup of water in a blender and process until smooth. Set aside.

4. Melt the butter in a large saucepan on medium heat.

5. Stir in the puréed onion/pepper mixture and cook for 2 to 3 minutes.

6. Stir in the marinated chicken and any remaining marinade and cook for 5 minutes.

7. Stir in the tomato sauce and continue cooking until the chicken is tender about 10 minutes.

8. Stir in the fenugreek leaves and more water as required and cook until they are soft—about 5 minutes.

9. Stir in the whipping cream (or half-and-half cream substitute) slowly. There should be enough gravy to just cover the chicken. Add more water or cream as required.

10. Simmer until heated through. Avoid letting it come to a boil as that might cause the cream to separate.

11. Enjoy with Saffron Rice (page 249) and Naan (page 266).

Variations:

BUTTER CHICKEN PI-NAAN-ZA: Karen's family loves leftover *Butter Chicken* spread on a pizza shell and baked with a few fresh chillies to garnish.

BUTTER CHICKEN SKEWERS: In summer thread the marinated chicken on metal skewers and cook them on the grill without the heavy sauce. Serve with a fresh green salad.

Cardamom Chicken

TIME	YIELD	GLUTEN-FREE
30 minutes	4 servings	

Cardamom, the Queen of Spices, lends its clean bite to the otherwise rich tomato sauce in this quick and easy supper dish.

3 Tablespoons	olive oil
1½ teaspoon	coarsely ground green cardamom seeds
2 lb	chicken breast, boneless and skinless, cut into strips
1 teaspoon	Indian chilli powder
½ teaspoon	turmeric
1 teaspoon	paprika
1 Tablespoon	tomato paste
1 teaspoon	salt
1 cup	Yogurt (page 46)
1 Tablespoon	finely cut coriander leaves

① Heat the olive oil in a wok on medium heat, add the cardamom and stir for one minute.

② Add the chicken and cook, stirring, for 5 minutes.

③ Stir in the ground chilli, turmeric and paprika, tomato paste and salt and cook until chicken is tender.

④ Stir in the Yogurt, 1 Tablespoon at a time, and simmer, stirring until all of the Yogurt has been added. The mixture should be quite thick. If not, remove the chicken with a slotted spoon and cook the sauce until it is a thick gravy and then replace the chicken.

⑤ Garnish with the coriander leaves just before serving.

⑥ Enjoy with Naan (page 266) and the chutneys of your choice.

Chicken Drumsticks with Coriander and Chilli Peppers

MARINATE	TIME	YIELD	GLUTEN-FREE
at least 2 hours or overnight	60 minutes	4 servings	

Watch for chicken drumsticks to go on sale and make this finger-licking treat for your family.

2 lb	chicken drumsticks, skinned
½ cup	fresh coriander leaves, firmly packed
2	fresh green chillies, or to taste
1 teaspoon	Garlic Paste (page 42)
1 teaspoon	Ginger Paste (page 43)
½ teaspoon	Garam Masala (page 29)
2 Tablespoons	lemon juice
1 Tablespoon	olive oil
1 teaspoon	salt

① Make cuts through the flesh on both sides of the drumsticks about 1-inch apart and down to the bone.

② Place the coriander leaves, chillies, garlic and ginger pastes, Garam Masala, lemon juice, olive oil and salt in a blender and pulse until smooth paste forms—adding water if needed.

③ Marinate drumsticks in the coriander paste—covered and refrigerated—for at least 2 hours or overnight.

④ Place the drumsticks on a baking tray. Bake uncovered in a preheated 350°F oven—turning after 20 minutes—for a total of 40 minutes. The chicken should be browned and the juices run clear when pierced with a knife.

⑤ Enjoy with salad and Naan (page 266).

Chicken Kalyo

RICH CHICKEN CURRY

MARINATE 3–4 hours minimum	**TIME** 60 minutes
YIELD 4 servings	*GLUTEN-FREE*

Put this chicken in the refrigerator to marinate in the morning, pick up some *Naan* on the way home from work and look forward to enjoying this sumptuous dish at day's end. It will take about an hour of cooking and simmering—time enough to do a few chores and make a crunchy salad to go along with it.

1 cup	Yogurt (page 46)
1 Tablespoon	lemon juice
6	strands saffron
1 teaspoon	salt
1 teaspoon	Garlic Paste (page 42)
2 teaspoons	Ginger Paste (page 43)
1 teaspoon	Green Chilli Paste (page 44)
2 ¼ lbs	bone-in chicken pieces
1	large peeled potato, cut into 6 wedges
1 Tablespoon	olive oil
2 Tablespoons	Ghee (page 43) or butter
3× 2-inch pieces	cinnamon bark
3	whole cloves
3	green cardamom pods, cracked
3	whole black peppercorns
2 teaspoons	ground cumin
½ teaspoon	Indian chilli powder
1 cup	canned crushed tomatoes
½ cup of	water (or more if needed)
3 Tablespoons	Crispy Fried Onion (page 42)
½ teaspoon	Garam Masala (page 29)
1 Tablespoon	finely cut coriander leaves

1. Stir the yogurt, lemon juice, saffron, salt, garlic, ginger and chilli pastes together in a large bowl or baking dish and then add the chicken pieces and coat them thoroughly.

2. Cover and marinate in the refrigerator for at least 3 to 4 hours.

3. Remove it from the fridge as you begin to prepare the rest of the dish.

4. Preheat the oven to 375°F and line a baking tray with parchment paper.

5. Place the potato wedges on the parchment paper and drizzle with the olive oil, tossing to coat them.

6. Separate the wedges on the baking tray and bake for 20 to 25 minutes or until crispy and golden.

7. Melt the ghee in a wok on medium heat, add the cinnamon, cloves, cardamom and peppercorns and cook on medium heat for 1 minute.

8. Stir in the marinated chicken and the cumin, chilli powder, tomatoes and tomato paste and water as needed—cook and stir as needed on medium heat until cooked through—about 15 to 20 minutes.

9. Stir in the oven-fried potatoes, the fried onion and Garam Masala and lower the heat so the dish will stay at a simmer for a further 10 to 15 minutes.

10. Sprinkle with coriander leaves just before serving.

11. Enjoy with fresh Naan (page 266).

Note: Advise your guests to remove the whole spices if any appear in their serving.

Chicken Kebabs

TIME	YIELD
30–40 minutes	2–3 servings

You can make the traditional kebab shape for this recipe or flatten them into patties and cook them on the grill to treat your family to a spicy chicken burger.

1 lb	ground chicken
1 Tablespoon	Yogurt (page 46)
¾ teaspoon	Garlic Paste (page 42)
¾ teaspoon	Ginger Paste (page 43)
½ teaspoon	Green Chilli Paste (page 44)
½ teaspoon	salt
½ teaspoon	ground cumin
1	egg
½ cup	bread crumbs
1 Tablespoon	finely cut coriander leaves

① Combine the ground chicken, yogurt, garlic, ginger, and chilli pastes, salt, cumin, egg, bread crumbs and coriander leaves in a bowl and mix well.

② Divide the mixture into golf ball size spheres and shape into 18 to 20 thumb-size elongated kebabs.

   TIP: If the mixture is soft you can add more bread crumbs to help shape the balls.

③ Arrange the kebab in a single layer on a lightly oiled baking tray, and spray the kebabs with oil.

④ Broil on high, 6 to 8 inches from the broiler, turning when required until both sides are broiled and cooked.

⑤ Enjoy with your choice of salad, chutneys, raita and Naan (page 266).

Chilli Flake and Honey Chicken

MARINATE	TIME	YIELD	*GLUTEN-FREE*
2 hours or overnigh	30–40 minutes	4 servings	

Delightful and easy—two words that are magic to a cook's ear when searching for dinner ideas on busy nights.

TIP: You could buy large batches of chicken, multiply this recipe, add the marinade in equivalent amounts to the portions you'd like and freeze them in bags and then thaw them as you need them to cope with your family's "fright night" of the week.

2 lbs	chicken breast, boneless and skinless

For the Marinade:

1 teaspoon	Garlic Paste (page 42)
1 teaspoon	Ginger Paste (page 43)
1 Tablespoon	honey
1 teaspoon	salt
1 teaspoon	chilli pepper flakes
4 teaspoons	olive oil
½ teaspoon	turmeric, optional
1 teaspoon	paprika

① Slice each chicken breast in half, horizontally, to reduce the thickness of the meat.

② Combine the marinade ingredients in a bowl, add the chicken and coat it with the mixture and marinate for 2 hours or overnight.

③ Place the chicken in a lightly oiled ovenproof pan and bake at 400°F for 10 minutes.

④ Reduce the oven to 350°F and bake for another 15 minutes and the chicken is cooked through but still moist.

⑤ Enjoy with Avocado, Mango and Almond Salad(page 56) and Cumin-Scented Rice (page 249) as a lovely dinner.

Jeera Chicken

CUMIN-SCENTED CHICKEN

TIME	YIELD	GLUTEN-
40–45 minutes	3–4 servings	*FREE*

Cumin is the second most consumed spice in the world after black peppercorns. Noorbanu uses both to create this warmly flavoured dish.

4 Tablespoons	butter or olive oil
1 cup	chopped onion (2 small)
2 ¼ lb	skinless chicken pieces
1½ cups	chopped tomatoes (2 medium)
2 teaspoons	Garlic Paste (page 42), or to taste
2 teaspoons	Ginger Paste (page 43), or to taste
4	finely chopped chilli peppers (jalapeños or Serranos), or to taste
1 Tablespoon	coarsely ground cumin seeds
½ teaspoon	coarsely ground peppercorns
1 Tablespoon	lemon juice
2 Tablespoons	finely cut coriander leaves
Salt	to taste

① Melt the butter (or heat the oil) in a wok on medium heat and cook the onions until they are soft and translucent.

② Stir in the chicken pieces and cook for 2 minutes.

③ Stir in the tomatoes, garlic and ginger paste.

④ Cook covered on medium heat until the chicken is cooked through and the fat separates. Add a little water from time to time if needed to prevent the sauce from sticking and burning.

⑤ Stir in the chilli peppers, cumin, peppercorns, lemon juice and coriander leaves and cook for 2 minutes more—the gravy should be fairly thick when ready.

⑥ Taste and season with salt to taste.

⑦ Enjoy hot with Naan (page 266), tossed salad and the chutneys of your choice.

w/ rice is good served.

Karai Chicken

CHICKEN COOKED IN A WOK

TIME	YIELD	GLUTEN-FREE
45–50 minutes	3–4 servings	

This is the perfect example of a recipe that's really easy when you have your own *Masala Daba* (spice box) containing most of these ingredients. Refer to Chapter One to learn more about this Indian cook's timesaver.

2 lbs to 2½ lb	chicken cut into 16 pieces
3 Tablespoons	butter or olive oil
4	cloves
4	cardamom pods
2× 1-inch pieces	cinnamon bark
10	black peppercorns
2	finely chopped chilli peppers, preferably Serrano, or to taste
2 teaspoons	Garlic Paste (page 42)
2 teaspoons	Ginger Paste (page 43)
1 teaspoon	Green Chilli Paste (page 44), or to taste
1 ½ teaspoon	salt, or to taste
1 teaspoon	coarsely ground cumin seeds
½ teaspoon	ground coriander
1 cup	canned crushed tomatoes
2 Tablespoons	finely cut coriander leaves

① Melt the butter or oil in a wok over medium heat and add the cloves, cardamom pods, cinnamon, black peppercorns and chopped chilli pepper and cook for 1 minute.

② Stir in the chicken pieces and cook for 2 to 4 minutes.

③ Stir in the garlic, ginger and chilli pastes, salt, ground cumin and coriander and cook, uncovered, for 7 to 10 minutes.

④ Stir in the tomatoes and a little water then simmer until chicken pieces are cooked through, about 25 minutes. The sauce should be thick. If not, remove the chicken pieces, increase heat and reduce the sauce until it is like a thick gravy.

⑤ Garnish with the coriander leaves.

⑥ Enjoy hot with Naan (page 266), or Parotha (page 269).

Kashmiri Masala Chicken

MARINATE	TIME	YIELD	*GLUTEN-FREE*
3 hours	60–75 minutes	4 servings	

Kashmir has the reputation of being the terrestrial paradise of India. The Wazwan food of this region is rich in spices—especially the highly sought after *saffron* which is the world's most expensive spice. When you make this dish you'll be rewarded with a great example of this complex cuisine.

1½ lbs	chicken pieces, skinned and washed

For the Marinade:

1½ teaspoon	Garlic Paste (page 42)
1½ teaspoon	Ginger Paste (page 43)
½ teaspoon	Green Chilli Paste (page 44)
1½ cups	Yogurt (page 46)

For the Sauce:

2 cups	water
1 teaspoon	salt, or to taste
1 Tablespoon	Kashmiri Masala (page 32)
2 Tablespoons	olive oil
4 Tablespoons	tomato paste
1½ teaspoons	ground cumin
1 large	red or green bell pepper, blended to a paste in a food processor
2	medium potatoes, each cut into 8 pieces then fried or roasted
1 Tablespoon	finely cut coriander leaves

① Mix the marinade ingredients in a glass bowl, add the chicken, coat well with the marinade and place covered in the refrigerator for at least 3 hours.

② Place the marinated chicken in a pot on medium-high heat. Add the water, salt and Kashmiri Masala paste and bring to a boil.

③ Reduce the heat to medium and simmer until the chicken is cooked through and tender, stirring occasionally.

④ Heat the olive oil in another pot, add the tomato paste and cumin and cook for 2 minutes.

⑤ Stir in the bell pepper paste and cook for 2 minutes, then add this mixture to the chicken.

⑥ Cook on low heat for 5 minutes and then add the pre-cooked potatoes and simmer for 5 minutes, adding water if needed. The sauce should cover the chicken.

⑦ Garnish with freshly chopped coriander leaves just before serving.

⑧ Enjoy with Naan (page 266), or your choice of rice dish.

PURI
(RECIPE, PAGE 236)

Kuku Paka

CHICKEN, POTATOES AND EGGS IN A COCONUT SAUCE

TIME	YIELD	GLUTEN-FREE
1 hour	6 servings	

This is a most beloved recipe. It's a great example of the fusion of flavours that resulted when the Ismaili people of the Gujarat in India immigrated to East Africa in the 1920s. They brought their knowledge of spices and adapted their use to the new ingredients they found. The combination of those spices with coconut, chicken, eggs and potatoes makes this one of the Nimji family's all time favourites. We hope it will be one of yours as well.

4	eggs
4	potatoes
2 Tablespoons	coconut oil
½ cup	finely chopped onion (1 small onion)
2 ¼ lbs	bone-in chicken pieces, skinned
1 cup	chopped tomato (1 medium)
½ teaspoon	Garlic Paste (page 42)
½ teaspoon	Ginger Paste (page 43)
½ teaspoon	Green Chilli Paste (page 44), or to taste
½ teaspoon	Indian chilli powder, or to taste
1 teaspoon	salt
½ teaspoon	ground cumin
½ teaspoon	ground coriander
⅛ teaspoon	turmeric
1	(14 ounce/398 mL) can coconut cream
1	(14 ounce/398 mL) can coconut milk
water	as necessary
½ cup	whipping cream (you can use more coconut cream if you want the dish to be dairy-free)
1 Tablespoon	finely cut coriander leaves
2-3 Tablespoons	lemon juice

1. Bring water to boil in a small saucepan, add the eggs, cook for 8 minutes (for hard-boiled eggs), drain the water and replace with cold water. Once the eggs have cooled enough, peel them; slice them in half lengthwise and set aside.

2. Peel and boil 4 medium sized potatoes in another pot on medium-high heat until firm but cooked—about 10 to 15 minutes, drain and set aside.

   TIP: You can prep the egg and potato a day ahead and keep them in the fridge.

3. Heat the oil in a large deep sided skillet, add the onion, cook and stir on medium heat until soft and translucent.

4. Stir in the chicken, tomatoes, garlic, ginger and chilli pastes, the chilli powder, salt, cumin, coriander and turmeric and cook on medium heat until the chicken is almost done—it will be tender when pricked and have pink juices flowing from it.

   TIP: Noorbanu speeds this process up by broiling the chicken pieces on a baking tray until lightly brown and then adding them to the onions with the spices.

5. Add the coconut cream and milk and enough water so that the gravy does not quite cover the chicken pieces. Cook until the chicken is done or the juices run clear when pierced.

6. Add the whipping cream (if using), eggs, potatoes, coriander leaves and lemon juice and cook until heated through—2 to 3 minutes.

7. Enjoy with a slice of Mikati Mimina (page 152) or Parotha (page 269).

Makati Mimina

COCONUT AND RICE BREAD
TO ACCOMPANY KUKU PAKA

TIME	YIELD	*GLUTEN-FREE*
5–7 hours	2 Makati	*& VEGETARIAN*

In Kiswahili (the language spoken in Kenya, Tanzania and Uganda), *Makati* means bread. *Makati Mimina* is traditional rice flour bread that seems to be designed to soak up the sauce of *Kuku Paka* that gets caught up in the lacy design formed by the rice flour while baking. Both *Kuku Paka* and *Makati Mimina* taste great on their own but together they're sensational.

TIPS: Make sure you have both an 8 and 10-inch non-stick (Teflon—not stainless steel) skillet on hand to cook them and follow the directions closely. The best results are achieved when your frying pan has straight sides, perpendicular to the base. Ensure the yeast is fresh.

4½ cups	cool water
1	(50 – 60 gram) package of coconut cream powder
1	(400 gram) package of rice flour (gluten-free)
1 teaspoon	instant yeast
1 teaspoon	sugar
Water to dissolve	
2 cups	sugar
½ cup	water
1 teaspoon	ground green cardamom seeds
3 Tablespoons	butter, divided
2 teaspoons	white poppy seeds, divided

1. Mix the coconut cream and rice flour in a large bowl and gradually add the water whisking until all lumps are gone.

2. Add the yeast and sugar and water to another bowl and mix until the sugar dissolves. Then place it in a toaster oven that's been turned on for a minute and then turned off. The heat will make the yeast frothy and double in volume very quickly.

3. Add the doubled yeast to the rice flour mixture, cover and set aside for 4 to 6 hours or overnight. The batter will be of liquid consistency.

4. Add the 2 cups of sugar, ½ cup of water and the *cardamom* to the yeast and flour mixture in the morning and stir well to dissolve the sugar and form a smooth homogenous batter.

5. Place an ovenproof 10-inch nonstick frying pan and a second 8-inch pan on the stove and add 2 Tablespoons of butter to the first and 1 Tablespoon of butter to the second and let them melt and bubble on medium-high heat before dividing the batter into the 2 pans.

6. Continue cooking—covered—on medium-high heat until the surface is covered with bubbles.

7. Sprinkle with the poppy seeds if desired at this point.

8. Reduce the heat to medium-low and continue to cook covered until the *Makati* is set (cooked through). Shake the pan to ensure there is no more liquid under the surface.

9. Broil under a preheated broiler until the top is golden.

10. Cool for a few minutes and then turn it out onto a plate. Flip onto another plate so that the top (poppy seed side) is exposed.

11. Repeat for the cooking and finishing process for the second cake.

12. Enjoy with Kuku Paka (page 150) or as a delicious treat on its own.

Persian Chicken

MARINATE	TIME	YIELD	*GLUTEN-FREE*
20 minutes	60 minutes	3–4 servings	

Before the Ismaili people lived in Africa or the Gujarat area of India, they were influenced by the ancient Persian culture. This dish with its apricots, prunes and almonds is an excellent example of those culinary influences.

3 lbs	bone-in chicken pieces
½ teaspoon	Garlic Paste (page 42)
1 teaspoon	Ginger Paste (page 43)
½ teaspoon	Green Chilli Paste (page 44)
½ teaspoon	coarsely ground black pepper
¾ teaspoon	salt
6 Tablespoons	unsalted butter
½ cup	dried apricots
½ cup	dried pitted prunes
½ cup	blanched almonds
1 cup	diced onion (1 medium)
2 cups	tomatoes, blended (2 large tomatoes)
½ cup	white vinegar
1 Tablespoon	brown sugar
¼ teaspoon	Indian chilli powder
½ cup	water

① Preheat the oven to 400°F.

② Marinate the chicken pieces in a large glass baking dish with the garlic, ginger and chilli pastes, black pepper and salt for at least 20 minutes.

③ Bake the chicken in the preheated oven for 45 minutes.

④ Heat the butter in a skillet on medium heat, add the apricots, prunes and almonds and cook and stir for about 1 minute—then remove them with a slotted spoon to a bowl and reserve.

⑤ Add the onions to the same skillet and cook and stir on medium heat until light brown—then stir in the tomatoes and cook for 3 to 4 minutes more.

⑥ Stir in the baked chicken, vinegar, brown sugar, chilli powder, the reserved fruit mixture and ½ cup of water (enough to cover the chicken) and simmer 15 minutes to combine the flavours.

⑦ Enjoy hot over Fluffy Basmati Rice (page 249).

Piri Piri Chicken

SPICY HOT CHICKEN

TIME	YIELD	GLUTEN-FREE
45 minutes	3-4 servings	

This is the Indian version of *Nando's*™. It's supposed to be a spicy hot dish but you can adjust the amount of chilli powder to your own taste.

4 Tablespoons	olive oil
4 chopped	garlic cloves
2-inch	chopped ginger piece
2 to 2½ lbs	skinless chicken, cut into 8 pieces
1 teaspoon	salt, or to taste
1 ½ teaspoons	Indian chilli powder
½ cup	lemon juice

① Heat the oil in a large saucepan, add the garlic and ginger and cook until fragrant.

② Stir in the chicken and salt and cook covered on low until the meat is cooked through and all the liquid is absorbed, about 25 to 30 minutes.

③ Stir in the chilli powder and lemon juice and cook for 5 more minutes.

④ Serve with French fries or rice and salad, and of course, some Ambli Ni Chutney (page 104) and more hot sauce if you like.

Nazlin's Better Butter Chicken

TIME	YIELD	GLUTEN-FREE
30 minutes	4–5 servings	

This is the favourite dish of Noorbanu's daughter, Nazlin. It is an original butter chicken recipe from *A Spicy Touch: Volume II* and we had to include it here because—for Nazlin—it is the "better butter chicken." She likes to add a little cream just before serving. The spicing is more complex than Noorbanu's other butter chicken recipe. Do make both and let us know which one's your favourite.

1 Tablespoon	oil
6 × 1 inch pieces	cinnamon bark
6	green cardamom pods (cracked)
6	cloves
1 ½ teaspoons	cumin seeds
1 ½ teaspoons	Garlic Paste (page 42)
1 ½ teaspoons	Ginger Paste (page 43)
1 teaspoon	Green Chilli Paste (page 44), or to taste
2 lbs	bone-in chicken, cut in pieces, skin removed
¼ cup	butter
2 cups	canned crushed tomatoes
5 Tablespoons	Crispy Fried Onions (page 42), ground to a powder
½ teaspoon	ground cumin
½ teaspoon	ground coriander
¼ teaspoon	turmeric
1 teaspoon	salt
½ cup	half-and-half cream
½ teaspoon	Garam Masala (page 29)
2 Tablespoons	finely cut coriander leaves

① Heat the oil in a wok on medium heat, add the cinnamon, cardamom, cloves and cumin seeds and cook until fragrant—about 30 to 60 seconds.

② Stir in garlic, ginger, and chilli pastes and—after about 30 seconds—add the chicken and butter and cook until the chicken is starting to change colour but is still pink on the inside—about 10 to 15 minutes. (Add a little more butter if the chicken does not have much fat of its own).

③ Stir in the tomatoes, ground onion, cumin, coriander, turmeric, salt and cook for 10 minutes or until the chicken cooks through and the oil separates.

④ Stir in ½ of the coriander leaves and cook until the chicken is tender and the oil separates. Add cream.

⑤ Stir in the Garam Masala and top with the other half of the coriander leaves just before serving.

⑥ Enjoy with Parotha (page 269) or Naan (page 266).

Fish and Seafood

JEERA PRAWNS (RECIPE, PAGE 165) ON
SHAVED FENNEL AND CUMIN SALAD
(RECIPE, PAGE 60)

Fish and Masala Chips

TIME	YIELD	GLUTEN-FREE
45 minutes	4 servings	

This is a delectable version of fish and chips with the brightness of an Indian-spiced tomato sauce.

1 ¼ lbs	halibut or any firm white fish, cut in 4–5 small pieces
½ teaspoon	salt
2 lbs	frozen French fries
4 Tablespoons	oil
1 cup	canned crushed tomatoes
2 teaspoon	Garlic Paste (page 42)
½ teaspoon	Green Chilli Paste (page 44), or to taste
½ teaspoon	Indian chilli powder, or to taste
1 teaspoon	ground cumin
½ teaspoon	ground coriander
½ teaspoon	salt
¼ teaspoon	turmeric
¼ cup	water
1 Tablespoon	finely cut coriander leaves

① Wash the fish, pat it dry with paper towel, sprinkle it with salt and set aside for 20 minutes.

② Preheat the oven to 425°F.

③ Spread the fish in a single layer on a baking tray lined with parchment paper and bake in the preheated oven until golden brown (10 minutes per inch of thickness).

④ Spread the French fries on another baking tray in a single layer and bake in the same oven until golden brown—about 20 minutes (or according to package directions).

⑤ Heat the oil in a frying pan on medium heat and add the tomatoes, garlic and chilli pastes, chilli powder, cumin, coriander, salt, turmeric and water.

⑥ Cook until most of the liquid has evaporated and the mixture is quite thick.

⑦ Put the French fries on a platter and arrange the cooked fish on top.

⑧ Drizzle the sauce over the fish and fries.

⑨ Garnish with the coriander leaves.

⑩ Enjoy with Rotli (page 268), Parotha (page 269) or Naan bread (page 266).

Fish Curry

TIME	YIELD	GLUTEN-
20 minutes	4 servings	*FREE*

This makes a nice quick supper with Rotli (page 268) or with Fluffy Basmati Rice (page 249) to soak up all the delicious sauce. We like to use a firm white fish like halibut or lingcod.

1 lb	fish (use steaks not fillets)
3 Tablespoons	olive oil
1 Tablespoon	Crispy Fried Onions (page 42)
½ cup	canned crushed tomatoes
½ cup	water
4	whole cloves
1 teaspoon	Garlic Paste (page 42)
1 teaspoon	ground cumin
¼ teaspoon	turmeric
½ teaspoon	Indian chilli powder, or to taste
1 teaspoon	salt, or to taste
2 cup	hot water
½ teaspoon	Garam Masala (page 29)
1 Tablespoon	finely cut coriander leaves
1 Tablespoon	lemon juice

① Wash the fish and cut it into 4 pieces—about the size of a deck of cards.

② Heat the olive oil in a medium-sized saucepan on low heat, add the onions and cook until golden brown—about 10 minutes.

③ Remove the onions from the oil using a slotted spoon and set aside in a separate bowl.

④ Add the cloves to the hot oil and cook covered for about 1 minute.

⑤ Place the onions and the tomatoes in a blender and process to a smooth purée, then add the purée to the spice mixture and cook for about 10 minutes.

⑥ Add the garlic, cumin, turmeric, chilli powder and salt and cook while stirring for 1 minute.

⑦ Stir in the water when the sauce starts to boil and then add the fish and simmer (without stirring—you don't want the fish to fall apart—you are actually poaching it in this sauce) until it is cooked.

⑧ Stir in the Garam Masala.

⑨ Enjoy served on a platter of rice topped with coriander leaves and lemon juice.

Fish Paka

FISH WITH COCONUT AND RICE

TIME	YIELD	
45 minutes	3-4 servings	*GLUTEN-FREE*

This is an easy alternative to fish biryani. In East Africa, where Noorbanu lived the first half of her life, coconuts were plentiful and coconut cream was often substituted in dishes that would have been made with cow's cream in India. The results were wonderful flavour adaptations and now that all the health benefits of coconut have come to light this geographical adaptation turns out to be quite healthy too.

1 lb	fish fillets (cod, haddock, halibut, lingcod)
½ teaspoon	salt
1 Tablespoon	lemon juice
¼ teaspoon	Indian chilli powder
½ teaspoon	Garlic Paste (page 42)
2 Tablespoons	coconut
1½ Tablespoons	finely cut coriander leaves, divided
½ cup	chopped tomato (1 small)
½ cup	chopped onion (1 small)
1	(14 ounce/398 mL) can coconut milk or cream, divided
1 Tablespoon	lemon juice
½ teaspoon	salt, or to taste
⅛ teaspoon	turmeric, optional

① Wash the fish, cut into 4 pieces and pat them dry with paper towels.

② Rub the fish with salt and lemon juice and marinate for 30 minutes.

③ Turn the broiler on in your oven.

④ Combine the chilli powder, garlic paste and oil and brush the mixture on both sides of the fish.

⑤ Place the fish on a baking tray lined with parchment paper and broil the fish on both sides until it is golden brown and flakes easily.

⑥ Save any pan juices.

⑦ Place 1 teaspoon of the cilantro leaves and the tomato, onion and ¼ cup of the coconut milk in a food processor and pulse to a fine purée.

⑧ Combine the remaining coconut milk with the tomato mixture and any fish pan juices in a medium saucepan and cook on low heat until the liquid is reduced by half—stirring frequently

⑨ Add the fish, lemon juice, salt, turmeric and the rest of the cilantro leaves.

⑩ Enjoy with Parotha (page 269) and Fluffy Basmati Rice (page 249).

Fish with Spinach and Cream

TIME	YIELD	GLUTEN-FREE
30 minutes	4-5 servings	

An elegant and vitamin-packed dish for dinner.

1 lb	fish fillets (cod, haddock, halibut, lingcod), washed, dried and cut in 2-inch cubes
½ teaspoon	salt
1 Tablespoon	lemon juice
1 Tablespoon	butter
½ cup	finely chopped onion (1 small)
½ cup	canned crushed tomatoes
½ teaspoon	salt
½ teaspoon	Garlic Paste (page 42)
½ teaspoon	black pepper
¼ teaspoon	turmeric
½ lb	finely chopped fresh spinach
1 cup	whipping cream
1 Tablespoon	lemon juice

① Preheat the oven to 425°F.

② Sprinkle the fish with salt and lemon juice and marinate for 15 minutes.

③ Place the fish pieces on a baking tray lined with parchment paper and bake for 10 minutes.

④ Melt the butter in a saucepan on medium heat, stir in the onions and cook until transparent.

⑤ Stir in the tomatoes, salt, pepper, garlic, turmeric and spinach and cook for 3 minutes then cover and cook until the spinach is wilted and water is reduced to a minimum—about 5 minutes more.

⑥ Add the whipping cream and fish and cook for another 3 minutes.

⑦ Stir in the lemon juice.

⑧ Enjoy with Naan (page 266) or Fluffy Basmati Rice (page 249).

Fish Bhajias

FISH FRITTERS

TIME	YIELD	GLUTEN-FREE
45 minutes	3-4 servings	

When we serve these the table is covered with all our favourite chutneys. Our plates look like an artist's palate as we dollop the chutneys on them and then dip each morsel of fish into a different one. Try Apple and Mint Chutney (page 105), Ambli Ni chutney (page 104), Coconut Chutney (page 107) or Lemon Chutney (page 111). You'll soon develop your own list of favourites.

Sunflower oil for frying

1 lb	fish fillets (cod, haddock, halibut, lingcod)
½ teaspoon	salt
1 Tablespoon	lemon juice
1 cup	chana flour
½ cup	warm water
½ teaspoon	Garlic Paste (page 42)
½ teaspoon	Ginger Paste (page 43)
½ cup	Green Chilli Paste (page 44) or Sambal Oelek
1 teaspoon	olive oil
¼ teaspoon	turmeric
½ teaspoon	salt
1 Tablespoon	chopped fresh fenugreek (*methi*) leaves (optional)
1 Tablespoon	finely cut coriander leaves
¼ teaspoon	baking powder
¼ teaspoon	freshly ground black pepper

① Cut the fish into small pieces (about 1½-inch × ½-inch thick) then wash and pat it dry with paper towels.

② Sprinkle the fish with salt and lemon juice and marinate for 30 minutes.

③ Sift the chana flour into a bowl and add enough water to make a pancake-like batter.

④ Stir in the garlic, ginger and chilli pastes, oil, turmeric, salt, fenugreek, cilantro, baking powder and pepper.

⑤ Wash the fish again and pat it dry with paper towels.

⑥ Heat the oil in a deep-fryer or wok to 350°F.

⑦ Dip the fish in the batter and then slip it directly into the oil.

⑧ Deep-fry a few pieces of fish at a time until they turn golden brown.

⑨ Remove the fish with slotted spoon to a paper towel-lined plate to absorb excess oil before serving.

⑩ Enjoy with your favourite chutneys.

Jeera Prawns

PRAWNS IN CUMIN SAUCE

TIME	YIELD	GLUTEN-FREE
15 minutes	4 servings	

Buying frozen or fresh raw prawns that are already peeled, deveined and ready to cook makes this recipe a breeze.

1 ¼ lb	raw, shelled and deveined large prawns (25–30 per pound)
1 Tablespoon	butter or Ghee (page 43)
2 – 3 finely	chopped chillies (preferably Serrano)
1 teaspoon	Garlic Paste (page 42)
1½ teaspoons	coarsely ground cumin seeds
½ teaspoon	salt
¼ teaspoon	turmeric
2 Tablespoons	lemon juice
1 Tablespoon	finely cut coriander leaves

① Rinse the prawns under cold running water, pat them dry and set aside.

② Melt the butter or ghee in a skillet on medium heat, add the chillies, garlic and cumin and stir-fry for 1 minutes.

③ Add the prawns, salt, turmeric and lemon juice and stir constantly until the prawns curl and turn pink.

④ Garnish with the coriander leaves.

⑤ Enjoy as a starter or or with Shaved Fennel and Cumin Salad (page 60) for a light meal.

JEERA PRAWNS ON SHAVED
FENNEL AND CUMIN SALAD
SEE PAGE 158

Prawns and Halibut in Coconut Cream

TIME	YIELD	GLUTEN-FREE
30–40 minutes	3–4 servings	*GLUTEN-FREE*

This is a favourite of Karen's family who love the combination of flavours in this light coconut dish.

½ lb	large shelled, deveined prawns (about 30 per lb)
½ lb	halibut cut in 2-inch pieces, bones removed

For the Marinade:

1 Tablespoon	coconut oil, divided into 1 teaspoon × 3
1 teaspoon	Garlic Paste (page 42)
½ teaspoon	Green Chilli Paste (page 44), or to taste
½ teaspoon	salt
1 Tablespoon	lemon juice
½ teaspoon	ground cumin

For the Sauce:

½	small spicy red pepper
½	small spicy green pepper
1	(14 ounce/398mL) can coconut cream
Pinch	turmeric
1 Tablespoon	finely cut coriander leaves

① Whisk 1 teaspoon of the coconut oil with the garlic and chilli pastes, salt, lemon juice and cumin in a large bowl and add the fish and prawns.

② Mix to coat thoroughly and marinate for at least 30 minutes.

③ Heat the next 1 teaspoon of oil in a wok on medium heat and cook the shrimp until they curl and turn pink. Remove the prawns from the wok and set aside.

④ Heat the remaining 1 teaspoon of oil and cook and stir the bell peppers until they begin to soften. Remove these and set them aside.

⑤ Add the coconut cream, turmeric and any remaining marinade to the wok and simmer until the sauce thickens.

⑥ Add the fish and poach it until it is cooked but still tender.

⑦ Add the reserved shrimp and peppers and cook until they are warmed through again.

⑧ Transfer to a serving dish, garnish with the freshly chopped coriander leaves and serve.

⑨ Enjoy with Fluffy Basmati Rice (page 249) and Coconut Chutney (page 107).

Prawns Masala

DRY PRAWN CURRY

TIME	YIELD	
30–35 minutes	6 servings	*GLUTEN-FREE*

The sprinkle of freshly ground Garam Masala at the end of this recipe enhances all of its delicious flavours.

2 lbs	large, shelled and deveined prawns (about 30 per lb)
½ teaspoon	salt, or to taste
1 Tablespoon	lemon juice
1 Tablespoon	butter
2 Tablespoons	olive oil
1½ cups	fresh blended tomatoes (2 medium)
1 Tablespoon	tomato paste
2 Tablespoons	Crispy Fried Onions (page 42)
1½ teaspoons	Garlic Paste (page 42)
½ teaspoon	Ginger Paste (page 43)
½ teaspoon	Indian chilli powder, or to taste
1 teaspoon	ground cumin
½ teaspoon	ground coriander
½ teaspoon	turmeric
½ teaspoon	salt, or to taste
¼ cup	water
½ teaspoon	Garam Masala (page 29)
1 Tablespoon	finely cut coriander leaves
6	lemon slices

① Marinate the prawns in the salt and lemon juice for 10 to 15 minutes. Drain and pat dry with paper towel.

② Melt the butter in a heavy-bottomed wok or pan and cook the prawns on both sides until they are just pink—be careful not to overcook.

③ Remove the prawns and their juices from the pan and set aside.

④ Add the olive oil, stir in the tomatoes and tomato paste, garlic and ginger pastes, crispy fried onions, chilli powder, cumin, coriander, turmeric, salt and water and cook until the oil separates from the mixture.

⑤ Add the prawns and reserved pan juices and cook until heated through before transferring to a serving platter.

⑥ Garnish with the Garam Masala (page 29) and coriander leaves.

⑦ Enjoy with a Naan (page 266) and a lemon wedge with each serving.

Spiced-up Fish Cakes

TIME
20–30 minutes (with precooked potatoes)

YIELD
12 fish cakes,
4–6 servings

Karen grew up on Canada's East Coast in the small town of St. Andrews-by-the-sea, New Brunswick. Her grandfather and father were both fishermen and fish cakes were a popular treat for a Friday night supper with the family. After making Noorbanu's recipe, Karen only had one question, why would I eat regular fish cakes when I could be eating these instead? Palates change with exposure to exciting ingredients.

1 lb	skinned and boned white fish
1 lb	boiled and mashed potatoes
2 Tablespoons	finely cut coriander leaves
3 Tablespoons	finely chopped green onion
1 Tablespoon	lemon juice
1 teaspoon	Garlic Paste (page 42)
1 teaspoon	Green Chilli Paste (page 44), or to taste
1 teaspoon	ground cumin
½ teaspoon	black peppercorns, freshly ground
1 teaspoon	salt
1 beaten	egg, reserved in a small bowl
1 cup	bread crumbs, for coating
4 Tablespoons	sunflower oil, to fry all 12 cakes

① Place the fish in a steamer over boiling water, cover with a lid and steam until it is cooked through—5 to 10 minutes.

② Flake the fish with a fork and mix with the potatoes, coriander leaves, green onion, lemon juice, garlic and chilli pastes, cumin, black pepper and salt.

③ Divide the mixture into 12 golf ball size spheres and flatten these into small patties.

④ Dip the patties into the egg and then coat both sides with the bread crumbs.

⑤ Heat the oil in a frying pan and fry the cakes until both sides are golden brown and crisp.

⑥ Enjoy with the salad of your choice and Coriander Chutney (page 108), or Ambli Ni Chutney (page 104).

Tandoori and Grilling

LAMBSICLES WITH
FENNEL CREAM
(RECIPE, PAGE 186)

Beef Shish Kebabs
with Homemade Barbecue Sauce

TIME	YIELD
40–50 minutes	4 servings

Karen loves this recipe but also thinks this mixture makes the best burger patties EVER. She likes to serve them on buns loaded with summer fresh tomatoes, sliced red onions and crisp lettuce dripping with a good dose of this homemade barbecue sauce and other chutneys from her fridge. If the sauces are rolling down your arm as you eat this—you know you're doing it right.

For the Kebabs:

1 lb	lean ground beef
1½ Tablespoons	finely cut coriander leaves, divided evenly
1 teaspoon	Garlic Paste (page 42)
1 teaspoon	Ginger Paste (page 43)
1 teaspoon	Green Chilli Paste (page 44), or to taste
1 Tablespoon	Worcestershire Sauce
2 Tablespoons	Ambli Ni Chutney (page 104)
1 teaspoon	Sambal Oelek, or to taste
½ teaspoon	salt
½ teaspoon	freshly ground pepper
2 teaspoons	ground cumin
1 Tablespoon	oil

For the Sauce:

5 Tablespoons	canned crushed tomatoes
1 teaspoon	tomato paste
1 Tablespoon	Worcestershire sauce
1 Tablespoon	soy sauce
½ teaspoon	Garlic Paste (page 42)
½ teaspoon	Ginger Paste (page 43)
½ teaspoon	Green Chilli Paste (page 44)
½ teaspoon	salt
1 Tablespoon	lemon juice
2 Tablespoons	finely cut coriander leaves
½	red and green bell pepper, cut into ½-inch slices

To Make the Kebabs:

① Mix the ingredients in a large bowl with your hands until well distributed.

② Divide into 24 balls.

③ Thread 1 ball onto a skewer and shape the meat mixture into a thumb length kebab around the skewer.

④ Repeat until there are 4 or 5 kebabs on each skewer.

⑤ Place the skewers on a hot grill and cook about 4 minutes each side, or until the juices run clear.

To Make the Sauce:

① Mix all of the sauce ingredients except the red and green peppers in a saucepan and simmer on medium heat until thick. Add the peppers and half a cup of hot water and cook a few minutes more— until the peppers are heated through.

② Stir in kebabs and simmer on low heat for 2 to 3 minutes.

③ Sprinkle with the remaining coriander leaves.

④ Enjoy with Lightly Spiced Rice (page 249), and Naan (page 266).

Chilli Lime Sauce

TIME	YIELD	*GLUTEN-FREE*
5 minutes	¾ cup	*& VEGETARIAN*

½ cup	butter
¼ cup	lime juice
3 teaspoons	Indian chilli powder
1 teaspoon	salt
½ teaspoon	freshly ground black pepper

① Melt the butter and stir in the lime juice, chilli powder, salt and pepper.

② Serve as a dipping sauce for the ribs or pour over the whole batch if all your guests can take some heat.

③ Enjoy the ribs with the chilli lime sauce and a side of cooling Cucumber Raita (page 108).

Barbecued Crosscut Beef Short Ribs

WITH CHILLI LIME SAUCE

MARINATE	TIME	YIELD	*GLUTEN-*
at least 8 hours	30 minutes	4 servings	*FREE*

This recipe is the specialty of Noorbanu's grandson Imran Mangalji. The ribs are quick and easy to make, addictively delicious and sure to be a legendary party pleaser. The crosscut rib might be unfamiliar to you. It is popular in Korean restaurants that feature L.A. Golbi ribs. Once you start to look for them, we're sure you'll find them or ask your butcher to cut the long thin strips of beef short ribs for you.

4 lbs	beef short ribs, long thin strips of crosscut ribs
¼ cup	Garlic Paste (page 42)
¼ cup	Ginger Paste (page 43)
3 Tablespoons	olive oil

① Place the ribs in a large bowl and coat them with the garlic and ginger paste and oil.

② Marinate overnight (or at least 8 hours) in the refrigerator in a covered container.

③ Place the ribs on a hot preheated grill and cook about 4 to 5 minutes per side or according to your preference.

④ Put the ribs on a platter and use kitchen shears or a sharp knife to cut them into serving size portions.

TIP: Cut between the bones.

⑤ Enjoy as an appetizer with the Chilli Lime Sauce or as a meal with your choice of salad, chutneys, potatoes and vegetables.

Boti Kabab
Meat Miskaki

BEEF, CHICKEN OR LAMB
ON SKEWERS

MARINATE	TIME	YIELD	GLUTEN
Overnight	20 minutes	4–6 servings	*FREE*

Noorbanu's son-in-law Nasir Mangalji has perfected this recipe over the years. One of his top secret tips (until now) for incredibly tender results is to marinate the meat with a quarter of a mashed up kiwi for 1 to 2 days in the fridge. Do this towards the end of the week and invite your friends over for a weekend barbecue. You'll be all the rage because, after all, everyone loves food on a stick.

2 lbs	meat (your choice), cut in 1-inch cubes
2 teaspoons	Garlic Paste (page 42)
2 teaspoons	Ginger Paste (page 43)
1 teaspoon	Green Chilli Paste (page 44), or to taste
1 Tablespoon	Sambal Oelek or to taste
2 teaspoons	ground cumin
1 teaspoon	ground coriander
½ teaspoon	salt
½ teaspoon	crumbled dried fenugreek (*Kasoori Methi*) leaves
1 Tablespoon	oil

① Combine all the ingredients in a glass bowl or baking dish, cover and marinate in the refrigerator overnight.

② Thread 6 to 7 cubes of meat onto each skewer and grill on high heat until cooked through.

③ Enjoy with Yogurt (page 46), Spicy Spuds (page 199), green salad, Ambli Ni Chutney (page 104), Coriander Chutney (page 108) and Naan (page 266).

Chicken Tikka

MARINATE	TIME	YIELD	GLUTEN-FREE
4 hours to overnight	30–40 minutes	4–5 servings	

Tikka is the Hindi word for *chunks of meat* cooked on skewers. It's a popular dish worldwide, and when the Nimji's lived in Nairobi it was the family's favourite snack at the drive-in movie theatre.

TIP: Make lots of this as the leftovers are delicious in sandwiches the next day or used to create another great meal Pi-Naan-Za (page 267).

2 lbs	boneless and skinless chicken breast, cut in 1-inch cubes

Marinade:

2 Tablespoons	Yogurt (page 46)
2 teaspoons	Garlic Paste (page 42)
2 teaspoons	Ginger Paste (page 43)
1 teaspoon	Green Chilli Paste (page 44)
2 Tablespoons	tomato paste
1 teaspoon	salt, or to taste
1 Tablespoon	olive oil
½ teaspoon	Indian chilli powder, optional

Bamboo skewers, soaked in water for a few hours

① Mix the yogurt, garlic, ginger, chilli, and tomato pastes, salt, oil and chilli powder (if used) in a bowl.

② Add the chicken to the marinade, mix thoroughly and cover. Refrigerate for about 4 hours or overnight.

③ Soak the bamboo skewers in water for at least 2 hours (or use metal skewers)

④ Thread 5 to 6 marinated chicken cubes onto each skewer.

⑤ Place on a hot grill and cook 5 to 6 minutes per side or until juices run clear.

⑥ Enjoy hot with your choice of salad, Ambli Ni Chutney (page 104), Cucumber Raita (page 108) and Naan (page 266).

Variation:

CHICKEN TIKKA WRAP: Noorbanu's granddaughter likes to spread Cucumber Raita (page 108) on a piece of hot Naan (page 266) with shredded lettuce and a pile of the hot *Chicken Tikka* cubes for an instant wrap and instant taste sensation.

Coconut Can Chicken

TIME	YIELD	GLUTEN-FREE
2 hours	4 servings	

This is a fun take on the popular "beer can chicken." Typically, a chicken is positioned butt-side down on a partially empty can of beer with the goal of even cooking and increased moisture retention. In our spin on this recipe, Karen adds a half a can of coconut milk and tropical flavours to a clean empty beer can. It was an instant hint when she and Noorbanu's grandson Imran were recipe testing for this chapter.

For the Chicken:

1–3 lb	whole chicken
1	(14 ounce/398 ml) can coconut milk
¼ cup	lime juice
1	shallot, cut in half
1	key lime, zest removed and both lime and zest reserved
1	finely diced shallot
1 teaspoon	Garlic Paste (page 42)
1 teaspoon	Ginger Paste (page 43)
1 teaspoon	Green Chilli Paste (page 44)
½ teaspoon	turmeric
1 teaspoon	cumin

For the Basting Marinade:

2 Tablespoons	melted Ghee (page 43)
1 Tablespoon	honey
1 teaspoon	paprika
1 teaspoon	Green Chilli Paste (page 44)
½ teaspoon	salt

1. Wash the chicken inside and out with cold water and then pat it dry with paper towel.

2. Open a can of coconut milk, without shaking it, and spoon the thick white coconut cream at the top of the can into a small bowl. Set aside.

3. Pour the remaining coconut milk into a clean, empty beer can and add the lime juice, shallot and key lime (slice as necessary to fit in the can).

4. Mix the lime zest, the diced second half of the shallot, garlic, ginger and chilli pastes, turmeric and cumin with the coconut cream in its bowl.

5. Pull the skin—gently—of the chicken breasts and thighs away from the meat without detaching it and slide the coconut and spice paste into the cavity between the skin and meat.

6. Slide the bottom of the chicken onto the beer can.

7. Heat 1 side of your grill on high and place the chicken on the other side.

8. Whisk the basting ingredients in a bowl and baste the exterior of the chicken at the start, at 1 hour and then 1 more time about 5 minutes before finishing.

   TIP: A 3 lb chicken will take about 1 ½ to 2 hours to cook. You'll know its done when the legs move easily and the juices run clear.

9. Remove the whole chicken and can from the barbecue to a tray, tent with foil for at least 5 minutes and then carefully remove the chicken from the can and carve.

10. Enjoy with Coconut Rice (page 249) and Spicy Green Beans (page 215) or Cassava Oven Fries (page 68) and a fresh green salad.

Grilled Salmon with Honey, Lime and Green Chilli Paste

TIME	YIELD	
40–50 minutes	4 servings	*GLUTEN-FREE*

It's always nicer to cook fish outside on the grill but if the weather doesn't cooperate this recipe can be baked in an oven preheated to 400°F for 10 to 15 minutes.

2 lbs	salmon fillet
2 teaspoons	olive oil
1 teaspoon	ground coriander
1 teaspoon	ground cumin
½ teaspoon	mustard powder
½ teaspoon	Garlic Paste (page 42)
1 teaspoon	Green Chilli Paste (page 44), or to taste
1 teaspoon	lime juice
Zest of 1 lime	
2 Tablespoons	honey
Salt and pepper, to taste	

① Place the fish fillet on a double layer of aluminum foil and fold the edges up to form a tray around the fish.

② Whisk the olive oil, ground coriander and cumin, mustard powder, garlic and chilli pastes, lime juice and zest, honey, salt and pepper together in a bowl and brush it on the salmon.

③ Cook on a hot grill for 10 minutes per inch of thickness of the fish.

④ Enjoy as shown here with Spinach Curry (page 218) or with Spicy Potatoes with Bell Peppers (page 217) and your choice of salad.

Variation:

Place the salmon on the foil and coat with olive oil then sprinkle with the A Spicy Touch Grilling Masala (page 32) and cook 10 minutes for each inch of thickness of the fish on high heat on the grill or in the oven.

Grilled Steak with Avocado Tomato and Coriander Salsa

TIME	PLUS	YIELD	GLUTEN-FREE
30 minutes	resting time for the meat	2–4 servings	

For the Steak:

2 lbs	grilling steak (T-bone, prime rib, sirloin)
1 Tablespoon	olive oil
1 teaspoon	A Spicy Touch Grilling Masala (page 32)

For the Salsa:

1	peeled and chopped avocado
1 cup	chopped tomato (2 small) or use grape tomatoes
¼ – ½ cup	Coriander Chutney (page 108)
Salt and pepper, to taste	

① Rub the steak with the olive oil and sprinkle both sides with the A Spicy Touch Grilling Mas*ala*. Let it rest for an hour on a plate on the counter to bring the meat to room temperature before grilling. It will cook more evenly this way.

② Heat the grill to high and place the steak on it for 4 to 5 minutes per side or to your desired doneness.

③ Remove it from the grill, place it on a rack and tent it with foil to rest.

④ Combine the avocado, tomato and Coriander Chutney in a bowl and season with salt and pepper to taste and serve with the steak.

⑤ Enjoy with a Spicy Spud (page 199) and extra Coriander Chutney (page 108).

Hot 'n' Spicy
Chicken Drumsticks

MARINATE	TIME	YIELD	GLUTEN-FREE
2 hours	30 minutes	4 servings	

Wings are great but Noorbanu's daughter Rosie loves to make a meatier drumstick version for family gatherings.

2 lbs	chicken drumsticks

Marinade:

1 teaspoon	Indian chilli powder
1½ teaspoons	Garlic Paste (page 42)
1½ teaspoons	Ginger Paste (page 43)
1 teaspoon	salt

Hot Sauce:

2 Tablespoons	melted butter or Ghee (page 43)
1 Tablespoon	finely cut coriander leaves
½ teaspoon	freshly ground black pepper
1½ cups	Louisiana Hot Sauce™

For the Drumsticks:

① Rinse the chicken and pat it dry with a paper towel.

② Mix the ingredients for the marinade in a bowl, add the chicken and toss to coat it well, then marinate for 2 hours.

③ Place the chicken on a hot grill and cook on medium heat for about 10 minutes per side or until juices run clear.

For the Hot Sauce:

① Melt the butter or ghee in a medium saucepan.

② Stir in the coriander, pepper, Louisiana Hot Sauce™ and cook for about 10 minutes or until the sauce thickens.

③ Spread the chicken on a platter and coat with the sauce.

④ Enjoy hot of the grill as an appetizer with the traditional wing sides of chopped celery, carrot sticks and ranch dressing for the hot drumsticks to take a cool dip in.

Lamb Chops

MARINATE	TIME	YIELD	*GLUTEN-FREE*
3 hours to overnight	40 minutes	4 servings	

These are just plain finger-licking, lip-smackingly good.

2 lbs	lamb chops

For the Marinade:

1½ teaspoons	Garlic Paste (page 42)
1½ teaspoons	Ginger Paste (page 43)
3 Tablespoons	soy sauce (substitute tamari for gluten-free)
2 Tablespoons	sweet chilli pepper sauce
1 Tablespoon	lemon juice
½ teaspoon	salt, or to taste
2 Tablespoons	olive oil

① Whisk all of the ingredients for the marinade in a glass bowl.

② Add the lamb chops, toss to coat them well and marinate for a minimum of 3 hours or overnight in the refrigerator.

③ Place on a hot grill and cook the chops on high about 4 to 5 minutes per side or to desired temperature.

④ Remove to a rack, tent with foil and let the meat rest for 5 minutes before serving.

⑤ Enjoy with Spicy Potatoes with Bell Peppers (page 217), and Naan (page 266), and your choice of salad.

Lambsicles with Fennel Cream

MARINATE	TIME	YIELD	GLUTEN-FREE
30 minutes minimum or overnight in the fridge	20–30 minutes	4 servings	

We love to eat at Vij's Restaurant when we visit Vancouver. Owners Vikram Vij and Meeru Dhalwala, are famous for many dishes and the restaurant is consistently named as the top Indian restaurant in the world. True to their generous spirit they share their signature Lamb Popsicle recipe in their bestselling cookbook, *Vij's: Elegant and Inspired Indian Cuisine* (Douglas and McIntyre, 2006). This recipe is our nod to Vij's recipe. We've kept the full flavour and cut back on some of the fat content. We are aware that heart disease is prominent in South Asians and Ismaili people. Karen's cardiologist husband Todd reminds us frequently!

For the Lambsicles:

2 lbs	lamb racks
1 Tablespoon	olive oil
1 teaspoon	honey
1 teaspoon	Garam Masala (page 29)
1 teaspoon	fennel seeds
1 teaspoon	Garlic Paste (page 42)
1 teaspoon	Ginger Paste (page 43)
1 teaspoon	Green Chilli Paste (page 44)

For the Fennel Cream:

1 Tablespoon	olive oil
1 teaspoon	fennel seeds
1 teaspoon	black mustard seeds
1 teaspoon	Garlic Paste (page 42)
½ teaspoon	Green Chilli Paste (page 44)
½ teaspoon	turmeric
½ teaspoon	paprika
½ cup	half-and-half cream
1 teaspoon	lime juice
1 teaspoon	Dried Fenugreek Leaves (*Kasoori Methi*)
½ teaspoon	salt

LAMBSICLES WITH FENNEL CREAM
SEE PAGE 187

For the Lambsicles:

① Cut between the bones of the rack of lamb to create chops. French the chops by cutting out the triangle of fat along the bone to where the bulk of the meat is located. This will create a Popsicle-shaped piece of meat at the end of the bone.

② Stir the oil, honey, Garam Masala, fennel seeds, garlic, ginger and chilli pastes in a bowl and then coat both sides of each chop with the paste.

③ Marinate the chops at room temperature for at least 30 minutes.

④ Heat the grill to medium-high heat and cook the chops for 3 to 4 minutes on each side for medium rare chops.

⑤ Remove and place on a rack to rest, then tent with foil for 5 minutes.

For the Sauce:

① Heat the olive oil, add the fennel and mustard seeds and then—once they pop—add the garlic and chilli pastes with the turmeric and paprika.

② Stir the spices and then slowly add the cream so it does not curdle.

③ Stir in the lime juice, *Kasoori Methi* and salt and cook on medium heat until the *methi* leaves are soft and the sauce is heated through.

④ Enjoy the chops on their own with the sauce in a little dipping bowl for each guest or place the chops on a platter filled with rice, drizzle with the sauce and serve family style.

Spatchcocked Chicken with A Spicy Touch Grilling Masala

TIME	YIELD	GLUTEN-FREE
2 hours	4 servings	

Spatchcocking is a fancy name for removing the backbone and cooking a chicken flat. This definitely speeds up the cooking time. To help the chicken stay moist, we place it on a clay pizza stone and the results are positively succulent.

1–3 lb	chicken
1 Tablespoon	olive oil
1 teaspoon	Garlic Paste (page 42)
1–2 teaspoons	A Spicy Touch Grilling Masala (page 32)

① Heat the grill on high and place a clay pizza stone in the centre.

② Wash the inside and outside of the chicken with running water and pat it dry with paper towel then cut the backbone out of the chicken with kitchen shears.

③ Flatten the chicken on a baking tray and rub the outside with the olive oil and garlic paste and then sprinkle it with the A Spicy Touch Grilling Masala.

④ Slide the chicken from the baking tray to the pizza stone on the grill and cook on medium-high heat for about 1½ hours.

⑤ Remove the chicken to a rack on a baking tray and tent with foil for 5 minutes before carving.

TIP: Taking the time to tent your meat will allow the juices to be reabsorbed and retained after carving, resulting in a juicier final product.

⑥ Serve with a green salad, Cabbage Salad with a Kick (page 58) or Shaved Fennel and Cumin Salad (page 60) and your choice of potato or rice.

Tandoori Chicken

SPICY BARBECUED CHICKEN

MARINATE	TIME	YIELD	*GLUTEN-FREE*
8 hours to overnight	45 minutes	2–4 servings	

This succulent dish is a favourite at backyard gatherings in the summer months in Canada. You can get up in the morning and put this chicken in the marinade, then cook that evening but the longer you leave it, the better it will taste (up to 2 to 3 days).

2 ¼ lbs	chicken pieces (thighs, legs, breasts with slits cut in the meat to allow more marinade to absorb)

For the Marinade:

1 small	onion, grated (optional)
1 Tablespoon	tomato paste
1 Tablespoon	Garlic Paste (page 42)
1 Tablespoon	Ginger Paste (page 43)
½ teaspoon	Green Chilli Paste (page 44)
½ teaspoon	Indian chilli powder
2 Tablespoons	yogurt (full fat or sour cream)
1 teaspoon	ground cumin
½ teaspoon	ground coriander
¼ teaspoon	Garam Masala (page 29)
1 Tablespoon	lemon juice
4–6	saffron strands, optional
2 Tablespoons	olive oil
1 Tablespoon	Ambli Ni Chutney (page 104)

① Place the marinade ingredients together in a plastic bag or glass dish and mix together.

② Add the chicken and marinate overnight or for 6 to 8 hours minimum.

③ Broil or cook on medium-high heat grill.

④ Enjoy with Spicy Spuds (page 199), green salad, Yogurt (page 46) and Ambli Ni Chutney (page 104).

Tandoori Prawns

MARINATE	TIME	YIELD	*GLUTEN-FREE*
minimum of 1 hour marinating time	15 minutes	2–3 servings	

In citrus season these prawns are a great treat layered on top of a salad of blood oranges or grapefruit, fennel and avocado.

1 lb	rinsed, peeled and deveined prawns (about 30 per lb)

For the Marinade:

½ cup	Yogurt (page 46)
1 teaspoon	fresh lemon juice
½ teaspoon	ground cumin
¼ teaspoon	turmeric
½ teaspoon	Indian chilli powder, or to taste
½ teaspoon	salt, or to taste
1 Tablespoon	olive oil

① Place prawns in a shallow glass baking dish.

② Mix the yogurt, lemon juice, cumin, turmeric, chilli powder, salt and olive oil in another bowl.

③ Pour half the marinade over the prawns, completely coating them and refrigerate for at least 1 hour.

④ Skewer or place the prawns directly on a hot grill, brush with the remaining marinade and cook them until they turn pink, about 3 minutes on each side.

⑤ Enjoy with rice, salad and Naan (page 266), or the fun Naa-co recipe that follows.

Tandoori Prawn and Mango Salsa Naa-cos

MAKE FIRST	TIME	YIELD
Tandoori Prawns (page 191)	15 minutes	4 Naa-cos

Mangoes are in season from May to September. They are the world's most consumed fruit and our favourite, so we're always looking for yet another way to enjoy them. This is a good one —our Tandoori Prawn recipe stuffed in fresh Naan and topped with a lively mango salsa.

For the Mango Salsa Topping:

1	chopped fresh mango
½ cup	chopped, seeded English Cucumber
1	finely chopped jalapeño
2 Tabelspoons	finely chopped red onion
1 Tablespoon	lime juice
2 teaspoons	olive oil
1 Tablespoon	finely cut coriander leaves

For the Garnish:

1 sliced	habanero chilli
1 red	Thai chilli, sliced in rings

For the Naa-cos:

1	Tandoori Prawns recipe (page 191)
4 pieces	Naan (page 266)

① Toss the mango, cucumber, jalapeño, red onion, lime juice, olive oil and coriander leaves in a bowl.

② Stuff the Naan with the Tandoori Prawns hot from the grill, top with the Mango Salsa and garnish with the habaneros and Thai chillies.

③ Enjoy with additional chutneys of your choice and a fresh salad.

Seasonal Sides for Grilled Dishes

We wanted to include these side dishes here because they go so well with the food in this chapter. However, we encourage you to check out the salads in Chapter 3 and Chutneys and such in Chapter 5 to round out all this grilling greatness.

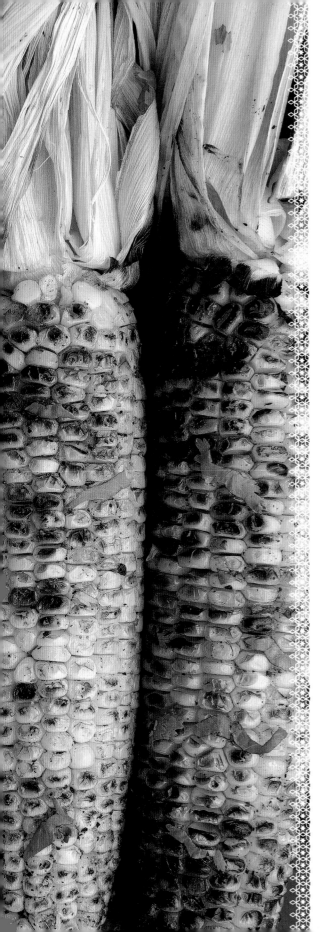

Barbecued Corn with Cumin-scented Butter

TIME	YIELD	
15 minutes	6 servings	*GLUTEN-FREE & VEGETARIAN*

Fresh corn dripping with butter is one of the joys of summer. Adding a little cumin just takes it up a "nob" or two.

6	fresh cobs of corn
4 Tablespoons	soft butter
2 teaspoons	ground cumin
2 teaspoons	freshly ground black pepper
¼ teaspoon	salt

① Boil corn until fork tender—about 7 minutes.

② Mix the butter, cumin, pepper and salt together.

③ Place the cooked corn on a hot grill, baste with the butter mixture and turn to coat and char all sides.

④ Serve hot with your favourite main.

Mixed Vegetables with A Spicy Touch Grilling Masala

TIME	YIELD	*GLUTEN-FREE*
20 minutes	4 servings	*& VEGETARIAN*

This is a healthy way to include more vegetables in your diet.

TIP: If you have leftovers save them to top a tasty Pi-Naan-Za (page 267).

2	zucchini, cut in half and then halved again and cut into strips
1	red bell pepper, cut in strips with core removed
1	yellow bell pepper, cut in strips with core removed
1	red onion, cut into strips lengthwise
2–3 Tablespoons	olive oil
2 teaspoons	Garlic Paste (page 42)
1 teaspoon	A Spicy Touch Grilling Masala (page 32)

① Combine all ingredients in a large bowl and toss the vegetables until they are thoroughly coated.

② Heat a grilling basket or grilling wok on the gas grill to high heat, add the vegetables and stir fry until they are slightly charred and cooked through.

③ Enjoy as a side with your favourite grilled meat.

Grilled Eggplant

TIME	YIELD	GLUTEN-FREE
20 minutes	4 servings	*& VEGETARIAN*

2	large eggplants
Olive oil as needed	
2 teaspoons	Garlic Paste (page 42)
1 – 2 teaspoons	A Spicy Touch Grilling Masala (page 32)

① Cut the eggplants in half and coat the flesh side with the olive oil and garlic paste then sprinkle them with A Spicy Touch Grilling Masala.

② Place the eggplant flesh side down on a hot grill and cook until browned and soft on that side.

③ Turn and heat the skin sides for 2 to 3 more minutes then remove to and arrange on platter.

④ Enjoy drizzled with Cucumber Raita (page 108), Ambli Ni Chutney (page 104) and Coriander Chutney (page 108).

Spicy Spuds

TIME	YIELD	MULTIPLY	*GLUTEN-FREE*
60 minutes (mostly baking time)	1 potato for 1 person	1 potato for 1 person, multiply as needed	*& VEGETARIAN*

This fun way to cook potatoes was invented at Sweden's *Scandic Hasselbacken Restaurant* but we think it fuses with Indian spicing very nicely. Besides, Noorbanu's favourite food is ANYTHING with potatoes.

1 large	Yukon gold, Russet, Agria, Kennebec or other great baking potato
1 Tablespoon	Ghee (page 43) or butter (melted), or olive oil, or coconut oil
½ teaspoon	A Spicy Touch Grilling Masala (page 32)
Dash	salt
Dash	pepper
Dash	paprika

Variations:

GARLIC SPUDS: Add ½ teaspoon of Garlic Paste (page 42) to the butter alone or in combination with a teaspoon of chopped fresh herbs.

CHILLI SPUDS: Baste the potato with 1 teaspoon of sweet chilli sauce at the halfway point of it's baking.

① Wash the potato and pat it dry.

② Set the potato on a cutting board and make crosswise slits with a sharp knife about ¼-inch apart – making sure to stop before you reach the cutting board. You want to leave the bottom of the potato intact and create a fan or accordion effect.

TIP: You may find it helpful to position the potato against a flat wooden spoon handle to help your knife stop cutting at the right depth.

③ Preheat the grill or oven to 425°F.

④ Set the potato on a parchment lined baking tray and using a pastry brush, baste the outside of the potato with half of the Ghee (or other choice), then sprinkle with the A Spicy Touch Grilling Masala and the salt and pepper.

⑤ Bake for 30 minutes and then baste with the remaining Ghee (or other choice) once the potato wedges have opened.

⑥ Continue baking until crispy on the outside and cooked through on the inside—about 20 minutes more—depending on the size of the potato.

⑦ Sprinkle with the paprika just before serving.

⑧ Enjoy drizzled with Cucumber Raita (page 108) and your favourite grilled meats.

CHAPTER 10

Vegetables

SPICY COCONUT
GREEN BEANS
RECIPE, PAGE 215

Bhinda Nu Saak

OKRA CURRY

TIME	YIELD	GLUTEN-FREE
45 minutes	4–5 Servings	& VEGETARIAN

This healthy and delicious curry is pure comfort food.

TIP: When using fresh okra do not wash it; just wipe it with a wet cloth to avoid stickiness.

1 lb	okra, fresh
2 Tablespoons	oil, divided
½ cup	chopped onion (1 small)
1 cup	finely chopped tomato (1 medium)
1 teaspoon	tomato paste
½ teaspoon	Garlic Paste (page 42)
½ teaspoon	ground coriander
½ teaspoon	ground cumin
⅓ teaspoon	salt, or to taste
⅓ teaspoon	turmeric
1 Tablespoon	water

① Cut the top and tail off the okra and then cut into 1 to 2 inch pieces.

② Put the okra in a plastic bag and add 1 Tablespoon of the oil.

③ Shake the bag until the pieces are coated and then arrange them on a baking tray in a single layer.

④ Broil on both sides until the okra turns golden in colour and crispy and then set aside—this is a healthier approach but the okra can also be shallow or deep-fried.

⑤ Heat the remaining 1 Tablespoon of oil and fry the onion until golden brown.

⑥ Stir in the tomato, tomato paste, garlic, coriander, cumin, salt and turmeric and cook until the tomatoes are soft—add the water only if necessary to prevent sticking.

⑦ Add the cooked okra, cover and simmer for 10 minutes—the gravy should be fairly dry.

⑧ Enjoy hot off the stove with Rotli (page 268) or Naan (page 266) and Yogurt (page 46).

Cauliflower, Peas and Potato Curry

TIME	YIELD	*GLUTEN-FREE*
20 minutes	2–3 servings	*& VEGETARIAN*

This makes a great lunch time sandwich stuffed in Naan or Rotli and drizzled with your favourite chutney.

2 teaspoons	olive oil
½ teaspoon	mustard seeds
½ teaspoon	cumin seeds
1 or 2	dried red chillies
1 cup	chopped fresh tomatoes
1 teaspoon	tomato paste
1 teaspoon	Garlic Paste (page 42)
½ teaspoon	turmeric
1 teaspoon	ground cumin
½ teaspoon	ground coriander
½ teaspoon	salt
½ cup frozen	peas
1 cup	potatoes, cut in 1-inch cubes
1 cup	chopped cauliflower
1 Tablespoon	finely cut coriander leaves

① Heat the olive oil in a saucepan, add the mustard and cumin seeds and the red chillies and cook covered until the seeds start to pop—about 1 minute.

② Stir in the tomato, tomato paste, garlic paste, turmeric, cumin, coriander, salt and cook for 5 minutes.

③ Stir in the potatoes and peas and simmer until the potatoes are almost cooked, adding water as needed if vegetables become too dry.

④ Add the cauliflower and cook until the mixture is fairly dry and the potatoes are cooked.

⑤ Sprinkle with the coriander leaves just before serving.

⑥ Enjoy with Rotli (page 268) or Naan (page 266).

Curried Corn

TIME	YIELD	GLUTEN-FREE
15 minutes	6–8 Servings	& VEGETARIAN

This is great hot but also makes a great "Indian Summer" salad when cooled and added to chopped tomatoes and diced bell peppers along with your favourite cooked Indian lentil or bean.

2	(12 ounce/341 mL) cans sweet corn niblets, drained
2 teaspoons	olive oil
½ teaspoon	mustard seeds
¼ teaspoon	cumin seeds
2 small	chillies, sliced lengthwise
4 fresh	curry leaves (optional)
¼ teaspoon	turmeric
1 ½ teaspoons	tomato paste
½ teaspoon	salt
½ teaspoon	ground cumin
½ teaspoon	Green Chilli Paste (page 44), or to taste
1 Tablespoon	lemon juice
1 Tablespoon	finely cut coriander leaves

① Heat the oil in a saucepan on medium heat and add the mustard seeds, cumin seeds, chillies and curry leaves .

② Cover and cook until the mustard seeds pop and splutter—about 1 minute.

③ Stir in the corn, turmeric, tomato paste, salt, cumin, chilli paste and continue cooking until the ingredients are heated through—about 5 minutes.

④ Stir in the lemon juice and garnish with coriander leaves just before serving.

⑤ Enjoy hot withTandoori Chicken (page 190), Beef Shish Kebabs (page 172) or other grilled meats.

Dudhi Nu Saak

CHINESE SQUASH CURRY

TIME	YIELD	GLUTEN-FREE
15–20 minutes	3–4 servings	*& VEGETARIAN*

Bottle gourd is another name for this neutral flavoured ancient form of squash that was once dried and used to carry water. It's popular in Gujarati dishes, low in calories and cooks up quickly.

2 Tablespoons	olive oil
½ teaspoon	mustard seeds
¼ teaspoon	cumin seeds
1 -2	Serrano chillies, split lengthwise or to taste
1 teaspoon	ground cumin
½ teaspoon	ground coriander
¼ teaspoon	turmeric
½ teaspoon	Indian chilli powder, or to taste
½ cup	canned crushed tomatoes
1 teaspoon	Garlic Paste (page 42)
½ teaspoon	salt
1 lb	peeled and diced, Chinese squash (dudhi)
½ cup	water, if needed
2 Tablespoons	Ambli Ni chutney (page 104)

① Heat the oil in a saucepan on medium heat and add the mustard and cumin seeds and Serrano chillies and cook covered until the seeds pop and splutter—about 1 minute.

② Stir in the cumin, coriander, turmeric, chilli powder, tomatoes, Garlic Paste, salt and water and cook for 5 minutes or until the oil separates from the sauce.

③ Stir in the diced squash (*dudhi*) and continue to cook until the squash is tender—adding water if needed to keep it from sticking and burning.

④ Add the Ambli Ni Chutney once the squash is cooked and tender when pierced with a fork.

⑤ Enjoy hot with Rotli (page 268) or Naan (page 266).

Eggplant Bhadthu

TIME	YIELD	
15–60 minutes	4–5 Servings	*GLUTEN-FREE*
(depending on cooking method)		*& VEGETARIAN*

Eggplant is indigenous to India but is a favourite worldwide with many cultures having a signature way to prepare it.

1–2 teaspoons	oil
1 large	eggplant
2 Tablespoons	chopped green onion
½ teaspoon	Garlic Paste (page 42) *or garlic*
½ teaspoon	Green Chilli Paste (page 44)
½ teaspoon	ground cumin
¼ teaspoon	salt, or to taste
1 Tablespoon †	olive oil

① Brush oil on the eggplant and cook it one of 2 ways: bake at 350° F for 45 to 50 minutes OR poke holes in the eggplant skin and then microwave until tender—about 10 minutes.

② Hold the cooked eggplant under cold running water to cool.

③ Cut the eggplant in ½ lengthwise, use the edge of a spoon to scrape the seeds away from the flesh and discard them (if there are too many for your liking), then scrape the flesh from the skin and chop it finely.

④ Mix the eggplant with the onion, garlic and chilli pastes, cumin, salt and oil in a bowl.

⑤ Enjoy with Rotli (page 268), Yogurt (page 46) and your favourite chutney on the side.

Variation:

BABA BHADTHU

If you add 1 Tablespoon of finely cut coriander leaves to the mix above this will taste very similar to *Mediterranean Baba Ghanoush* and you can enjoy it as brightly flavoured dip for vegetables, as a spread on Naan (page 266) or Rotli (page 268) or as a spread for a sandwich filled with Mixed Vegetables with A Spicy Touch Grilling Masala (page 196).

Eggplant Curry

TIME	20–30 minutes
YIELD	4–6 servings
GLUTEN-FREE & VEGETARIAN	

We have a favourite little take-out restaurant in Calgary called *Mirchi* (the *Punjabi word for Chilli*). Karen likes to pop in on her way to Noorbanu's to pick up *kebabs* and *Naan* straight from their clay oven. One day, Karen mentioned to Noorbanu that she'd love the recipe for a particularly tasty eggplant dish they'd tried and the next time she showed up for lunch, Noorbanu had recreated it. No surprise – it was every bit as good and is now one of Karen's all-time favourite dishes.

2× 8-inch long	Japanese eggplant
¼ cup	olive oil
1 teaspoon	mustard seeds
1½ cup	canned crushed tomatoes
½ teaspoon	Garlic Paste (page 42)
½ teaspoon	Ginger Paste (page 43)
1 teaspoon	Green Chilli Paste (page 44)
1 Tablespoon	finely ground Crispy Fried Onion (page 42)
¼ teaspoon	turmeric
½ teaspoon	ground coriander
½ teaspoon	ground cumin
¼ teaspoon	Garam Masala (page 29)
1 Tablespoon	finely cut coriander leaves

① Cut the top and bottom off the eggplant, then cut it in cubes and set aside.

② Heat the oil in a saucepan on medium heat, add the mustard seeds and cook covered until they pop and splutter—about 1 minute.

③ Add the tomatoes, garlic, ginger and chilli pastes, Crispy Fried Onion, turmeric, coriander and cumin and cook for another 2 to 3 minutes.

④ Stir in the eggplant and cook for about 10 minutes—or until soft when pierced with a fork—and the oil is separating from the sauce.

⑤ Sprinkle with Garam Masala and coriander leaves.

⑥ Enjoy with fresh Rotli (page 268).

Ghisoda

RIDGE GOURD CURRY

TIME	YIELD	GLUTEN-FREE
20–30 minutes	4 servings	*& VEGETARIAN*

This is one of those vegetables that you might walk by at the market and wonder what to do with. Finally – here's a very tasty answer.

1 lb chopped	ghisoda (*Si Gua* in Chinese)
2 Tablspoons	olive oil
½ teaspoon	mustard seeds
¼ teaspoon	cumin seeds
2	dried or fresh red or green chillies
½ cup	finely chopped tomatoes
1 teaspoon	tomato paste
1 teaspoon	Garlic Paste (page 42)
¼ teaspoon	Green Chilli Paste (page 44)
¼ teaspoon	paprika
½ teaspoon	turmeric
½ teaspoon	salt, or to taste
2 Tablespoons	chopped fresh dill leaves (optional)
Water, if needed	

① Wash and then peel the ridges off the *ghisoda*.

② Quarter the *ghisoda* lengthwise and slice into ½-inch pieces.

TIP: Do not rinse again.

③ Heat the olive oil in a saucepan on medium-high heat, add the mustard and cumin seeds, and the dried or fresh chillies and cook covered until the seeds pop and splutter—about 30 seconds.

④ Stir in the ghisoda and cook for 2 minutes.

⑤ Stir in the tomatoes and tomato paste and continue cooking until tomatoes are soft.

⑥ Stir in the garlic and chilli pastes, paprika, turmeric, and salt and cook for 2 minutes.

⑦ Reduce the heat to low and cook until the *ghisoda* is tender.

⑧ Add the fresh dill leaves (if desired) and simmer on low heat for a few more minutes to allow the flavours to mingle.

TIP: The gravy should be just covering the mixture—adjust by adding a little water as necessary.

⑨ Enjoy with Rotli (page 268).

Ghor Wara Marcha

STUFFED SWEET PEPPERS

TIME	YIELD	*GLUTEN-FREE*
35–40 minutes	8–10 servings	*& VEGETARIAN*

These are a treat to eat.

8–10	banana peppers
1¼ cups	sifted chana flour
3 ounce	jaggery (*Gur*)
1 teaspoon	ground cumin
1 teaspoon	turmeric
1 teaspoon	Indian chilli powder
1 teaspoons	salt, or to taste
½ teaspoon	Garlic Paste (page 42)
2 Tablespoons	lemon juice
1 Tablespoon	finely cut coriander leaves
2 Tablespoons	water
4 Tablespoons	olive oil, divided
½ teaspoon	mustard seeds
¼ teaspoon	cumin seeds

① Preheat the oven to 350°F.

② Make a slit on one side of the peppers and remove their seeds.

③ Mix together the chana flour, jaggery, cumin, turmeric, chilli powder, salt, garlic, lemon juice, coriander leaves, water and 2 Tablespoons of the olive oil and evenly stuff the peppers with the mixture.

④ Layer the peppers in a steamer or double boiler and steam for 15 to 20 minutes, or until soft.

⑤ Place the steamed peppers in a baking dish.

⑥ Heat remaining 2 Tablespoons of olive oil in a saucepan, add the mustard and cumin seeds and cook covered until the seeds start to pop.

⑦ Pour the oil and spices over the peppers and bake at 350° F for 10 minutes.

⑧ Enjoy as an accompaniment to any main course.

Jagu Wari Makai

CORN CURRY
IN PEANUT SAUCE

TIME	YIELD	*GLUTEN-FREE*
20 minutes	4–6 servings	*& VEGETARIAN*

Noorbanu updated this recipe by using peanut butter instead of ground peanuts and we both love the ease and taste of the way it turned out.

4 cups	water
4	cobs of corn, cut into quarters or thirds so each is 2–3 inches long
1 cup	peanut butter (substitute coconut milk for peanut allergies)
¾ teaspoon	salt
½ teaspoon	Green Chilli Paste (page 44)
½ teaspoon	ground cumin
Pinch	turmeric
2 Tablespoons	lemon juice
1 Tablespoon	finely cut coriander leaves

① Bring the water to boil in a large pot on high heat and boil the corn until it is cooked—about 5 minutes.

② Drain the corn and reserve the water for later use.

③ Combine 1 cup of the reserved corn water with the peanut butter in a saucepan on medium heat and stir to a smooth paste.

④ Stir in the corn, salt, chilli paste, cumin, and turmeric and cook on medium heat for 5 minutes. Use the remaining corn water to adjust the gravy so that it is just covering the corn in the pot.

⑤ Add the lemon juice and coriander leaves and cook for another 5 minutes.

⑥ Enjoy as a side dish or on its own with Fluffy Basmati Rice (page 249).

Karela Nu Saak

BITTER MELON CURRY

TIME	PLUS	YIELD	GLUTEN-FREE
20 minutes	salting time	2–3 servings	& VEGETARIAN

Don't let the name put you off, the bitterness of the melon disappears with cooking and imparts a subtle blend of flavours.

1 lb	peeled karela (bitter melon)
1–2 teaspoons	salt
3 Tablespoons	olive oil
1 large	sliced onion
½ cup	canned crushed tomatoes
1 teaspoon	ground cumin
1 teaspoon	ground coriander
½ teaspoon	Indian chilli powder, or to taste
2 teaspoons	Garlic Paste (page 42)
½ teaspoon	turmeric

① Peel the outer layer of skin off the *karela*.

② Cut the peeled *karela* into strips 1-inch wide and 2-inches long and rub salt into the pieces.

③ Set aside for 30 minutes to reduce the bitterness, then wash them under cold running water to remove salt and the seeds. Drain well.

④ Heat the oil in a saucepan on medium, stir in the *karela* and cook until it turns pale green, approximately 7 to 10 minutes.

⑤ Add the onion and cook until it softens.

⑥ Reduce the heat to minimum and add the tomatoes, cumin, coriander, chilli powder, Garlic Paste and turmeric and a little water if necessary.

⑦ Cook on low heat until the *karela* is tender.

⑧ Enjoy with Naan (page 266) or Rotli (page 268).

Variation:
¼ lb of lean ground beef can be added to this dish when you are adding the onion.

Matar Paneer

PEAS AND CHEESE

TIME	YIELD	GLUTEN-FREE
30 minutes	4 – 6 servings	*& VEGETARIAN*

Great –
made spinach
variation 3/22

Paneer is an Indian cheese that is great in curries because—unlike other cheese—it doesn't melt at normal cooking temperatures. This *paneer* dish is a nice way to add something bright and green to your plate. Karen likes the variation of this with spinach as much as the original.

TIP: You can buy paneer at Indian grocers but, we prefer to make our own. Then we can control the quality of the milk and avoid additives used in commercial processing facilities—see Paneer (page 45).

2 Tablespoons	Ghee (page 43)
½ teaspoon	mustard seeds
¼ teaspoon	cumin seeds
3 curry	leaves
1 or 2	dried red chillies
3 Tablespoons	canned crushed tomato
1 teaspoon	Garlic Paste (page 42)
1 Tablespoon	sweet chilli sauce
¾ teaspoon	ground cumin
¼ teaspoon	turmeric
¾ teaspoon	salt, or to taste
2¼ cups	frozen green peas

¼ cup	water
¾ lb	Paneer (page 45), cut into cubes
1 Tablespoon	finely cut coriander leaves

① Heat the Ghee in a pot. Add the mustard and cumin seeds, curry leaves and the dried red chillies. When the seeds start to pop, add the tomato, garlic paste, sweet chilli sauce, ground cumin, turmeric, and salt, and cook for 2 minutes more.

② Stir in the water and peas, then cook until the peas are tender. *brown first*

③ Stir in the *paneer* and cook for 2 minutes.

④ Add the coriander leaves just before serving.

⑤ Enjoy with Rotli (page 268) or Naan (page 266).

Variation:

PALAK PANEER – SPINACH AND CHEESE
Follow the directions above but add 8 cups of freshly chopped spinach instead of the frozen peas.

TIP: The spinach will release a lot of water. You can remove the spinach from the pan with a slotted spoon when it's bright green, then cook down the fluids to a thick sauce and add the spinach back at that point. Stir in the *paneer* and the coriander leaves to finish.

Potato Curry

TIME	YIELD	GLUTEN-FREE
25–30 minutes	4–5 servings	*& VEGETARIAN*

This is a versatile side dish and speaks to Noorbanu's love of all things potato. This is definitely one of Noorbanu's favourite recipes.

1 ½ lbs	potato, cut into ½-inch cubes
2 Tablespoons	oil
½ teaspoon	mustard seeds
1–2	chillies, jalapeño or Serrano, slit on each side
4–5	curry leaves (optional)
1 cup	canned crushed tomatoes
1 teaspoon	Garlic Paste (page 42)
¼ teaspoon	turmeric
1 teaspoon	ground cumin
½ teaspoon	ground coriander
Salt, to taste	
1 Tablespoon	finely cut coriander leaves

① Parboil the potato cubes until almost cooked—about 10 minutes.

② Heat the oil in a saucepan on medium heat, add the mustard seeds, chillies, curry leaves and cook until the seeds pop and splutter—about 30 to 60 seconds.

③ Stir in the tomatoes, garlic, turmeric, cumin, coriander and salt and cook for 2 minutes.

④ Stir in the potatoes and cook on low until they are fork tender but not falling apart.

⑤ Transfer to a serving dish and garnish with the coriander leaves.

⑥ Enjoy with Rotli (page 268) or Puri (page 236).

Spicy Coconut Green Beans

TIME	YIELD	GLUTEN-FREE
30 minutes	3 – 4 servings	*& VEGETARIAN*

This is wonderful as a side with fish and reminds Karen of all the coconut-inspired dishes she's experienced in South India.

1 lb	green beans
Pinch	baking soda
½ teaspoon	salt
2 teaspoons	coconut oil
½ teaspoon	mustard seeds
½ teaspoon	cumin seeds
1 clove	finely chopped garlic
1 Tablespoon	finely chopped ginger
1 teaspoon	dry chilli flakes
½ cup	coconut milk
1 Tablespoon	finely cut coriander leaves
2 teaspoons	sesame seeds
2 teaspoons	coconut flakes

① Top and tail the beans and cut them in half.

② Blanch the beans in water with baking soda and salt until still crispy and bright green. Drain and plunge in cold water to stop the cooking at this point.

③ Heat the coconut oil in a wok, add the mustard and cumin seeds and cook until the seeds start to pop and splutter.

④ Stir in the garlic, ginger and chilli flakes.

⑤ Add the beans and then the coconut milk and cook, stirring until all the liquid evaporates.

⑥ Enjoy sprinkled with coriander leaves, sesame seeds and coconut flakes.

SPICY COCONUT
GREEN BEANS
SEE PAGE 200

Spicy Potatoes and Bell Peppers

TIME	YIELD	GLUTEN-FREE
30–40 minutes	6 servings	*& VEGETARIAN*

These are a great accompaniment to any dish and Noorbanu enjoys them with Meat Cutlets (page 129) and a green salad.

2 lbs	potatoes
2 teaspoons	olive oil
½ teaspoon	black mustard seeds
½ teaspoon	cumin seeds
1 teaspoon	Garlic Paste (page 42)
1 teaspoon	Ginger Paste (page 43)
¼ teaspoon	Green Chilli Paste (page 44), or to taste
½ teaspoon	ground cumin
½ teaspoon	ground coriander
¼ teaspoon	turmeric
1 teaspoon	paprika
¾ teaspoon	salt
¼ teaspoon	black peppercorns, coarsely ground
½ cup	green bell pepper, cut into strips
½ cup	red bell pepper, cut into strips
1 Tablespoon	lemon juice
1 Tablespoon	finely cut coriander leaves

① Peel and cut potatoes into bite-size cubes and then boil them in salted water until cooked. Drain.

② Heat the olive oil in a saucepan, add the mustard and cumin seeds, garlic, ginger, and chilli pastes and cook covered for 1 minute.

③ Stir in the ground cumin and coriander, turmeric, paprika, salt and black pepper, and cook for 1 minute. Add a little water if needed.

④ Add the bell peppers, and stir for 2 minutes.

⑤ Add the potatoes, lemon juice and coriander leaves and mix well.

⑥ Enjoy with any barbecued meats or as a savoury accompaniment to any other dish.

Variation:

SPICY SMASHED POTATOES

① Bake 2 lbs of baby potatoes (skins on) at 375°F for 30 minutes after coating them with olive oil.

② Smash them when you remove from the oven.

③ Follow the rest of the above recipe.

Spinach Curry

TIME	**YIELD**	*GLUTEN-FREE*
15–20 minutes	4 servings	*& VEGETARIAN*

Noorbanu's granddaughter, Tahira, loves this curry simply because it is so easy to make, delicious to eat and healthy for the body. Multiply as you like or add cubes of paneer for a quick and easy version of Palak Paneer (page 212).

6 cups	spinach, tightly packed
¼ cup	butter
2 teaspoons	Garlic Paste (page 42)
2	puréed tomatoes
2 teaspoons	tomato paste
¾ teaspoon	salt
¼ teaspoon	turmeric
½ teaspoon	Indian chilli powder, or to taste
1 teaspoon	ground cumin

① Wash, drain and finely chop the spinach.

② Melt the butter in a saucepan on medium heat, add the Garlic Paste and cook until fragrant—about 30 seconds.

③ Stir in the tomato purée and paste, salt, turmeric, Indian chilli powder and cumin and cook for 2 to 3 minutes.

④ Add the spinach and cook until most of the water is absorbed.

⑤ Enjoy as a side dish or with Rotli (page 268).

SEE PHOTO AS ACCOMPANIMENT TO GRILLED SALMON WITH HONEY, LIME AND GREEN CHILLI PASTE PAGE 181

Vegetable Curry

TIME	**YIELD**
30 minutes	8 servings

GLUTEN-FREE & VEGETARIAN

An extremely tasty way to eat lots of vegetables.

4 Tablespoons	oil
1 teaspoon	mustard seeds
½ teaspoons	cumin seeds
4	curry leaves
2 ¼ lb	(1-inch) cubed mixed vegetables*
2 cups	chopped tomatoes (2 medium)
2 Tablespoons	water
1 ½ teaspoons	tomato paste
2 teaspoons	Garlic Paste (page 42)
2 teaspoons	Ginger Paste (page 43)
1 teaspoon	Green Chilli Paste (page 44), or to taste
1 teaspoon	Indian chilli powder, or to taste
1 teaspoon	ground cumin
1 teaspoon	ground coriander
½ teaspoon	turmeric
1 Tablespoon	finely cut coriander leaves

*Use any combination of peas, lima beans, spinach, Japanese eggplant, potatoes, cauliflower or zucchini.

① Heat the oil on medium heat in a wok, add the mustard seeds, cumin seeds and curry leaves cook covered until the seeds pop and splutter—30 to 60 seconds.

② Stir in the vegetables, tomatoes, water, tomato paste, garlic, ginger and chilli pastes, the chilli powder, cumin, coriander and turmeric and cook until the vegetables are tender. Add water if necessary.

③ Garnish with the fresh coriander leaves.

④ Enjoy as a side dish or with rice and *dal* for a vegetarian meal that covers all your bases.

Whole Roasted Paneer Stuffed Cauliflower

TIME	PLUS	YIELD	*GLUTEN-FREE*
1 hour	Paneer preparation (page 45)	6 – 8 servings as a main, 12 as a side	*& VEGETARIAN*

Noorbanu's son Akbar asked us to try this idea. Cauliflower or *Gobi* is a beloved vegetable in India. It's fun to try out a new way to eat it.

TIP: You will need to make your own fresh paneer for this recipe and instead of setting something heavy on it to press it into a firm cheese, just gather it in the cheese cloth and give it a squeeze and then use it in its lighter fluffier form for the stuffing of this delicious cauliflower dish.

6 cups of	water
3 Indian	Bay leaves
4	cloves
3	green cardamom pods
6 pieces	cinnamon bark
1 head	cauliflower, outer leaves and most of the core removed
1 ½ cups	fresh Paneer (page 45)
¼ cup	Greek yogurt
1 Tablespoon	olive oil
1 Tablespoon	lime juice
1 teaspoon	Garlic Paste (page 42)
1 teaspoon	Ginger Paste (page 43)
2 Tablespoons	honey
1 teaspoon	salt, or to taste
1 teaspoon	Sambal Oelek
1 teaspoon	ground cumin
¼ teaspoon	turmeric
1 teaspoon	Garam Masala (page 29)

1. Place the water and whole Bay leaves, cloves, cardamom pods and cinnamon bark in a large pot with the water and bring it to a boil and then simmer for 5 minutes.

2. Set the cauliflower in the spice infused water, cover the pot with a lid and steam it for about 10 minutes.

3. Lift it from the pot and let it cool.

4. Preheat the oven to 400°F

5. Stir the Paneer, Yogurt, oil, lime juice, Garlic and Ginger Pastes, honey, salt, Sambal Oelek, cumin and turmeric in a bowl and then—once the cauliflower has cooled—use your hands to stuff the underneath cavities with the paneer mix, then turn it top side up and stuff in between the florets —as best you can.

6. Save enough filling to coat the top of the cauliflower.

7. Place the cauliflower in a shallow oven-proof dish and bake in a preheated oven for 30 minutes or until golden brown on top.

   TIP: You may want to broil the top to help it become golden at the end of the cooking time.

8. Sprinkle the top with Garam Masala.

9. Serve from the baking dish and slice in wedges.

10. Enjoy drizzled with a little Coriander Chutney (page 108).

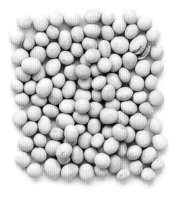

TOP

LEFT TO RIGHT: Moong beans, Moong dal split with skins on, Moong dal split and skins removed

MIDDLE

Rajma (Whole Kidney Beans)

BOTTOM

LEFT TO RIGHT:
Whole Urad, Urad Dal

TOP

Black-Eyed Peas

MIDDLE

LEFT TO RIGHT: Kala Chana (black chickpeas), Chana Dal

BOTTOM

Whole Dried Peas

TOP

LEFT TO RIGHT:
Whole Masoor, Masoor Dal

MIDDLE

Chickpeas

BOTTOM

LEFT TO RIGHT:
Whole Tuvar,
Tuvar Dal split and oiled

Dal

Bharazi

PIGEON PEAS IN COCONUT CREAM

TIME	PLUS	YIELD	*GLUTEN-FREE*
30–40 minutes	soaking time if using dry peas	4 servings	*& VEGETARIAN*

This dish is easy to make and is especially delicious with the *Mandazi* recipe for sweet coconut donuts that follows. When the Nimji family lived in Africa, vegetable peddlers went door to door to sell their freshly shelled pigeon peas. Noorbanu would buy them and make *Bharazi* and *Mandazi* for the family's breakfast— which is when this dish is traditionally eaten.

TIP: If you remember to soak dried pigeon peas overnight, the recipe will come together quickly or you can keep canned pigeon peas on hand. Though the dish will cost a little more to make, it's still very inexpensive.

1 cup OR	dry pigeon peas
1	(19 ounce/540 mL) can pigeon peas (use black pigeon peas)
1 Tablespoon	sunflower oil
1 Tablespoon	finely chopped onion
½ cup	finely chopped tomato (1 small)
1	(14 ounce/398 mL) can coconut milk or cream
¼ teaspoon	Indian chilli powder
⅛ teaspoon	turmeric, optional
1 whole	chilli, slit down the sides (jalapeño or Serrano)
¼ teaspoon	Garlic Paste (page 42) *(optional)*
½ teaspoon	Green Chilli Paste (page 44) (and/or Sambal Oelek), or to taste
1 Tablespoon	lemon juice
1 Tablespoon	finely cut coriander leaves

① Soak the dry pigeon peas in water overnight then rinse in several changes of water, drain, then add 2 cups of fresh water and the peas to a saucepan and boil on high until tender—about 20 minutes. Drain and set aside.

② Heat the oil in a saucepan and fry the onion until light gold, then add the tomatoes and cook until soft and mushy.

③ Stir in the coconut milk or cream, chilli powder, turmeric (if using), whole chilli, garlic and chilli paste and lemon juice together and cook on medium-high heat until it comes to a boil.

④ Stir in the cooked (or canned) pigeon peas, lower the heat to medium and simmer for 10 minutes.

⑤ Add the coriander leaves and continue to simmer for another 10 minutes.

⑥ Enjoy with Mandazi (page 226) for an amazing breakfast treat or as a vegetarian meal with Coconut Rice (page 249).

Mandazi

EAST AFRICAN COCONUT DOUGHNUTS

TIME	PLUS	YIELD	VEGETARIAN
1 hour and 15 minutes	overnight rest	12 large doughnuts	

No matter what you think when you read this recipe, if you've never tried these light fluffy donuts, we promise you they are worth the effort. *Mandazi* are a great snack on their own but we love them with the *Bharazi* in the preceding recipe. *Mandazi* are the perfect vehicle for soaking up every last bit of the delicious *Bharazi* sauce.

¼ cup	warm water
½ teaspoon	sugar
½ teaspoon	dried yeast
50 grams	pure creamed coconut
¼ cup	water
1 ½ cups	all-purpose flour
½ cup	sugar
⅓ teaspoon	coarsely ground green cardamom seeds

Sunflower oil for frying

① Place the warm water in a bowl and sprinkle with the sugar and yeast and let it develop for 10 minutes.

② Dissolve the coconut cream in the water.

③ Combine the flour, sugar, cardamom and yeast mixture.

④ Stir the coconut cream into the mixture gradually and then knead it to make pliable dough.

⑤ Let the dough rest, covered, overnight.

⑥ Divide the dough into 3 equal parts and roll each into a 6-inch circle about ¼-inch thick.

⑦ Cut each circle into quarters.

⑧ Let the dough rest on a floured surface or on a tray for about 1 hour or until the dough doubles in size.

⑨ Deep-fry the pieces in the sunflower oil on medium heat—about 375°F—until golden brown.

⑩ Remove the donuts with a slotted spoon to a waiting paper towel-lined baking tray.

⑪ Enjoy these with Bharazi (page 224) or on their own.

Chana Wagharia

CHICKPEAS AND EGGPLANT IN A SPICY SAUCE

TIME	YIELD	
20–25 minutes	4 servings	*GLUTEN-FREE & VEGETARIAN*

Noorbanu made this for our lunch when we were doing the photo shoot for the book and it has become a "go-to" recipe for our busy photographer Pauli-Ann Carriere ever since.

1 Tablespoon	olive oil
5–6	curry leaves
½ teaspoon	mustard seeds
1 cup	canned crushed tomatoes
1	Chinese eggplant (10–12 inches long), cut into bite-size cubes
½ teaspoon	salt
½ cup	water
1½ teaspoons	ground cumin
¼ teaspoon	turmeric
1 teaspoon	ground coriander
½ teaspoon	sugar
½ teaspoon	Indian chilli powder
1	(19 ounce/540 mL) can chickpeas
1 Tablespoon OR	Ambli Ni Chutney (page 104)
1 Tablespoon	lemon juice
1 Tablespoon	finely cut coriander leaves

① Heat the olive oil in a saucepan on medium heat and add the curry leaves and mustard seeds. Cook covered until the seeds pop—about 1 minute.

② Stir in the tomato, eggplant and salt and cook on medium-low heat—adding a little water if necessary—until eggplant is almost cooked, about 10 minutes.

③ Stir in the cumin, turmeric, coriander, sugar and chilli powder and cook for 4 to 5 minutes more or until the eggplant cubes are cooked and tender when pierced with a fork.

④ Stir in the chickpeas, Ambli Ni Chutney OR lemon juice and simmer for another 5 minutes. The gravy should just cover the chickpeas and eggplant.

TIP: If you really like an authentic *Wagharia*, add about 4 Tablespoons of oil and simmer for a few more minutes. It will be richly satisfying.

⑤ Stir in the coriander leaves just before serving.

⑥ Enjoy hot with Jardo (page 252) or Biryani (page 246).

Chana Dal

TIME about 10 minutes	**YIELD** 4 servings	*GLUTEN-FREE & VEGETARIAN*

This is a delicious *dal* for busy people that still want to eat well. Canned chickpeas are a real timesaver—just rinse them well before use.

1	(19 ounce/540 mL) can chickpeas
½ cup	water
1 Tablespoon	olive oil
¼ teaspoon	cumin seeds
½ teaspoon	mustard seeds
10	curry leaves
Pinch	ajwan (*omum*) seeds
½ cup	diced tomato (1 medium)
½ teaspoon	Garlic Paste (page 42)
½ teaspoon	Ginger Paste (page 43)
½ teaspoon	Green Chilli Paste (page 44)
¼ teaspoon	ground cumin
½ teaspoon	turmeric
1	(19 ounce/540 mL) can of boiling water
½ teaspoon	salt, or to taste
1 teaspoon	lemon juice
¼ teaspoon	Garam Masala (page 29) (optional)
1 Tablespoon	finely cut coriander leaves

① Rinse the canned chickpeas and add them to the bowl of a food processor with the ½ cup of water and blend until smooth. Set aside.

② Heat the oil in a saucepan on medium heat and add the cumin seeds, mustard seeds, curry leaves and *ajwan* seeds and cook covered until the seeds start to pop and splutter—about 30–60 seconds.

③ Stir in the tomato, garlic, ginger and chilli pastes, cumin and turmeric and simmer 5 minutes.

④ Stir in the chickpea blend and a can of boiling water and cook for 5 minutes more.

TIP: You can adjust the thickness of the *dal* to your liking by adding more water if needed.

⑤ Stir in the salt, lemon juice, Garam Masala and coriander leaves.

⑥ Enjoy with Cumin Rice (page 249) and Carrot Pickle (page 106).

Chana Dal Curry

TIME	PLUS	YIELD	GLUTEN-FREE
1 hour	1 hour soaking time	4–6 servings	& VEGETARIAN

This is an inexpensive nutritional powerhouse with flavour galore.

1 cup	chana dal
3	eggs
1 Tablespoon	olive oil
½ cup	chopped onion (1 medium)
1 teaspoon	Garlic Paste (page 42)
1 teaspoon	Ginger Paste (page 43)
½ teaspoon	Green Chilli Paste (page 44)
½ cup	canned crushed tomato
½ teaspoon	turmeric
1 teaspoon	ground cumin
½ teaspoon	ground coriander
1½ teaspoon	salt, or to taste
2 cups	water
1½ Tablespoon	finely cut coriander leaves, divided
½ teaspoon	Garam Masala (page 29)
2 teaspoons	lemon juice
1 teaspoon	sugar

① Soak the *dal* in hot water for one hour, rinse and drain.

② Place the eggs in a pot of boiling water, cook for 8 minutes, drain, fill the pot with cold water to chill the eggs then peel and cut in half. Set aside.

③ Heat the olive oil in a saucepan on medium heat, stir in the onion and cook until golden brown.

④ Mix the garlic, ginger and chilli pastes with the crushed tomato, turmeric, ground cumin and coriander and salt in a small bowl and then stir it into the onions and cook for 5 minutes.

⑤ Add the drained *dal* and cook for 3 to 4 minutes or until heated through.

⑥ Stir in the 2 cups of water and simmer until the dal is tender (about half an hour). The gravy should cover the dal.

⑦ Stir in half of the coriander leaves, the Garam Masala, lemon juice and sugar, transfer to a serving dish and garnish with the egg halves and remaining coriander leaves.

⑧ Enjoy with Fluffy Basmati Rice (page 249), or Cumin-scented Rice (page 249), and Rotli (page 268).

Chuti Khichadi

RICE AND SPLIT PIGEON PEAS
(TUVAR DAL)

TIME	PLUS	YIELD	*GLUTEN-FREE*
30 minutes	90 minutes soaking time for the dal	5–6 servings	*& VEGETARIAN*

This dish featuring *Tuvar dal* is often the first solid food introduced to Ismaili children.

TIP: If you press down on the cardamom pods with your thumb on a hard surface until they crack—before adding them to a dish—they will release more flavour while cooking.

½ cup	split pigeon peas (you may substitute Moong dal, without husks)
1 cup	basmati rice
1 Tablespoon	olive oil
3–4 small	pieces of cinnamon bark
3 green	cardamom pods
1 teaspoon	Garlic Paste (page 42)
3 cups	water
1 teaspoon	salt
¼ teaspoon	turmeric

① Clean the *dal* under running water and soak them in lots of water for at least 90 minutes.

② Clean the *dal* again by changing the water several times. During the process, use your hands to rub away any skins.

③ Clean the rice and soak it for at least 10 to 15 minutes.

④ Heat the oil in a saucepan on medium heat and add the cinnamon, cardamom, cumin seeds and garlic and cook stirring—about 30 seconds.*

⑤ Add the water, salt and turmeric and bring to a boil.

⑥ Stir in the drained *dal* and boil for 5 minutes with the pot half covered to prevent it boiling over.

⑦ Stir in the drained rice, reduce the heat and cook covered until all the water is absorbed—about 20 minutes

⑧ Fluff with a fork before serving.

⑨ Enjoy this with Khadhi (page 233) or Eggplant Curry (page 207).

*Advise your guests to set the whole spices contained in this dish aside when eating the finished product.

Khadhi

A WARM YOGURT DRINK

TIME	YIELD	GLUTEN-FREE
15 minutes	2–3 servings	& VEGETARIAN

This is a great accompaniment to Chuti Khichadi. Some people strain it to remove the seeds before serving but Noorbanu likes how they look in the soft yellow color of the drink.

1 ¼ cups	Yogurt (page 46)
1 ½ cups OR	water
2 cups	buttermilk
¾ cups	water

Plus

1 ½ teaspoon	chana flour (you may double this if you like a thicker soup)
¾ tsp	salt
1 Tablespoon	sunflower oil
¼ teaspoon	mustard seeds
¼ teaspoon	cumin seeds
⅛ teaspoon	ajwan (omum), optional
1 small	chilli, cut in strips
5 or 6	fresh curry leaves (Limdho)
2	cloves
¼ teaspoon	ground cumin
½ teaspoon	Garlic Paste (page 42)
½ teaspoon	Ginger Paste (page 43)
¼ teaspoon	Green Chilli Paste (page 44)
¼ teaspoon OR	citric acid powder
1 teaspoon	lemon juice
Dash	turmeric
½ teaspoon	jaggery or sugar
2 Tablespoons	finely cut coriander leaves

① Place the yogurt and water (or buttermilk and water), chana flour and salt in a blender and combine until smooth.

② Heat the oil in a saucepan on medium high heat and add mustard and cumin seeds, *ajwan* (if you'd like a bit of liquorice taste), chilli, curry leaves and cloves and cook covered until the seeds pop and splutter.

③ Add the yogurt mixture and stir continuously until the mixture starts to boil—the stirring will prevent it from separating.

④ Reduce the heat and stir in the cumin, garlic, ginger and chilli pastes, citric acid or lemon juice and turmeric.

⑤ Continue boiling the mixture gently until enough water has evaporated to make it look like thick cream.

⑥ Add the *jaggery* or sugar and the coriander leaves.

⑦ Enjoy with the Chuti Khichadi recipe on the preceding page.

Dal with Coconut

LENTILS WITH COCONUT

TIME	PLUS	YIELD	*GLUTEN-FREE*
75 minutes	1 hour soaking time	4 servings	*& VEGETARIAN*

Most of the cooking time for this recipe is boiling time for the lentils so this is much easier than the time suggests. If you own a pressure cooker, you can prepare this dish—with less water—in about 30 minutes.

TIP: It's important to note that moong dal is green when the husks are on and yellow when they are removed. If you are not sure, refer to the photos on page 222 or check with your Indian grocer.

1 cup	moong dal, without husks
3 cups	water
½ teaspoon	salt
1 cup	diced tomato (2 medium)
1	(14 ounce/398 mL) can coconut milk
½ teaspoon	Green Chilli Paste (page 44), or to taste
½ teaspoon	ground cumin
½ teaspoon	turmeric
1 Tablespoon	lemon juice, or to taste
1–2 Tablespoons	finely cut coriander leaves

① Wash the dal and soak in warm water for 1 hour.

② Combine drained dal, 3 cups of water, salt and tomatoes in a saucepan and cook on very low heat until the dal is tender, about 45 to 60 minutes.

③ Place the dal in the bowl of a food processer and blend until smooth.

④ Return the dal to the saucepan and stir in the coconut milk, chilli paste, cumin, turmeric and lemon juice.

⑤ Cook for 10 to 15 minutes on medium-low heat or until the consistency of the *dal* is like a thick cream soup. If necessary, add boiling hot water to thin it.

⑥ Enjoy hot with Fluffy Basmati Rice (page 249).

Dry Moong Dal Curry

SUKI MUG NI DAL

TIME	PLUS	YIELD	*GLUTEN-FREE*
1 hour	½ hour soaking time	4 servings	*& VEGETARIAN*

This is a delicious dal that takes very little time to prepare.

1 cup	moong dal without husks
½ cup	finely chopped onion (1 medium)
2 Tablespoons	olive oil
½ cup	finely chopped tomato (1 medium)
2 teaspoons	tomato paste
1 teaspoon	ground cumin
½ teaspoon	turmeric
¼ teaspoon	Indian chilli powder, or to taste
½ teaspoon	salt
1 cup	water
1 Tablespoon	lemon juice
1 Tablespoon	finely cut coriander leaves

① Soak the moong dal for 30 minutes in hot water, then drain.

② Heat the olive oil in a saucepan on medium heat, add the onion and cook until it is just transparent (before it starts to brown).

③ Stir in the tomatoes and cook for 1 minute.

④ Stir in the tomato paste, ground cumin, turmeric, chilli powder, salt and the moong dal and cook on high heat stirring continuously for 2 minutes.

⑤ Reduce the heat to medium-high heat, add the 1 cup of water and bring to a boil.

⑥ Reduce to low heat, cover and simmer until the *dal* is cooked—about 15 minutes— and most of the water has evaporated.

⑦ Add the lemon juice and garnish with the coriander leaves just before serving.

⑧ Enjoy with Puri (page 236) and Mango Juice (page 277).

Puri

DEEP-FRIED PUFFED BREAD

TIME	YIELD	GLUTEN-FREE
60 minutes	20–24 puffs of bread	*& VEGETARIAN*

Puri is thin, round and flat unleavened bread made from whole wheat or all-purpose flour, water, salt and oil. It is usually deep-fried in oil, puffs up during frying and is eaten immediately. We made this once during a cooking lesson for a youth group and they couldn't wait to use it to scoop up the Dry Moong Dal Curry (page 235) we made. We always thought if we had told them they'd be having bread and beans for lunch they wouldn't have liked it—but when they saw the puri puff up in the pan, they knew it was something special and they loved it. They also loved spending time with Noorbanu and receiving her gentle guidance.

1 cup	whole wheat flour
1 cup	all-purpose flour
½ teaspoon	salt
2 Tablespoons	sunflower oil
¾ cup (approximately), warm water	
Sunflower oil for frying	
¼ teaspoon	turmeric

① Rub the flour, salt and oil together with your fingers until the mixture resembles fine crumbs.

② Add the water—as needed—and knead lightly to pull it into a dough.

③ Divide into 20 to 24 equal-size balls and cover with a damp cloth.

④ On a lightly oiled surface, roll each of these balls into a circle about 4 to 5-inches in diameter.

TIP: By using oil rather than flour to roll out the puris, you avoid the problem of excess flour burning in the oil when frying.

⑤ Deep-fry in hot oil, topside first (this is important to get it to puff).

⑥ Tap each of the puri lightly with a slotted spoon and gently push it down into the oil. The puri should puff up within seconds.

⑦ Turn the puri over and continue frying until golden brown.

⑧ Enjoy hot with honey, butter and jam, yogurt or vegetable curry, or Dry Moong Dal Curry (page 235), and Mango Juice (page 277).

PURI
SEE PHOTOS, PAGE 149

Gosh Wari Dal

DAL WITH MEAT

TIME	YIELD	GLUTEN-FREE
2 hours	6 servings	

1 cup	moong dal or chana dal or a mix of each
1¼ lbs	beef OR lamb, cubed, preferably with bones
1 teaspoon	salt
1½ teaspoons	Ginger Paste (page 43), divided
6 cups	water
1 Tablespoon	olive oil
½ cup	chopped onion
1 cup	chopped tomato (2 medium)
1 teaspoon	Garlic Paste (page 42)
½ teaspoon	Green Chilli Paste (page 44) or Sambal Oelek
1 teaspoon	ground cumin
¼ teaspoon	turmeric
2 Tablespoons	lemon juice
1 Tablespoon	finely cut coriander leaves
½ teaspoon	Garam Masala (page 29)

① Wash the dal and then soak for 1 hour.

② Drain the dal and combine with the meat, salt, half a teaspoon (as the first addition) ginger paste and water in a saucepan.

③ Cook on medium heat until the meat is very tender—about 90 minutes

TIP: If you have a pressure cooker this will take about 30 to 45 minutes.

④ Heat the oil in a separate saucepan on medium heat, add the onion and cook until soft and transparent.

⑤ Stir in the tomato, garlic paste, remaining ginger paste, chilli paste, cumin and turmeric and continue to cook for 4 or 5 minutes.

⑥ Remove the meat from the *dal* mixture using a slotted spoon and add it to the tomato sauce mixture and cook for 5 minutes.

⑦ Transfer the dal to the meat and tomato mix and simmer a further 10 to 20 minutes or to your desired thickness.

⑧ Stir in the lemon juice, coriander leaves and Garam Masala just before serving.

⑨ Enjoy hot with Fluffy Basmati Rice (page 249).

Lasi Khichadi

BOILED RICE AND LENTILS

TIME	YIELD	GLUTEN-FREE
30 minutes	2–3 servings	*& VEGETARIAN*

This is Noorbanu's son, Akbar's favourite comfort food. He loves the pure simplicity of its taste.

½ cup	split green moong dal lentils
½ cup	short grain rice
3 cups	water
½ teaspoon	salt
1 Tablespoon OR	butter
¼ cup	milk

① Clean the moong dal of any stones then wash both moong dal and rice.

② Put cleaned moong dal, rice, water and salt in a pot and bring to a boil.

③ Reduce the heat to low, cover and let simmer until the rice and the lentils are very soft and all the water is absorbed. Add more water if moong dal or rice is not soft and continue to cook.

④ Remove from the heat and add butter OR milk, then mix thoroughly.

⑤ Enjoy with Khadhi (page 233), Spinach Curry (page 218) or Eggplant Curry (page 207).

Moong Beans Curry

TIME	PLUS	YIELD	GLUTEN-FREE
40 minutes	soaking time	4 servings	& VEGETARIAN

This is another easy and inexpensive vegetarian dish. Just remember to soak the beans overnight in lots of water.

1 ½ cups	moong beans
4 cups	water
½ teaspoon	salt
3 Tablespoons	olive oil
4 whole	cloves
¼ teaspoon	cumin seeds
4	curry leaves
½ cup	canned crushed tomato
½ teaspoon	Garlic Paste (page 42)
½ teaspoon	Ginger Paste (page 43)
½ teaspoon	ground cumin
½ teaspoon	ground coriander
½ teaspoon	Indian chilli powder
½ teaspoon	salt
¼ teaspoon	Garam Masala (page 29)
2 teaspoons	sugar
1 Tablespoon	lemon juice
1 Tablespoon	chopped coriander leaves

① Wash the beans and soak them in lots of cold water overnight.

② Drain the moong beans and rinse to release the skins that have loosened.

③ Put the moong beans in a large pot with the water and salt and bring to a boil then lower the heat and cook partially covered over medium heat—about 30 minutes or, until they are cooked.

④ Drain the beans and reserve the liquid.

⑤ Heat the oil in a saucepan, add the cloves, cumin seeds and curry leaves and cook until the cumin seeds pop—about 1 minute.

⑥ Stir in the tomato, garlic and ginger pastes, cumin, coriander, chilli powder and salt and cook on medium heat until pools of oil separate from the paste.

⑦ Add the moong beans and ¼ cup of the reserved liquid, stir, reduce the heat and simmer for 10 minutes.

⑧ Stir in the Garam Masala, sugar, lemon juice and chopped coriander just before serving.

⑨ Enjoy hot with Rotli (page 268) or Puri (page 236).

Tuvar Dal

LENTIL CURRY

TIME	PLUS	YIELD
20 minutes	at least 1 hour of soaking time	3 servings

GLUTEN-FREE & VEGETARIAN

Tuvar dal—split pigeon peas—are the most widely used lentil. They form the base of the South Indian breakfast lentil and vegetable soup known as *sambhar* and are prominently used in dals of Gujarati origin which feature the sweet and sour taste notes you'll find in this dish.

TIP: *Tuvar take a little longer to cook than moong or masoor dal.*

1 cup	tuvar dal (or equal mixture of moong and tuvar dal)
4 cups	water
½ teaspoon	salt
1 teaspoon	olive oil
¼ teaspoon	mustard seeds
¼ teaspoon	cumin seeds
Dash	ajwan (omum) seeds
5–6	curry leaves
3–4	dried red chillies or ½ a fresh jalapeno pepper, cut into long strips
½ cup	pureed fresh tomato
1 teaspoon	Garlic Paste (page 42)
1 teaspoon	Ginger Paste (page 43)
1 Tablespoon	Green Chilli Paste (page 44), or to taste
1 teaspoon	ground cumin
½ teaspoon	turmeric
½ teaspoon	salt
½ cup	boiling water
1 teaspoon	sugar
1 Tablespoons	finely cut coriander leaves
4 teaspoons OR 2 Tablespoons	lemon juice OR Ambli NI Chutney (page 104)

① Wash the dal and soak in water overnight or for at least 1 hour.

② Rinse and rub the dal between your fingers to remove as many of the skins as possible then place the drained dal in a pot and add the 4 cups of water and salt.

③ Boil the dal until tender and soft, about 1½ hour.

   TIP: This only takes 30 minutes in a pressure cooker.

④ Place the cooked dal with its water in a blender and pulse until smooth. Set aside.

⑤ Heat the oil in a saucepan on medium heat and add mustard, cumin, and ajwan (omum) seeds, curry leaves and chillies and cook covered until the seeds start to pop and splutter—about 1 minute.

⑥ Stir in the tomato, garlic, ginger and chilli pastes, ground cumin, turmeric, salt and boiling water and cook for 2 to 4 minutes.

⑦ Stir in the blended dal and cook for 10 minutes more. The dal texture should be like a thick cream soup. If it is too thick, you can add up to another cup of boiling water until you achieve your desired consistency.

⑧ Stir in the sugar, lemon juice or Ambli Ni Chutney and coriander leaves and add salt to taste just before serving.

⑨ Enjoy hot with Cumin-scented Rice (page 249).

Urad Dal

CREAMY SPLIT BEAN CURRY

TIME	YIELD	
30 minutes	4 servings	*GLUTEN-FREE & VEGETARIAN*

Urad dal are also known as black lentils or black gram. They are popular in the North of India where they are much loved for their creamy texture. Remember to soak the *dal* overnight or at least 2 hours.

1 cup	urad dal (split and hulled)
5 cups	water
2 Tablespoons	olive oil
1 Tablespoon	finely chopped onion
½ teaspoon	Garlic Paste (page 42)
½ teaspoon	Ginger Paste (page 43)
½ teaspoon	Green Chilli Paste (page 44)
¾ teaspoon	salt
⅛ teaspoon	turmeric
½ teaspoon	ground cumin
2 cups	buttermilk
1 Tablespoon	finely cut coriander leaves

① Clean the dal and soak overnight.

② Wash the dal in three changes of cold water, drain and then place in a pot with 5 cups of fresh water.

③ Cook until tender—about 15 minutes, and then place in a food processor or blender with their liquid and blend until smooth.

④ Heat the oil in a large pot on medium heat, add the onion and cook until soft.

⑤ Stir in the garlic, ginger and chilli pastes, salt, turmeric, and cumin and cook for 2 to 3 minutes.

⑥ Add the dal to this pot and stir to mix well.

⑦ Stir in the buttermilk, increase the heat to medium-high and cook until the mixture boils.

⑧ Lower the heat and simmer for 15 minutes or until the consistency resembles a thick cream soup.

⑨ Garnish with the coriander leaves just before serving.

⑩ Enjoy with fresh Rotli (page 268).

Urad Dal Makhani

BUTTERY WHOLE BLACK BEAN DAL

TIME	YIELD	GLUTEN-FREE
2–6 hours	4–5 servings	& VEGETARIAN

This recipe uses the whole—and most nutritious— form of *urad*. It does take awhile to cook them but it's worth it because you end up with the *Makhani* (buttery) texture and flavour this dish is famous for. Plan on soaking the *dal* overnight but if you forget to do so, soak them for at least 2 hours.

1½ cups	whole urad
8 cups	water
1 cup	chopped onion (1 large)
½ cup	canned crushed tomato
½ cup	Ghee (page 43)
1 Tablespoon	finely chopped ginger
8	finely chopped garlic cloves
1 teaspoon	salt, or to taste
1 teaspoon	ground cumin
2	chopped fresh chillies (jalapeño or Serrano), or to taste
2 teaspoons	lemon juice
2 Tablespoons	finely cut coriander leaves
½ cup	whipping cream

① Soak the urad dal in lots of cold water overnight.

② Wash the soaked dal in three changes of water and drain.

③ Put the dal in a saucepan with water, onion and tomato and bring to a boil on high heat.

④ Reduce the heat and simmer for about 5 hours or until the dal are tender. Stir and check at intervals adding more water as necessary.

TIP: If you have a pressure cooker this will only take about 1 hour.

⑤ Melt the Ghee in a saucepan over medium heat, add the ginger and garlic and cook until fragrant—about 30 seconds.

⑥ Add the Ghee mixture, salt, cumin, chillies, coriander and lemon juice to the dal and cook for another hour or until it is the consistency of a thick soup.

⑦ Stir in the cream just before serving.

⑧ Enjoy with Naan (page 266) or Rotli (page 268).

Urad Ni Kadhi

TANGY BLACK BEANS

TIME	YIELD	
3–4 hours	4–5 servings	*GLUTEN-FREE & VEGETARIAN*

Buttermilk adds bright tangy notes to this über healthy dish.

1 cup	urad dal
5 cups	water
1 teaspoon	salt, divided
3 Tablespoons	olive oil
2 Tablespoons	finely chopped onion
1 Tablespoon	finely chopped ginger
½ cup	chopped tomato (1 medium)
½ teaspoon	ground cumin
½ teaspoon	turmeric
1 teaspoon	Garlic Paste (page 42)
½ teaspoon	Ginger Paste (page 43)
¼ teaspoon	Green Chilli Paste (page 44), or to taste
1 ½ cups	buttermilk
1 Tablespoon	finely cut coriander leaves

1. Soak the urad overnight with lots of water —make sure the beans are covered by at least 2-inches.

2. Wash the urad thoroughly in several changes of water to remove loose skins and place the dal in a large pot with 5 cups of water and a ½ teaspoon of the salt.

3. Cook for 3 to 4 hours on medium heat— or until the beans are tender, mushy and easily broken with a fork. Add more water as necessary.

4. Heat the oil in a heavy-bottomed saucepan, add the onion and cook until golden brown.

5. Add the chopped ginger and stir.

6. Stir in the tomatoes, cumin, turmeric, garlic, ginger and chilli pastes, salt and cooked urad and cook on low until the tomatoes are soft.

7. Add the buttermilk and stir continuously until the mixture starts to bubble.

8. Simmer for 5 to 7 minutes and add chopped coriander leaves just before serving.

9. Enjoy with Rotli (page 268) or *Naan* (page 266).

Rice, Biryani and Pilau

CHICKEN BIRYANI
RECIPE, PAGE 246

Biryani

CHICKEN, BEEF OR LAMB

TIME	YIELD	*GLUTEN-*
Lots, but it's worth it	6 servings	*FREE*

Biryani originated in Persia and is a layered rice and meat main course traditionally prepared for weddings and special occasions. Cooks for the Moghul emperors in India transformed the dish into a delicacy by adding spices and other exotic ingredients. Saffron gives *biryani* a characteristic flavour and aroma. It may seem a bit complicated at first but if you look at it as cooking several separate things—that overlap a bit—it somehow seems easier. In any case, it's worth it. Your guests will be wowed by the flavours.

TIP: It's important to read through all the directions of this recipe before you begin cooking. There are a few things you'll want to prepare ahead like Crispy Fried Onion (page 42), Garam Masala (page 29) and the boiled potatoes. You can also cook the rice while doing some of this prep work. Suddenly everything will be ready and you'll simply combine it and pop it in the oven.

2 ¼ lbs	skinless bone-in chicken pieces or cubed beef or lamb

For the Marinade:

4 small	pieces cinnamon bark
6	cloves
6	black peppercorns
6	green cardamom pods
1½ cups	Yogurt (page 46)
1 cup	chopped tomato
1 Tablespoon	tomato paste
1 cup	finely chopped onion
1½ Tablespoons	finely chopped jalapeño, or to taste
1½ teaspoons	Garlic Paste (page 42)
1½ teaspoons	Ginger Paste (page 43)
½ teaspoon	cumin seeds
½ teaspoon	Indian chilli powder, or to taste
1 ¼ teaspoon	salt, or to taste
2 Tablespoons	lemon juice
¼ – ½ cup	olive oil or butter
25	saffron strands

CHICKEN BIRYANI
SEE PAGE 244

For the Potatoes:

6	small potatoes, peeled and fried
1 Tablespoon	sunflower oil
1 teaspoon	paprika
¼ teaspoon	salt
½ teaspoon	Garam Masala (page 29)
6 Tablespoons	Crispy Fried Onions (page 42)
2 Tablespoons	finely cut coriander leaves

For the Rice:

2 cups	basmati rice
4 cups	water
1 ½ teaspoon	salt, or to taste
2 Tablespoons	olive oil or butter

For the Assembly:

¼ teaspoon	yellow food colouring powder
10	saffron strands
¼ cup	hot water
2 Tablespoons	melted butter

For the Meat:

① Combine the meat with the well-mixed marinade ingredients and marinate 4 to 5 hours or overnight in the refrigerator.

② Cook the mixture in a large saucepan on medium heat until the meat is tender and fully cooked. Set aside.

For the Potatoes:

① Toss the boiled potato pieces with oil, paprika and salt and bake on a parchment lined baking tray at 375°F—until crispy— about 20 minutes OR deep fry the uncooked potato pieces in sunflower oil until golden brown.

② Combine the crispy potatoes and cooked meat in a large ovenproof casserole dish and sprinkle the Garam Masala, Crispy Fried Onion and coriander leaves over the top.

For the Rice:

① Wash and soak rice for 15 minutes, drain and add to a saucepan with 4 cups fresh water, salt and oil or butter. Bring to a boil, then lower heat and simmer covered until the rice is cooked. Set aside.

For the Assembly:

① Preheat the oven to 300°F.

② Mix the food colouring and *saffron* strands with the hot water.

③ Top the meat mixture with ½ the cooked rice.

④ Sprinkle ½ of the saffron and food colour mixture over the top.

⑤ Repeat these layers and then top with the melted butter.

⑥ Place the casserole dish in a preheated oven and bake for about 20 minutes.

TIP: The biryani can be served in the same ovenproof dish. If you'd prefer a more formal presentation, carefully transfer the rice first on a plate and then top it with the meat and potatoes.

⑦ Enjoy with Kachumber (page 59) and Cucumber Raita (page 108).

Chicken Pilau

TIME	YIELD	GLUTEN-
75 minutes	5–6 servings	*FREE*

This is a one pot wonder.

½ cup	sunflower oil
1 cup	chopped onion (1 large)
4	cloves
4	(1-inch) pieces cinnamon bark
4	green cardamom pods
6	black peppercorns
2	jalapeños, split on one side
1 teaspoon	cumin seeds
2 ¼ lb	skinless bone, in chicken pieces
2 teaspoons	salt, divided
1 teaspoon	Garlic Paste (page 42)
2 teaspoons	Ginger Paste (page 43)
½ teaspoon	Green Chilli Paste (page 44)
1 large	finely chopped tomato
½ cup	Yogurt (page 46)
1 Tablespoon	lemon juice
water	
2 cups	basmati rice, washed and soaked for 10 minutes
6 small	potatoes, cut in 2-inch cubes
1 Tablespoon	finely cut coriander leaves

① Preheat the oven to 300°F.

② Heat the oil on medium heat, add the onion and cook and stir until golden brown.

③ Add the cloves, cinnamon, cardamom, black pepper and split jalapeños and cook for 1 minute.

④ Stir in the chicken pieces, the first addition of 1 teaspoon of salt, then the garlic, ginger and chilli pastes, tomato, yogurt and lemon juice and simmer until the chicken is cooked through.

⑤ Add enough water to make 4½ cups of liquid in the pot and when the liquid starts to boil add the drained rice, potatoes, coriander and the final addition of 1½ teaspoons of salt. Cook on medium heat, partially covered until water is absorbed and rice is cooked.

⑥ Transfer to the preheated oven and bake for 15 minutes.

⑦ Serve hot with Kachumber (page 59), tossed salad and yogurt.

TIP: Advise your guests to set the whole spices aside as they enjoy the dish.

Fluffy Basmati Rice

TIME	YIELD	GLUTEN-FREE
30 minutes	4–5 servings	& VEGETARIAN

Look for aged basmati rice when you are shopping. It will be the most fragrant.

1½ cups	basmati rice
3 cups	water
1 teaspoon	salt
2 teaspoons	olive oil

① Wash and soak the rice in cold water for 10 to 15 minutes. Drain.

② Put the fresh water, rice, salt and oil in a saucepan on high heat and bring to a boil.

③ Boil for 2 to 3 minutes and then reduce the heat to low.

④ Simmer covered until all the water is absorbed. This will take 20 minutes.

TIP: Even though the water is gone, you still need to check to see if the rice is cooked. If not, add a sprinkle of water.

⑤ Fluff the rice with a fork before serving—each grain should separate easily.

⑥ Enjoy with your favourite curries or dal.

Variations:

COCONUT RICE: Add 1 Tablespoon of coconut powder to the Fluffy Basmati Rice recipe as you combine the ingredients and cook as above.

SAFFRON RICE: Add 2 pinches of saffron to the Fluffy Basmati Rice recipe as you combine the ingredients and cook as above.

DILL RICE: Add ½ cup of chopped fresh dill and ¼ cup of finely cut coriander leaves to the Fluffy Basmati rice recipe when you combine the ingredients and cook as above.

CUMIN-SCENTED RICE: Heat 2 teaspoons of olive oil in a saucepan, add ½ teaspoon of cumin seeds and cook 30 seconds then add the rice, water and salt as per the Fluffy Basmati Rice recipe above.

LIGHTLY SPICED RICE: Heat 2 teaspoons of olive oil in a saucepan, add ½ teaspoon cumin seeds, 2 green cardamom pods (cracked) and 2× 1-inch pieces of cinnamon bark and cook for 1 minute then add the water, rice and salt as per the Fluffy Basmati Rice recipe above.

Fish Bhath

FISH IN COCONUT CREAM
WITH RICE

MARINATE	TIME	YIELD	*GLUTEN-FREE*
20 minutes	30 minutes	4 servings	

Halibut, cod or haddock are all heart healthy fish that taste great in this dish.

TIP: Put the rice to soak before doing your other prep. Boil the potatoes ahead.

1 lb	white fish, cut into 2-inch squares

For the Marinade:

½ teaspoon	Garlic Paste (page 42)
½ teaspoon	Green Chilli Paste (page 44) or Sambal Oelek
1 Tablespoon	lemon juice
½ teaspoon	salt, or taste
2 Tablespoons	olive oil

For the Rice:

1¼ cups	basmati rice
1 Tablespoon	coconut oil
½ teaspoon	Garlic Paste (page 42)
1 teaspoon	chopped onion
2 ½ cups	coconut milk
1 teaspoon	salt

For the Sauce:

2 Tablespoons	coconut oil
1 cup	fresh tomatoes, blended in a food processor
1 teaspoon	tomato paste
1 teaspoon	Garlic Paste (page 42)
½ teaspoon	Green Chilli Paste (page 44) or Sambal Oelek
⅛ teaspoon	turmeric
½ teaspoon	ground cumin
½ teaspoon	Indian chilli powder, or to taste
½ teaspoon	salt
1	(14 ounce/394 mL) can coconut cream
1½ teaspoons	lemon juice
2	boiled potatoes, cut into 3 pieces each
2 Tablespoons	finely cut coriander leaves, divided

For the Fish:

① Preheat the oven to 450°F.

② Marinate the fish in the garlic and chilli pastes, lemon juice and salt for 20 minutes.

③ Brush a baking tray with oil, place the fish on the pan and brush the top of the fish with more oil.

④ Place in the oven and bake until golden brown and cooked through. Set aside.

For the Rice:

① Wash the rice then soak it for 10 to 15 minutes.

② Heat the coconut oil in a medium-size saucepan on medium heat; add the garlic and onion and cook until fragrant—about 1 minute.

③ Stir in the coconut milk and bring to a boil. Add drained rice and salt.

④ Drain the rice and add it and the salt to the coconut milk and cook on low heat, partially covered until all the liquid is absorbed and the rice is cooked.

TIP: You may need to add some water if the rice is not cooked.

For the Sauce and Assembly:

① Heat the coconut oil in a heavy-bottomed pan and add the tomatoes, garlic and chilli pastes, turmeric, cumin, chilli powder and salt and cook until the oil separates.

② Stir in the coconut cream until blended and reduced.

③ Stir in the lemon juice, potatoes, fish, half the cilantro leaves and cook long enough to heat through. Set aside.

④ Enjoy the dish by filling a platter with the rice and topping it with the fish and coconut cream sauce. Garnish with the remaining cilantro leaves.

Jardo

AROMATIC SWEET YELLOW RICE

TIME	YIELD	
40 minutes	3–4 servings	*GLUTEN-FREE & VEGETARIAN*

At festival times, in Noorbanu's family, it was traditional to have this sweet starter to balance savoury dishes like samosas or kebabs.

Syrup:

¾ cup	sugar
½ cup	water
⅛ teaspoon	yellow food colouring (powder)
2–3	saffron strands

For the Rice:

1 cup	basmati rice
1–2 Tablespoons	Ghee (page 43) or butter
3	(1-inch) pieces of cinnamon bark
3	green cardamom pods
1 teaspoon	golden raisins
1½ cups	water
⅛ teaspoon	yellow food colouring (powder)
1 Tablespoon	slivered, blanched almonds

For the Syrup:

① Add the sugar, water, food coloring and saffron to a saucepan and bring to a boil on medium-high heat. Then, lower the heat and simmer for 5 minutes—until slightly thickened and sticky. Set aside.

For the Rice:

① Clean, wash and soak the rice for 15 minutes.

② Heat the Ghee in a saucepan on medium heat and add the cinnamon, cardamom and raisins. When the raisins puff add the water, food colouring and drained rice.

③ Cook on medium heat until all the water is absorbed—about 15 minutes.

④ Add the syrup and almonds to the rice and cook, covered, on low heat for approximately 20 minutes—until the liquid is absorbed and the rice is cooked.

⑤ Enjoy hot with Chana Wagharia (page 229) or alone as a starter.

Mayai Khavo

EGG AND POTATO BIRYANI

TIME	YIELD	GLUTEN-FREE
60 minutes	4 servings	& VEGETARIAN

This recipe comes together quickly, once you've got the eggs and potatoes ready. Keeping some high quality store-bought Crispy Fried Onions on hand as another timesaver.

For the Rice:

1½ cups	basmati rice
3 cups	water
1 teaspoon	salt
2 teaspoons	sunflower oil

For the Biryani:

4	hard-boiled and peeled eggs
4	small peeled and boiled potatoes
3 Tablespoons	sunflower oil
½ cup	fresh tomato (1 small), blended in a food processor
1 Tablespoon	water
1 teaspoon	tomato paste
½ teaspoon	salt
1 teaspoon	Garlic Paste (page 42)
½ teaspoon	Green Chilli Paste (page 44)
¼ teaspoon	Indian chilli powder, or to taste
¼ teaspoon	turmeric
½ teaspoon	ground cumin
1 Tablespoon	Yogurt (page 46)
½ teaspoon	Garam Masala (page 29)
3 Tablespoons	Crispy Fried Onions (page 42)
1 Tablespoon	finely cut coriander leaves

For the Rice:

① Wash and soak the rice for 15 minutes then drain and cook on medium heat with the fresh water, salt and oil—until the water is absorbed and the rice is cooked. Set aside.

For the Biryani:

① Preheat the oven to 300° F.

② Heat the oil in a saucepan on medium heat and stir in the tomatoes, water, tomato paste, salt, garlic and chilli pastes, chilli powder, turmeric, cumin and yogurt. Cook until the tomatoes are soft.

③ Stir in the *Garam Masala*, Crispy Fried Onions and coriander leaves.

④ Add the eggs and potatoes and simmer for 5 minutes.

⑤ Transfer the mixture to an ovenproof serving dish, top with the cooked rice then bake, covered in preheated oven for 15 minutes.

⑥ Enjoy with Kachumber (page 59).

Machi Biryani

FISH AND RICE

TIME	YIELD	GLUTEN-FREE
60 minutes	3–4 servings	*& VEGETARIAN*

This is an exciting and exotic way to eat fish.

1 lb	halibut steak or firm white fish, cut in pieces

For the Marinade:

½ teaspoon	salt
1 Tablespoon	lemon juice
¼ teaspoon	chilli powder

For the Rice:

1¼ cups	basmati rice
1 teaspoon	sunflower oil
½ teaspoon	Garlic Paste (page 42)
2	jalapeños, slit along the sides
2 ½ cups	water
1 teaspoon	salt
⅛ teaspoon	yellow food colouring powder dissolved in 2 Tablespoons water
1 Tablespoon	Crispy Fried Onions (page 42)

For the Masala Sauce:

1 Tablespoon	oil
3	(1-inch) pieces cinnamon bark
3	cloves
3	black peppercorns
3	green cardamom pods
½ teaspoon	cumin seeds
1½ cups	fresh tomatoes, blended in a food processor
2 teaspoons	tomato paste
1 teaspoon	Garlic Paste (page 42)
1 teaspoon	salt, or to taste
1 teaspoon	ground cumin
¼ teaspoon	turmeric
2 Tablespoons	ground Crispy Fried Onions (page 42)
⅓ teaspoon	Garam Masala (page 29)
1 Tablespoon	lemon juice
1 Tablespoon	finely cut coriander leaves

For the Fish:

① Combine the marinade ingredients, add the fish and marinate for 30 minutes.

② Broil on both sides until slightly brown.

For the Rice:

① Wash then soak the rice for 10–15 minutes.

② Heat the oil in a saucepan, add the garlic and jalapeños and cook until fragrant—about 30 seconds.

③ Add the water and salt and bring to a boil, reduce heat to low and simmer until the rice is cooked and all the water is absorbed.

④ Sprinkle the yellow food colouring and Crispy Fried Onion over the rice and let it stand on very low heat or in a preheated oven at 300°F for 10 to 15 minutes.

For the Masala Sauce:

① Heat the oil in a saucepan at medium heat, add the cinnamon, cloves, cardamom, peppercorns and cumin seeds and cook until the seeds pop—about 30 seconds.

② Stir in the tomatoes, tomato paste, garlic, salt, cumin and turmeric and cook, stirring occasionally, until the tomatoes are soft and cooked.

③ Add the crushed Crispy Fried Onion and the broiled fish and cook for 3 to 4 minutes.

④ Stir in the Garam Masala, lemon juice and coriander leaves.

⑤ Spoon the rice onto a platter and enjoy topped with the fish and sauce.

Pea or Mixed Vegetable Pilau

TIME	YIELD	GLUTEN-FREE
60 minutes	4 servings	& VEGETARIAN

This is a reason to "give peas a chance" if there ever was one. This is an easy and delicious dish that we all have great affection for.

1 cup	basmati rice
3 Tablespoons	olive oil
½ cup	onion (1 small)
3	(1-inch) pieces cinnamon bark
3	cloves
5	black peppercorns
1	small green chilli, jalapeño or Serrano
½ teaspoon	cumin seeds
½ cup	chopped tomato (1 small)
1 cup	peas or frozen mixed vegetables
1 teaspoon	Garlic Paste (page 42)
1¼ teaspoons	salt, divided
Pinch	turmeric
½ teaspoon	cumin powder
2 cups	water

① Wash and soak the rice for 20 minutes.

② Heat the oil in a saucepan on medium heat. Add the onions and cook until they start to turn golden.

③ Stir in the cinnamon, cloves, black pepper, green chilli and cumin seeds and cook until the seeds pop and splutter—about 30 seconds.

④ Add the tomato, peas or vegetables, garlic, half of the salt, turmeric and cumin and cook on low heat until the tomatoes are soft and the vegetables are cooked, about 10 minutes.

⑤ Add water, drained rice and remaining salt. Bring to a boil and then lower the heat to minimum and cook covered until rice is tender and all the water is absorbed.

⑥ Enjoy with Cucumber Raita (page 108) or Yogurt (page 46) and Kachumber (page 59).

Prawns Biryani

TIME	YIELD	GLUTEN-FREE
60 minutes	4 servings	& VEGETARIAN

This is a special treat. Noorbanu's grandson, Zaakir says that *biryanis* are delicious and timeless in their appeal and because the flavours come together so well, one could always have another bowl – or two.

For the Prawns:

1 lb	jumbo shelled and deveined prawns
½ teaspoon	salt
1 Tablespoon	lemon juice

For the Rice:

1½ cups	basmati rice
1 Tablespoon	sunflower oil
1 Tablespoon	finely chopped onion
½ teaspoon	Garlic Paste (page 42)
1	chilli, jalapeño or Serrano, slit
3 cups	water
½ teaspoon	salt, or to taste
⅛ teaspoon	turmeric

For the Masala:

2 Tablespoons	sunflower oil
½ teaspoon	cumin seeds
1 cup fresh	tomato (1 medium), blended in a food processor
1–2 teaspoons	tomato paste
4 Tablespoons	Yogurt (page 46)
1½ teaspoons	Garlic Paste (page 42)
1 chopped	Serrano chilli
⅛ teaspoon	turmeric
½ teaspoon	ground cumin
1 Tablespoon	finely cut coriander leaves
3 Tablespoons	Crispy Fried Onions (page 42)
1 Tablespoon	lemon juice
½ teaspoon	salt, or to taste
½ teaspoon	Garam Masala (page 29)

For the Prawns:

Marinate the prawns in a mixture of the salt and lemon juice for 30 minutes. Drain in a colander, pat dry and set aside.

For the Rice:

① Wash then soak the rice for 10 minutes.

② Heat the oil in a saucepan, add the onion, garlic, and whole chilli and cook for about 30 seconds.

③ Add the water, drained rice, salt and turmeric, bring to a boil then reduce heat to medium and continue to cook until the water is absorbed and the rice is tender.

④ Leave on very low heat or in a preheated oven at 300°F for 10 to 15 minutes.

For the Masala:

① Heat the oil in a separate saucepan, add the cumin seeds and cook for 30 seconds. Add the prawns and fry until the prawns start to turn pink and curl.

② Remove the prawns from the oil and set aside.

③ Stir in the tomatoes and cook over medium heat for 5 minutes.

④ Add the yogurt 1 Tablespoon at a time, mixing it in thoroughly between each addition, until all the yogurt has been added.

⑤ Add the garlic, turmeric, cumin, crispy fried onion and chopped chilli and cook until the *masala* thickens.

⑥ Stir in the reserved prawns, coriander leaves, lemon juice, salt and Garam Masala.

⑦ Enjoy the hot rice topped with the prawns masala.

Tuvar Dal Bhath

LENTILS AND RICE

TIME	YIELD	
60 minutes	6 – 8 servings	*GLUTEN-FREE & VEGETARIAN*

Tuvar dal are yellow split pigeon peas. You can find them at Indian grocers.

For the Dal:

1 cup	tuvar dal
4 cups	water
¾ cup	sunflower oil
½ teaspoon	cumin seeds
6	(1-inch) pieces cinnamon bark
4	cloves
4	green cardamom pods
1	whole chilli, jalapeño or Serrano, slit lengthwise along the sides
½ cup	canned crushed tomato
1 teaspoon	tomato paste
½ teaspoon	Garlic Paste (page 42)
½ teaspoon	Ginger Paste (page 43)
½ teaspoon	Green Chilli Paste (page 44) or Sambal Oelek, or to taste
¼ teaspoon	turmeric
½ teaspoon	ground cumin
½ teaspoon	Garam Masala (page 29)

2 Tablespoons	lemon juice
2 Tablespoons	finely cut coriander leaves
½ teaspoon	salt, or to taste
½ cup	Crispy Fried Onions (page 42)
2	potatoes, cooked and cut into 2-inch pieces (optional)

For the Rice:

2 cups	rice
1 Tablespoon	sunflower oil
½ teaspoon	cumin seeds
4 cups	water
1½ teaspoon	salt, or to taste
⅛ teaspoon	turmeric

For the Dal:

① Clean and soak the *dal* in lots of water for 2 hours.

② Drain and add 4 cups of fresh water and cook until tender but firm.

③ Drain and reserve.

④ Soak the rice in cold water for 20 minutes—while you prepare the rest of the *dal* recipe.

⑤ Heat the oil in a heavy-bottomed saucepan, add the cumin seeds, cinnamon, cloves, cardamom pods and chilli and cook until the seeds pop—about 30 seconds.

⑥ Stir in the tomatoes, tomato paste, garlic, ginger and chilli pastes, turmeric, cumin, Garam Masala, lemon juice, and coriander leaves and cook for 5 to 7 minutes.

⑦ Add the drained *dal*, salt, Crispy Fried Onions, and potatoes (if using) and cook another 2 to 5 minutes. Set aside.

For the Rice:

① Heat oil in a saucepan on medium heat, add cumin seeds, water, salt and turmeric and cook for 30 seconds.

② Drain the soaked rice, stir it into the saucepan with the water and spices and cook on medium heat until all the water has evaporated, about 15 to 20 minutes.

③ Enjoy the rice hot topped with the *Tuvar dal* and with Khadhi (page 233) on the side.

Vegetable Biryani

Good.
9/21

TIME	YIELD	GLUTEN-FREE
35–40 minutes	6–8 servings	*& VEGETARIAN*

This is as pretty to look at—as it is enjoyable to eat.

2 Tablespoons	olive oil
8 chopped	fresh curry leaves
1 teaspoon	cumin seeds
2	chillies, Jalapeños or Serranos, slit along the sides lengthwise
¾ cup	peas
¾ cup	cauliflower florets
¾ cup	eggplant, cut in 1-inch cubes
1 cup	potato, cut in 1-inch cubes
1 cup	chopped tomatoes (1 medium)
2 teaspoon	tomato paste

1 teaspoon	salt, or to taste
1 cup	Yogurt (page 46)
1 teaspoon	Garlic Paste (page 42)
1 teaspoon	Ginger Paste (page 43)
1 teaspoon	Green Chilli Paste (page 44), or to taste
1 teaspoon	coarsely ground fennel seeds
1 teaspoon	sugar
½ cup	green bell peppers, cut in 1-inch cubes
½ cup	red bell peppers, cut in 1-inch cubes
½ teaspoon	Garam Masala (page 29)
1 teaspoon	finely cut coriander leaves
1 Tablespoon	lemon juice
3 Tablespoons	Crispy Fried Onions (page 42)

① Heat the oil in a saucepan on medium heat. Add the curry leaves, cumin seeds and chillies and cook until the seeds pop—about 30 seconds.

② Stir in the peas, cauliflower, eggplant and potato and cook for 2 minutes.

③ Stir in the tomatoes, tomato paste, salt, yogurt, garlic, ginger and chilli pastes and fennel seeds. Cover and cook, stirring occasionally, until the potatoes and eggplant are almost cooked.

TIP: Add water a little at a time — Careful. (when necessary) to keep the mixture from sticking.

④ Stir in the green and red bell peppers, Garam Masala, sugar and coriander leaves and cook until the vegetables are tender when pierced with a fork.

⑤ Add the lemon juice. There should be about a cup of gravy—if not, add hot water to make about 1 cup.

⑥ Add the Crispy Fried Onions last.

⑦ Enjoy hot over Fluffy Basmati Rice (page 249).

ROTLI
RECIPE, PAGE 268

Naan

TANDOORI BREAD

TIME	PLUS	YIELD	
60 – 70 minutes	rising time	4 pieces	*VEGETARIAN*

We tested several Naan recipes for this book. This was the simplest and it always turned out the best. Check out the fun *Pi-Naan-Za* variation that follows.

¼ cup	warm water
½ teaspoon	sugar
½ teaspoon	instant yeast (quick rise)
1½ teaspoons	all-purpose flour
1½ cups	all-purpose flour
½ teaspoon	salt
2 Tablespoons	sunflower oil or melted butter
½ cup	Warm water

① Combine the water, sugar, yeast and the first addition of flour in a bowl, cover and let stand until foamy.

② Add the rest of the flour, salt and oil or butter and mix with a ½ cup of warm water to make a soft pliable dough.

③ Cover the dough and let it rest in a warm place for about 1 hour or until the dough doubles in size. Punch the dough down and let it rest again for another 30 minutes.

④ Divide the dough into 4 balls and flatten each slightly.

TIP: If dough is slightly sticky, it helps to put a bit of oil on your hands when working with it.

⑤ Dust your counter with a bit of flour to prevent it from sticking and use a rolling pin to roll each portion into a 5-inch oval shape.

⑥ Rest the Naan for 10 minutes on a lightly oiled tray.

⑦ Heat a cast iron pan or griddle on medium-high heat, sprinkle the tops of the Naan with a bit of water and then cook top side down first. Wait for bubbles to appear, flip and then cook until golden brown spots appear underneath.

⑧ Turn the Naan again and cook until golden brown spots appear on the top side, and the Naan is well cooked.

TIP: You can also bake the Naan on a baking tray or clay pizza stone in a preheated 500°F oven or on a gas grill. Heat the pizza stone before placing the bread on it.

⑨ Pile the cooked pieces on a plate and keep the plate covered until you have finished cooking the whole batch.

⑩ Enjoy with any curry or on its own with butter and Chai.

Pi-Naan-Za

ITALY MEETS INDIA WITH THIS FUN IDEA

You can have endless fun creating these Naan breads (whether you make your own or buy them already prepared) treated as pizza crusts. Eat them as meals or snacks. We loved the ones we made with leftover Boti Kebab (page 176) for this photo. You could also use the Curry in a Hurry Sauce (page 48) as your base and then pile on grilled vegetables or canned chickpeas, red pepper, onion and zucchini as another delicious option. Finish by sprinkling the top with a little fresh cilantro and a drizzle of yogurt. Enjoy hot from the oven.

Rotli

CHAPATTI

TIME	YIELD	*VEGETARIAN*
20 minutes	8 Rotli	

Rotli are unleavened breads made with whole wheat flour and they are a true mainstay in Indian cuisine. They come together very quickly and are usually served at every meal. As a bonus, they double as a great edible utensil to carry food, especially dal, from dish to mouth.

2 cups	whole wheat flour
2–3 Tablespoons sunflower oil	
½ teaspoon	salt
1 cup boiling	water

① Rub the flour, sunflower oil and salt together with your hands and add the boiled water slowly, kneading it a little until you make a soft, pliable (but not sticky) dough.

② Divide the dough into 8 equal portions and cover.

③ Roll each portion into a circle, 6 to 7-inches in diameter, on a lightly floured surface.

④ Heat a griddle or regular cast iron frypan on medium-high heat and cook the rotli one at a time—placing the top side down first.

⑥ Cook until little bubbles appear, then turn and continue cooking for 1 to 2 minutes.

⑦ Turn the rotli over again and continue cooking until both sides are brown.

TIP: Pressing lightly with a spatula will cause the rotli to puff up.

⑧ Spread a little butter on the top side of the cooked rotli and stack them together to keep them soft.

⑨ Enjoy with any curry dish or with eggs for breakfast. Noorbanu also likes it with butter and jam, or sprinkled with sugar, or Yogurt (page 46) and Carrot Pickle (page 106).

TIP: Rotli can be wrapped in foil and frozen for future use. Reheat in an oven at 350°F or you can warm them up individually in a toaster oven.

Variation:
MASALA ROTLI

½ teaspoon	turmeric
½ teaspoon	ground cumin
1 teaspoon	Garlic Paste (page 42)
1 teaspoon	Green Chilli Paste (page 44)
½ teaspoon	ajwan
1 Tablespoon	finely cut coriander leaves

① Knead the dough as above with these additional ingredients.

② Roll and cook each rotli as above, using 1 or 2 teaspoons of sunflower oil when cooking each.

ROTLI
SEE PAGE 264

Masala Parotha

TIME	YIELD	*VEGETARIAN*
60 minutes	15 parotha	

Eating fresh—hot from the pan—parotha is a remarkable treat.

3 cups	whole wheat flour
¾ cup	chana flour
¼ cup	olive oil
1½ teaspoon	Garlic Paste (page 42)
½ teaspoon	turmeric
1 teaspoon	ground cumin
2 teaspoon	Green Chilli Paste page 44, or to taste
1 teaspoon	salt, or to taste
¼ cup	finely chopped coriander leaves
Warm water	
Sunflower oil for shallow frying	

1. Mix the whole wheat and chana flour in a bowl.
2. Stir in the oil and mix well.
3. Add the garlic paste, turmeric, cumin, chilli paste, salt and coriander leaves, then mix well.
4. Knead into pliable dough by adding just enough warm water to help the dough come together.
5. Cover the dough and let it rest for 15 minutes.
6. Divide the dough into 15 balls.
7. Flatten each ball into a small patty.
8. Rub a couple of drops of oil into the middle of the patty. Then sprinkle the oil with a little flour.
9. Draw the dough into the centre, resealing it over the oil and flour. Turn the patty over onto a board for rolling.
10. Use a rolling pin to roll it into a circle about 7-inches in diameter.
11. Heat a griddle or cast iron pan on high heat.
12. Cook the Parotha one at a time, placing them top side down, onto the griddle.
13. Wait for little bubbles to appear on the Parotha, then turn over and cook for 1 to 2 minutes more—adding 1 to 2 teaspoons of oil as needed.
14. Flip again, so the Parotha is again, top side down (adding more oil as needed) to ensure both sides are cooked.
15. Stack the Parothas together as you cook them to keep them soft.
16. Enjoy for breakfast with Yogurt (page 46) and chutney or eggs, or with any curry dish.

TIP: Once cool, the parothas can be wrapped in foil and stored in the freezer. Reheat wrapped in foil and placed in the oven or individually in a toaster oven.

Spinach Parotha

SPINACH STUFFED BREAD

TIME	YIELD	*VEGETARIAN*
75–90 minutes	13 parotha	

Parotha are an all-time favourite street food in India. Eating stuffed parotha—hot from the pan—is a double treat.

TIP: You can stack the parotha on each other and either freeze or store them, wrapped in foil for future use.

1	(10 ounce/300 gram) package thawed, chopped frozen spinach
3½ cups	whole wheat flour
6 Tablespoons	sunflower oil
1 teaspoon	salt
3 Tablespoons	Yogurt (page 46)
1 teaspoon	ground cumin
1 teaspoon	Garlic Paste (page 42)
1 teaspoon	Green Chilli Paste (page 44). or to taste
2 Tablespoons	finely cut coriander leaves
2 Tablespoons OR	cooked rice
2 slices	brown bread, soaked in water with excess water squeezed out
Water—if needed—to make dough	
Sunflower oil for frying	

① Gently squeeze some of the water from the spinach.

② Place the spinach in the bowl of a food processor and pulse to a paste.

③ Add the flour, oil, salt, yogurt, ground cumin, garlic and chilli pastes, coriander and boiled rice or bread to the food processor and pulse until a soft dough comes together. Add water only if needed.

④ Divide the dough into 13 balls.

⑤ Roll each ball into a small patty and spread a few drops of oil on each. Sprinkle flour over the oil. Fold edges of each patty to the middle and pinch to seal so that the oil and flour stay inside the ball.

⑥ Flatten each patty to a disc.

⑦ Use a rolling pin to roll them into a circle about 6 to 7-inches in diameter, with the folded side facing down.

⑧ Place each parotha, top side first, onto a hot griddle. When bubbles start to appear on the top, turn the parotha over.

⑨ Drizzle 1 to 2 teaspoons of oil on each side when cooking.

⑩ Cook the parotha on the bottom side and flip it over again.

⑪ Press the parotha with a spatula so it cooks evenly. This will also help it puff up.

⑫ Place cooked parotha on a paper towel-lined baking tray until they are all cooked.

⑬ Enjoy with your favourite curry or Yogurt (page 46), and the chutney of your choice.

Stuffed Bateta Parotha

POTATO STUFFED BREAD

TIME	YIELD	*VEGETARIAN*
60 minutes	4 servings	

If you ever get the chance to visit Chandni Chowk—the world's largest spice bazaar—in Old Delhi, there is a place Karen loves called *Parawthe Walla*. Five generations of the same family have made their famous stuffed parotha since 1875. A man, his one leg folded under him on the table where he sits, stuffs and flattens the breads. He has a box of prepped fillings beside him. His boss, the owner, fries each parotha as the *walla* finishes them. The pace is fast and furious and the results so delicious that Presidents of countries line up to eat here. Maybe you'll go someday or maybe you'll just enjoy how Noorbanu's recipe for these potato stuffed parotha can transport you there through your taste buds.

1½ lbs	cooked and mashed potatoes (about 5 medium)
1 teaspoon	Green Chilli Paste (page 44)
½ teaspoon	salt
1 teaspoon	ground cumin
2 teaspoons	lemon juice
1 Tablespoon	finely cut coriander leaves
1½ cups	whole wheat flour or all-purpose flour
3 Tablespoons	oil
½ teaspoon	salt
½ cup	warm water
Sunflower oil, For frying	

① Combine the mashed potato, chilli paste, salt, cumin, lemon juice and coriander. Set aside.

② Combine the flour, salt and oil and rub until it resembles crumbs.

③ Make pliable dough by adding the warm water and kneading until smooth.

④ Divide into 4 portions.

⑤ Using a rolling pin to roll each portion into a 6-inch circles—rolling the edges thinner than the centre.

⑥ Place a quarter of the potato mixture in the centre of the circle.

⑦ Bring the edges of the circle into the centre and pinch the dough to seal it together. Next, flatten slightly then roll very gently on a lightly floured surface to a 7-inch circle. Repeat with remaining 3 portions.

⑧ Fry the parotha on both sides until golden brown.

⑨ Enjoy with Yogurt (page 46) and your favourite fresh chutneys.

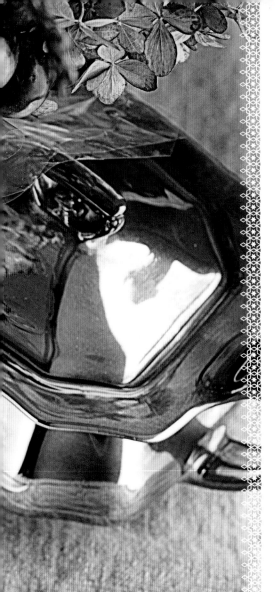

CHAI MASALA
RECIPE, PAGE 274

Chai Masala

TEA WITH MILK AND SPICES

TIME	YIELD	GLUTEN-FREE
15 minutes	4 servings	& VEGETARIAN

Stopping for *Chai* when you travel in India is a wonderful break from the rigours of driving on the roads. In India you order tea one of three ways. Black tea is just that. *Chai* is tea with milk and *Chai Masala* is tea with milk and a special spice blend. Tea stall workers—*chai wallas*—have their own blend of roasted, ground spices and the best have loyal patrons who return day after day. This is Noorbanu's Masala Chai.

3 cups	water
1 teaspoon	Chai Masala (page 31)
4	tea bags, use black tea bags
3 cups	milk
Sugar to taste	

① Boil the water, *chai masala* and teabags for 5 minutes.

② Add the milk and sugar and boil for another 3 to 5 minutes.

③ Strain and serve hot.

④ Enjoy at teatime, after dinner and on cold winter days.

Kadho

SAFFRON MILK

TIME	YIELD	GLUTEN-FREE
15 minutes	6–7 servings	& VEGETARIAN

Traditionally a wedding drink, this is also an excellent cold remedy.

4 cups	milk
1	(13½ ounce/370 mL) can evaporated milk
⅔ cup	sweetened condensed milk
6–8	strands of saffron, crumbled
¼ cup	chopped almonds
2 Tablespoons	chopped unsalted pistachios
¼ teaspoon	ground cardamom
⅛ teaspoon	nutmeg

① Bring the milk to a boil in a saucepan on medium-high heat, stirring continuously.

② Stir in the evaporated and condensed milk, the saffron, almonds, pistachios, cardamom and nutmeg and cook on medium heat, stirring continuously for about 5 minutes.

③ Enjoy hot.

CHAI MASALA
SEE PHOTO, PAGE 272

Kashmiri Faludo

TIME	YIELD	GLUTEN-FREE
30 minutes	4 servings	& VEGETARIAN

This is a wonderful treat on a hot summer day.

For the Drink Base:

2 teaspoons	agar agar powder
1 cup	hot water
1 teaspoon	tukmaria seeds (*faludo*)
18 Tablespoons	grenadine syrup, divided
2 cups	vanilla ice cream
4 cups	chilled milk (2%) OR Sherbet (page 279)

For the Garnish:

¼ cup chopped pistachios

① Add the agar agar to the hot water. Once dissolved, then microwave on high for 1 minute.

② Stir in 3 Tablespoons of the grenadine and return the mixture to the microwave for 1 minute. Set this liquid aside to cool to room temperature, then refrigerate it for about 15 minutes or until it sets. When set, grate it into fine slivers and set aside.

③ Soak the *tukmaria* in 2 cups of water for 15 minutes. They will double in size.

④ Drain the water from the tukmaria and any debris that has floated to the top.

⑤ Add more water and soak again—until the tukmaria settles to the bottom. Then drain the water again. Strain through a fine mesh sieve and set aside in a clean container.

⑥ Add 1½ Tablespoons of grenadine, 1 table spoon of tukmaria and 1½ Tablespoons of the grated *agar agar* to a 10-ounce glass.

⑦ Add 2 scoops of vanilla ice cream and fill the glass with milk (or the Sherbet).

⑧ Add ½ a Tablespoon of grenadine on top of the ice cream.

⑨ Enjoy garnished with chopped pistachios and serve with a dessert spoon and straw.

Lassi

SALTY OR SWEET YOGURT DRINK

TIME	YIELD	
5 minutes	1–2 servings	*GLUTEN-FREE & VEGETARIAN*

Lassi is a traditional beverage made by blending buttermilk or yogurt and water or other fruits, juices and spices until frothy. It is enjoyed chilled, as either sweet or salty hot-weather refreshment. It's also consumed to cool the palate when eating spicy foods.

¾ cup	Yogurt (page 46)
1 cup	water
⅛ teaspoon	salt
⅛ teaspoon	freshly ground black pepper
⅛ teaspoon	ground cumin

① Combine all the ingredients in a blender and process until smooth.

② Enjoy in a tall, chilled glass

Variation:

SWEET LASSI
Substitute sugar to taste in place of the salt and pepper.

Mango Lassi

TIME	YIELD	
10 minutes	1 serving	*GLUTEN-FREE & VEGETARIAN*

Mangoes are the world's most consumed fruit. We love them and eat as many as possible in season—May to September. Thanks to high quality cans of mango pulp we can make this delicious *lassi* anytime of the year. It keeps us going until the fresh season comes back around.

1 cup	buttermilk or Yogurt (page 46)
½ cup	mango pulp
¼ teaspoon	ground green cardamom seeds, optional
½ pinch	saffron (optional)
1 teaspoon	sugar
½ cup	ice cubes

① Combine the buttermilk or yogurt, mango pulp, ground cardamom—if using, saffron, and sugar and blend well.

② Enjoy in a tall glass with crushed ice or ice cubes and sprinkled with ground cardamom if desired.

Variation:
Instead of ground cardamom, try ground ginger.

Pistachio Lassi

TIME	YIELD	GLUTEN-FREE & VEGETARIAN
5 minutes	1 serving	

This is as nourishing as it is refreshing.

1½ cups	buttermilk
5 or 6	unsalted pistachios
1½ teaspoons	sugar, or to taste
¼ teaspoon	ground green cardamom seeds, optional
1 cup	crushed ice

① Combine the pistachios and buttermilk in a blender and process until the pistachios are crushed in the liquid.

② Add the sugar, cardamom and ice.

③ Blend for another 30 seconds—until the liquid is light and frothy.

③ Enjoy in a cold, frosted glass.

Mango Juice

TIME	YIELD	GLUTEN-FREE & VEGETARIAN
15 minutes	5–6 servings	

1	(28 ounce/796 mL) can mango pulp
1 Tablespoon	jaggery or demerara sugar
2 cups	milk
Pinch	saffron
½ teaspoon	ground ginger, optional

① Bring the milk to a boil, add the sugar or jaggery and stir the milk until the sugar is dissolved. Let it cool down and strain.

② Mix all of the ingredients and keep in the refrigerator until you are ready to serve.

③ Enjoy on its own or with Dry Moong Dal Curry (*Suki Mug Ni Dal*) (page 235) and Puri (page 236).

Sherbet

A TRADITIONAL WEDDING DRINK

TIME	YIELD	GLUTEN-FREE
10 minutes	8 – 10 servings	*& VEGETARIAN*

This pretty pink drink is like a very exotic strawberry milkshake.

4 cups	milk (2%)
1	(13½ ounce/370 mL) can evaporated milk
⅔ cup	sweetened condensed milk
1 cup	strawberry ice cream
¼ cup	chopped almonds
2 Tablespoons	chopped unsalted pistachios
1 teaspoon	vanilla
4 - 6 drops	rose essence
Dash	red or pink food colouring
Ice	

① Place all the ingredients in a blender and pulse to combine.

② Garnish with almonds and nuts. Enjoy in chilled glasses.

Tamarind Drink

TIME	YIELD	GLUTEN-FREE
15 minutes	5 – 6 servings	*& VEGETARIAN*

This is an ideal drink on a hot summer day.

4 ounce	tamarind pulp
4 cups	water
¼ teaspoon	ground cumin
¼ cup	sugar
½ teaspoon	salt
Crushed ice	

① Place the tamarind in a saucepan with the 4 cups of hot water. Soak it for 2 to 3 hours and then bring it to a boil on high heat. Lower the heat and simmer the tamarind for a few minutes.

② Let the tamarind cool, then strain it by pressing it through a sieve using a potato masher.

③ Put the remaining pulp back in the bowl. Then add more water, mix thoroughly and press it through the sieve again. Discard the remaining pulp.

④ Stir the sugar, salt and cumin into the tamarind juice.

⑤ Enjoy over crushed ice.

LEFT TO RIGHT BACK:
KADHO, LASSI, MANGO JUICE
FRONT:
KASHMIRI FALUDO

Desserts

282
Banana Fritters
GF · UEG

283
**Chai Masala
Biscuit Pudding**
Variation:
Chocolat Biscuit Pudding
UEG

285
**Double Ginger
Chai Log**
UEG

286
Cornflake Torte
GF · UEG

287
Gajar Ni Kheer
Carrot pudding
GF · UEG

288
Jardelau
Apricot pudding
Variation:
Butterscotch Jardelau
GF · UEG

289
Kheer
Rice pudding
GF · UEG

290
Ras Malai
Ricotta cheese and
saffron dessert
GF · UEG

291
Rich Fruitcake
UEG

Kulfi

293
Rich Indian Ice Cream

Classic Pistachio

Cardamom

**Toasted Coconut
with Candied Ginger**

Mango

Chai Masala

 CLOCKWISE FROM UPPER LEFT:
BADAMI HALVA, JUGU PAAK,
DATE HALVA

Desserts, Kulfi and Indian Sweets

Banana Fritters

TIME	YIELD	GLUTEN-FREE
15 minutes	24 fritters	& VEGETARIAN

Once you discover how easy these are to make, they may become your new way to "wow" friends and family. Especially if you whip up the quick and easy caramel sauce like Noorbanu suggests at the end of the recipe.

1 cup	sunflower oil for frying
¼ cup	cornstarch
¾ cup	flour
¼ teaspoon	salt
1 teaspoon	baking powder
2 Tablespoons	sugar
¼ teaspoon	ground green cardamom seeds
¾ cup	water
4	bananas

① Heat the oil to 350°F in a deep-fryer.

② Sift the cornstarch, flour, salt and baking powder together in a medium-size bowl and add the sugar and cardamom.

③ Stir the water in gradually and mix to make a smooth pancake-like batter.

④ Peel and slice the bananas in half then slice each half lengthwise into 2 to 3 pieces.

⑤ Dip the banana slices into the batter and then slide them gently into the oil. Deep-fry in small batches until golden brown.

⑥ Drain the fritters on a paper towel-lined baking tray.

⑦ Enjoy piping hot along side ice cream and a little caramelized sugar.*

*Bring a little butter, brown sugar and water to a boil in a saucepan until it bubbles and becomes a slightly thick caramel coloured sauce.

Chai Masala Biscuit Pudding

TIME	PLUS	YIELD	*VEGETARIAN*
20 minutes	overnight in the refrigerator	6 servings	

Start this recipe the day before you want to serve it. It's really easy to make—just a few nuts to chop and little cream to whip. Once assembled, the pudding should be covered and put in the fridge. Decorate just before serving.

½ lb	arrowroot, tea biscuits or Marie biscuits
1½ cups	evaporated milk
2 Tablespoons	sweetened condensed milk, divided
½ cup	chopped walnuts
¼ cup	chopped cashews
1 cup	whipping cream
2 teaspoons	icing sugar
1–2 teaspoons	Chai Masala (page 31)

Cherries, pistachios or chopped walnuts for decoration

① Place a layer of cookies on the bottom of a pretty serving dish, approximately 7-inches square.

② Pour half a cup of the evaporated milk and 1 Tablespoon of the condensed milk over the cookies and sprinkle with a third of the walnuts and a third of the cashews.

③ Repeat these layers twice.

④ Whip the cream and add the icing sugar and Chai Masala at the point where soft peaks are begin to form.

⑤ Spread the whip cream over the top of the biscuit layers and sprinkle the cherries, pistachios and walnuts on top.

⑥ Refrigerate overnight.

⑦ Enjoy cold—cut into desired serving sizes.

Variation:

CHOCOLATE BISCUIT PUDDING
Grated milk chocolate may be added to each layer.

Double Ginger Chai Log

TIME	YIELD	
30 minutes	4 servings	*VEGETARIAN*

Ginger cookies, candied ginger and Chai Masala complement each other in this light and easy to prepare dessert.

TIP: This needs at least 8 hours in the fridge prior to serving so that the cream has a chance to soften the cookies.

2 cups	whipping cream
2 Tablespoons	icing sugar
1 teaspoon	Chai Masala (page 31)
1	(6 ounce/150 gram) package of thin ginger cookies
½ cup	finely diced candied ginger, divided equally
6 – 8 pieces	whole candied ginger

① Beat the whipping cream and add the icing sugar and Chai Masala just as soft peaks are beginning to form. Continue beating until thick. Reserve two-thirds of the whipped mixture for later use.

② Line a baking tray with plastic wrap.

③ Add half the diced candied ginger to the one-third of the whipped cream mixture. Use it to coat 1 side of each cookie with and then stack them together to form a log on the plastic wrap.

④ Wrap the plastic wrap around the finished log and then place the log in tin foil and refrigerate it (and the reserved whipped cream) overnight or for at least 8 hours.

⑤ Place the log on a serving dish and remove the foil and wrap, just before serving.

⑥ Spread the reserved whip cream to coat the log and sprinkle with remaining ¼ cup of candied ginger.

⑦ Cut in diagonal slices—so that each piece has multiple layers of cookies and cream showing—and decorate with a piece of whole ginger.

⑧ Enjoy a slice with *chai* or coffee.

Cornflake Torte

TIME	PLUS	YIELD	*VEGETARIAN*
30 minutes	overnight in the refrigerator	8–10 servings	

This is a very simple dessert that comes together easily and Noorbanu and her family like it as much now as when she first started making it many years ago.

½ cup	butter
4 ounces	milk chocolate
4 Tablespoons	golden corn syrup
8 cups	corn flakes
2 cups	whipping cream, whipped (reserve 1 cup of the finished whipped cream)
2 cups	strawberries or other fresh fruit

① Melt the butter in a large saucepan on very low heat and stir in the chocolate and golden syrup.

② Stir in the cornflakes when the chocolate is melted and mix until they are thoroughly coated.

③ Divide and press the batter into 3 greased cake pans. Use 4, 6 and 9-inch pans to create tiers.

④ Refrigerate for a few hours or overnight.

⑤ Turn the 3 layers of your torte out on to a platter, stacking them on top of each other with the largest on the bottom and the smallest on the top.

⑥ Decorate with the whipped cream and fruit.

⑦ Place a dollop of the reserved whip cream on each plate and enjoy.

Gajar Ni Kheer

CARROT PUDDING

TIME	PLUS	YIELD	GLUTEN-FREE
30 minutes	soaking time	8–10 servings	& VEGETARIAN

Find *Hunza* apricots at an Indian grocer and soak them for at least 2 to 3 hours prior to making this recipe. It comes together quickly at that point.

20–25	Hunza apricots
4 cups	milk
2 cups	grated carrots
2 ounces	chopped cashews
4 Tablespoons	sweetened condensed milk
1 cup	evaporated milk
2 teaspoons	Bird's Eye custard powder
1 Tablespoon	water
1 cup	whipped cream
Grated chocolate for decoration	

① Soak the apricots for at least 2 to 3 hours or overnight, then pit and dice them.

② Bring the milk to boil in a saucepan on medium heat.

③ Add the carrots and cook for 5 minutes.

④ Stir in the apricots and cashews and cook for 5 minutes more.

⑤ Stir in the sweetened condensed milk and evaporated milk.

⑥ Mix the custard powder and water before adding it to the milk and carrot mixture Stir constantly until it thickens.

⑦ Pour the pudding into a 3-quart shallow dish. Cover and place in the refrigerator to chill.

⑧ Spread the top of the pudding with whipped cream and garnish with grated chocolate.

⑨ Enjoy served by the spoonful.

Jardelau

APRICOT PUDDING

TIME	YIELD	GLUTEN-FREE
10 minutes	6 servings	& VEGETARIAN

Look for *Hunza* apricots at Indian grocers.

1 lb	small dried pitted and quartered Hunza apricots
½ cup	water
4 teaspoons	sugar
1 cup	evaporated milk
2 Tablespoons	walnuts or cashews, chopped
1½ cups	whipping cream
2 Tablespoons	icing sugar

① Place the apricots in a saucepan with the ½ cup of water and cook on low heat until all the water is absorbed.

② Stir in the sugar and milk and cook until thick.

③ Pour the mixture into a shallow 2-quart dish and sprinkle with nuts.

④ Whip the cream, add the icing sugar as peaks start to form and beat until it thickens.

⑤ Spread the whip cream over the apricots, adding another sprinkle of nuts if desired.

⑥ Enjoy by the scoopful as a delectable treat alongside Nan Khatai (page 308) and *Chai* or coffee.

Variation:

BUTTERSCOTCH JARDELAU: You can use 3½ ounces of instant butterscotch pudding mix for another layer of flavour in this pudding. Just prepare it according to the package instructions and add it to the apricots instead of the sugar and milk.

Kheer

RICE PUDDING

TIME	YIELD	
30 minutes	4 cups	*GLUTEN-FREE & VEGETARIAN*

Puddings became part of Indian cuisine during the British Raj. They are part of a cooking legacy known as "Butler Cuisine" where Indian house staff learned the British recipes and adapted them with their own spicing and accents. No matter the origin, this recipe is pure comfort food.

½ cup	short grain rice
3 cups	water
5 cups	whole milk
1 cup	sweetened condensed milk
½ cup	evaporated milk
½ teaspoon	ground green cardamom seeds
Pinch	saffron
20	slivered almonds, divided
20	slivered unsalted pistachios, divided

① Clean and wash the rice in several changes of water.

② Add the drained rice and water to a saucepan and cook until the water is absorbed and the rice is soft and mushy.

③ Stir in the milk and bring to a boil, then reduce the heat to low.

④ Cook for approximately 20 minutes, stirring frequently to prevent burning.

⑤ Stir in the condensed milk, evaporated milk, cardamom and saffron.

⑥ Stir in half of the almonds and pistachios and simmer for a few minutes more, then pour into a 3-quart bowl.

⑦ Garnish with the remaining almonds and pistachios.

⑧ Enjoy with Puri (page 236), Potato Curry (page 214) and a main dish or serve on its own as a dessert.

Ras Malai

RICOTTA CHEESE AND SAFFRON DESSERT

TIME	PLUS	YIELD	
60 minutes	chilling time	6–8 servings	*GLUTEN-FREE & VEGETARIAN*

This dessert involves baking and chilling the ricotta cheese pieces and then making a separate sauce. Each step is fairly easy and the results are well worth the effort.

For the Squares:

1 lb	ricotta cheese
½ cup	sugar
Pinch	saffron
¼ teaspoon	ground green cardamom seeds
⅛ teaspoon	ground nutmeg
½ cup	whipping cream
1 teaspoon	icing sugar

For the Sauce:

1½ cup	milk
1½ cup	evaporated milk
1 Tablespoons	sugar
¼ teaspoon	ground green cardamom seeds

For the Garnish:

1 teaspoon	finely slivered almonds
1 teaspoon	finely slivered pistachios
Pinch	saffron

① Preheat the oven to 325°F.

② Whip the cream and add the sugar once peaks start to form and beat until thick. Store in the refrigerator until needed.

③ Stir the ricotta, sugar, saffron, cardamom and nutmeg in a bowl. Mix well.

④ Transfer the mixture to a greased 9-inch square dish and bake 30 minutes or until a wooden toothpick comes out clean when inserted.

⑤ Spread the whipped cream over the baked pudding while it is still hot.

⑥ Chill, then cut into desired shapes and sizes. Refrigerate for 4 to 5 hours.

⑦ Make the sauce for the pieces while they are chilling.

⑧ Combine the milk, evaporated milk, sugar and cardamom in a saucepan and bring to a boil, stirring for 5 minutes. Remove from heat, let cool and then chill in the refrigerator.

⑨ Pour the sauce into a decorative serving dish and arrange the Ras Malai pieces in the sauce.

⑩ Enjoy garnished with slivered almonds and pistachios and a pinch of saffron on top.

Rich Fruitcake

TIME	PLUS	YIELD	*VEGETARIAN*
3 hours	2–3 days for the fruit to soak	1 cake	

When Karen visited India in November of 2014, she was surprised when her group was invited to join the annual fruitcake making ritual at—not one, but—several hotels throughout South India. This is another example of India's "Butler Cuisine." Many traditional British foods that were loved enough by Indians were adopted and now are a part of their cuisine. Noorbanu's family also enjoyed fruitcake in the former British colony of Kenya. Her recipe is a classic.

TIP: Allow a few days for your fruit to soak before beginning this recipe and you'll reap the rewards in flavour for this extra step.

10 ounces	currants
5 ounces	raisins
5 ounces	cherries
5 ounces	mixed peel
½ cup	fruit juice or brandy
½ lb	butter
1 cup	brown sugar
5	eggs
12 ounces	all-purpose flour
1 ½ teaspoons	baking powder
½ lb	combination of chopped walnuts, cashews and almonds
1 Tablespoon	treacle (use molasses if you can't find treacle)
½ lb	almonds and cherries for decoration

① Soak the fruit in the fruit juice or brandy for 2 to 3 days.

② Drain the fruit and discard any juices.

③ Preheat the oven to 225°F.

④ Beat the butter and sugar until fluffy but not creamy in the bowl of a mixer.

⑤ Add 1 egg at a time, mix well and scrape down the sides of the bowl with each addition.

⑥ Stir in the flour, baking powder and mix on low speed to blend, then add the fruits, nuts and treacle and blend until ingredients are well distributed.

⑦ Line a 9-inch square or round cake pan with greased waxed paper and pour the batter into the pan.

⑧ Decorate as desired with almonds and cherries.

⑨ Bake for 2½ hours or until golden brown and a cake tester inserted in the centre comes out clean.

⑩ Enjoy this with a nice cup of *chai*.

Kulfi

RICH INDIAN ICE CREAM

TIME	YIELD	
45 minutes with an ice cream maker	4–5 cups	*GLUTEN-FREE & VEGETARIAN*

Kulfi traditionally took two days to make with one whole day spent condensing (boiling down) South Asia's widely available and incredibly rich tasting water buffalo milk to form the base of this heavenly treat. This recipe comes together quickly with the use of canned condensed milk and an electric ice cream maker.

TIP: If you don't have an ice cream maker, after you've beaten the ingredients together in a mixer, simply pour them into a shallow dish and freeze until set. Remove from the freezer 20 minutes before serving, as the end product will have a firmer consistency.

For the Ice Cream Base:

1	(13½ ounce/370 mL) can evaporated milk

TIP: keep a can of this in the freezer and you'll be able to make ice cream any time you like.

1	(10½ ounce/300 mL) can sweetened condensed milk, chilled in the fridge
1 cup	whipping cream, whipped

TIP: Use the best quality whipping cream you can find—avoid anything that says, "milk ingredients"— you want real cream only.

For the Ice Cream Base:

① Remove the evaporated milk from the freezer and place it in a bowl of boiling hot water for a few minutes. Once the frozen milk loosens from the sides of the can, add it to the bowl of an electric stand mixer. Break the frozen log of milk up with a knife and then beat it until creamy and smooth.

② Add the chilled sweetened condensed milk and beat until well mixed.

③ Add the whipped cream and mix again. Now you are ready to create flavours.

For the Flavours:

Tropical flavours like Pistachio, Ginger, Chai, Mango, Toasted Coconut and Cardamom are an excellent note to end an Indian meal with. Try the combinations below or change it up with seasonal flavours to create your own favourites.

TIP: You can find Kulfi forms at Indian Grocers. We used a variety of paper cups to make our fun shapes and sizes.

FROM TOP TO BOTTOM:
MANGO KULFI, CHAI MASALA,
COCONUT WITH CANDIED GINGER,
CLASSIC PISTACHIO

Kulfi

Classic Pistachio:

2 teaspoons	lemon juice
½ teaspoon	ground green cardamom seeds
Pinch	saffron, soaked in 1 teaspoon of water
¼ cup	chopped unsalted pistachios

① Add the lemon juice, cardamom and saffron to the base ingredients in the mixing bowl and beat until thoroughly distributed.

② Pour the mixture into the bowl of an electric ice cream maker and operate for 20 minutes—adding the pistachios in the last 5 minutes of processing.

③ Transfer to a storage container and freeze until ready to serve.

Cardamom:

2 teaspoons	ground green cardamom seeds
1 teaspoon	vanilla

① Add the cardamom and vanilla to the base ingredients in the mixing bowl and beat until thoroughly distributed.

② Pour the mixture into the bowl of an electric ice cream maker and operate for 20 minutes.

③ Transfer to a storage container and freeze until ready to serve.

Toasted Coconut with Candied Ginger:

1 teaspoon	vanilla or coconut extract
¼ cup	finely shredded lightly toasted
¼ cup	diced candied ginger

① Add the vanilla or coconut extract to the base ingredients in the mixing bowl and beat until thoroughly distributed.

② Pour the mixture into the bowl of an electric ice cream maker and operate for 20 minutes—adding the coconut and candied ginger in the last 5 minutes of processing.

③ Transfer to a storage container and freeze until ready to serve.

Mango:

1 teaspoon	lemon juice
Pinch	saffron
1½ cup	mango pulp
½ cup	finely diced fresh mango

① Add the lemon juice, saffron and mango pulp to the base ingredients in the mixing bowl and beat until thoroughly distributed.

② Pour the mixture into the bowl of an electric ice cream maker and operate for 20 minutes—adding the fresh mango in the last 5 minutes of processing.

③ Transfer to a storage container and freeze until ready to serve.

Chai Masala:

1 teaspoon	vanilla
1 teaspoon	ground cinnamon
1 Tablespoon	Chai Masala (page 31)

① Add the vanilla, cinnamon and *Chai Masala* to the base ingredients in the mixing bowl and beat until thoroughly distributed.

② Pour the mixture into the bowl of an electric ice cream maker and operate for 20 minutes.

③ Transfer to a storage container and freeze until ready to serve.

Badam Paak

SWEET ALMOND SQUARES

TIME	YIELD	
30 minutes	3 dozen pieces	*GLUTEN-FREE & VEGETARIAN*

Gum Arabic (*Gund*) is usually sold already chopped at Indian Grocers. You will only need to chop it if it is older and has clumped together. Be sure to fry it just half a Tablespoon at a time.

1 cup	sunflower oil for frying
2–4 ounces	chopped Gum Arabic (*Gund*)
¼ teaspoon	saffron
1 teaspoon	ground green cardamom seeds
½ teaspoon	ground nutmeg
1 lb salted	butter
1 lb	semolina (*sooji*)
½ cup	evaporated milk
1	(10 ½ ounce/300 mL) can sweetened condensed milk
1 lb	chopped almonds
4 ounces	chopped pistachios

For the Garnish:

2 ounces	finely slivered almonds
2 ounces	finely slivered pistachios
1 teaspoon	white poppy seeds

① Heat the oil in a wok and deep-fry ½ Tablespoon of Gum Arabic at a time until the pieces pop. Remove them—with a slotted spoon—to a plate or bowl and reserve for later use. Repeat until all pieces are fried.

NOTE: Discard any Gum Arabic that doesn't pop.

② Add the saffron, cardamom and nutmeg to the fried Gum Arabic.

③ Melt the butter in a saucepan on medium heat, add the semolina and cook stirring constantly until golden.

④ Remove the saucepan from the heat, and gradually add the evaporated milk, stirring all the time.

⑤ Add the condensed milk and stir well.

⑥ Add the almonds, pistachios and the fried Gum Arabic mixture and cook for 2 minutes more, stirring vigorously.

⑦ Spread the mixture evenly in a 15 × 10 × 2-inch pan.

⑧ Sprinkle the surface with the remaining slivered almonds, pistachios and poppy seeds and press them into the warm mixture firmly with the back of a metal spatula.

⑨ Cut the mixture into square or diamond shapes and sizes while still warm.

⑩ Enjoy at teatime.

Burfi

INDIAN FUDGE

TIME	YIELD	
30 minutes	16 pieces	*GLUTEN-FREE & VEGETARIAN*

Burfi is a traditional Indian and Pakistani dessert—very much like fudge. It's often served at birthday and wedding celebrations.

1 cup	whipping cream
1½ cups	sugar
4 ounces	butter
½ teaspoon	ground green cardamom seeds
¼ teaspoon	grated nutmeg
4 cups	powdered skim milk

For the Garnish:

2 Tablespoons	chopped almonds
2 Tablespoons	chopped pistachios
Pinch	saffron

① Combine the cream, sugar, butter, cardamom and nutmeg in a glass container and microwave on high power for 5 minutes.

② Remove from the microwave and stir.

③ Return to the microwave, and cook on high power for a further 5 minutes.

④ Remove the mixture, add the powdered skim milk, stir and then microwave the mixture for 2 more minutes.

⑤ Remove from the microwave and mix thoroughly.

⑥ Transfer the mixture to a lightly greased 8-inch square pan and press it down with the back of a spoon.

⑦ Garnish with almonds, pistachios and saffron while still warm in the pan.

⑧ Cut it into the desired number of pieces once the burfi has cooled completely.

Variation:

CHOCOLATE BURFI

① Proceed as above, but instead of garnishing with nuts, spread 4 ounces of melted milk chocolate over the burfi.

② Melt the chocolate by placing it in a glass bowl in a microwave.

③ Cook it at half-power for 2 to 3 minutes (depending on the power of your microwave you may need to stir it and give it another minute or more).

Badami Halva

ALMOND SWEETMEAT

TIME	YIELD	GLUTEN-FREE
30 minutes	10 – 12 servings	*& VEGETARIAN*

Noorbanu's daughters Khadija, Rosie and Nazlin all use this recipe and it turns out well for all three. Now that's a well-tested recipe.

1¼ cups	tapioca starch
2½ cups	water
1¼ cups	slivered almonds
¼ cup	chopped pistachios
2 cups	sugar
¼ teaspoon	yellow food colour
¼ teaspoon	orange food colour
1 teaspoon	ground cardamom
8 saffron	strands
2 teaspoons	lemon juice
¾ cup OR ½ cup	Ghee (page 43) melted butter

① Whisk the tapioca and water together until smooth.

② Stir in the almonds, pistachios, sugar, food colouring, cardamom, saffron and lemon juice until mixed well.

③ Stir in the Ghee or butter (if using) and mix well.

④ Cook in the microwave on high heat for 5 minutes, remove and stir.

⑤ Return to microwave for 5 minutes more, remove and stir.

⑥ Repeat 2 more times—until the *halva* is transparent and not sticky.

OR

① Cook on medium-high heat on the stove-top, stirring constantly until mixture starts to boil and becomes thick.

② Lower the temperature and cook until the mixture is transparent and no longer sticky.

③ Transfer to an 8-inch round cake pan and bake at 250°F until set.

④ Enjoy as a sweet appetizer before your meal or on its own with tea.

Date Halva

TIME	YIELD	
30 minutes	2 rolls or about 24 slices total	*GLUTEN-FREE & VEGETARIAN*

This stores well in the freezer and makes a delicious treat that you can pull out for your guests to enjoy with coffee after dinner.

1 cup	whipping cream
1 Tablespoons	brown sugar
1 lb chopped	pitted dates
2 cups	mixed unsalted nuts (almonds, cashews, pistachios)
½ cup	desiccated coconut

① Combine whipping cream, sugar and dates in a saucepan on medium heat. Cook, stirring constantly until thick and shiny (about 10 minutes) when patted with a spoon.

② Stir in the nuts and cook another 5 minutes.

③ Cool the mixture to a temperature where you can handle it and divide the mixture into 2 equal parts.

④ Make 2 rolls (2-inches in diameter each) by rolling each half on a flat surface with the centre of your palm.

⑤ Finish by rolling each log in the desiccated coconut.

⑥ Wrap them separately in foil and freeze for at least 5 hours.

⑦ Remove the logs from the freezer about 10 minutes before you want to serve them and cut into ¾-inch thick slices to serve.

⑧ Enjoy with tea or coffee.

Gulab Jamon (Gulab Jambu)

SWEET DOUGH BALLS
IN SYRUP

TIME	YIELD	
60 – 90 minutes	45 jamon	*VEGETARIAN*

4 litres	sunflower oil for deep-frying
3 cups	skim milk powder
1 cup	all-purpose flour
¾ teaspoon	baking powder
2 Tablespoons	butter
1 Tablespoon	Yogurt (page 46)
Dash	cardamom
Dash	nutmeg
Dash	saffron
1 cup	whipping cream

For the Garnish:

45	small pieces of edible silver paper (*optional*)
¼ cup	finely slivered almonds
¼ cup	finely slivered pistachios

For the Syrup:

3 cups	sugar
3 cups	water
1 teaspoon	vanilla
Few strands	saffron
Dash	yellow food colouring powder
½ cups	water

① Combine the powdered milk, flour and baking powder and rub in the butter with your fingers until the mixture resembles bread crumbs.

② Add the yogurt, cardamom, nutmeg and saffron.

③ For soft dough, add the whipping cream and a little milk if necessary for it to all come together.

④ Knead for about 5 minutes – until the dough is no longer sticky.

⑤ Shape into 45 small balls.

⑥ Deep-fry the balls on medium heat in a deep-fryer or wok filled with sunflower oil. They should be evenly browned.

   TIP: If the Gulab Jamon turn in the oil by themselves, the dough is considered to be the right texture. You can test this with one ball and if not correct, knead a little more milk into the dough and test again.

⑦ Place the cooked balls on a paper towel-lined baking tray and prick each one with a toothpick.

⑧ Make syrup by boiling the sugar, the first addition of water, vanilla, saffron and food colouring until the mixture is just sticky.

⑨ Place the balls in the warm syrup; add the second addition of water and boil gently for about 5 minutes or place in a preheated 200°F oven for 15 minutes.

⑩ Spoon all the balls–very gently—into a serving dish.

⑪ Enjoy garnished with almonds, pistachios and edible silver paper if you can find it at an Indian Grocer or Bakery.

Gund Paak

GUM ARABIC SQUARES

TIME	YIELD	*VEGETARIAN*
60–90 minutes	20 pieces	

Of all the Indian sweets, this is Noorbanu's daughter Khadija's favourite.

She says, "Mom's Gund Paak is the best that I've had and I enjoy it down to the last crumb. With the combination of rich almonds and pistachios, the crunch from the 'Gum Arabic' (*gund*) and the flavours from the spices and jaggery—no other square even comes close." Karen agrees. She thinks it tastes like pure love.

1 cup	sunflower oil or Ghee (page 43) (for frying Gum Arabic)
5 ounces	Gum Arabic
¾ lb	coarsely chopped almonds
4 ounces	chopped pistachios
1 Tablespoon	ground green cardamom seeds
1 Tablespoon	coarsely ground fennel seeds
1 teaspoon	ground nutmeg
½ teaspoon	saffron
1 lb	salted butter
1 lb	unsalted butter, divided
1 lb	whole wheat flour
¾ cup	semolina (*sooji*)
¾ cup	chana flour OR urad flour
¾ cup	medium flake coconut
¾ cup	powdered milk
½ cup	milk (2%)
¼ teaspoon	yellow food colouring powder
1 lb	chopped jaggery
1	(10 ½ ounce/300 mL) can sweetened condensed milk
2 ounces	finely slivered almonds
2 ounces	finely slivered pistachios
1 teaspoon	white poppy seeds

① Heat the oil or Ghee in a wok.

② Deep-fry the Gum Arabic pieces over medium heat, ½ a Tablespoon at a time, until they pop and then remove them with a slotted spoon and set them aside on a paper towel covered plate. Repeat until all are fried, discarding any Gum Arabic that do not pop.

③ Combine the chopped nuts, cardamom, fennel, nutmeg and saffron. Set aside.

④ Melt 1 lb of salted butter and ¾ of a lb of unsalted butter in a saucepan on medium heat.

⑤ Add the whole wheat flour, semolina and chana or urad flour and fry until a very light golden colour, stirring continuously.

⑥ Add the coconut and fry for a few minutes, remove from heat and add the powdered milk and stir for a few minutes. Set aside.

⑦ Heat the ½ cup of milk and food colour in another saucepan on medium heat and mix well.

⑧ Melt the remaining ¼ pound of butter in another saucepan, add the jaggery and cook until all the jaggery is melted and starts bubbling.

⑨ Remove from heat and pour the jaggery—through a strainer—into the milk mixture and then return to heat and cook for another 2 to 3 minutes.

⑩ Add the chopped nut mixture to the flour mixture and return to low heat.

⑪ Blend in the jaggery mixture now and cook until well mixed, stirring continuously.

⑫ Stir in the condensed milk and lastly add the fried Gum Arabic and mix well.

⑬ Pour the mixture into a 2 × 10 × 15-inch pan and spread evenly.

⑭ Garnish the top with the slivered almonds and pistachios while still warm, and press them firmly into the top with the back of a firm metal spatula.

⑮ Enjoy sprinkled with the poppy seeds last and cut into diamond shapes or squares.

Jugu Paak

PEANUT BRITTLE

TIME	YIELD	GLUTEN-FREE
30 minutes	15–20 pieces depending on the size you prefer	& VEGETARIAN

This is Noorbanu's daughter Nazlin's favourite treat.

TIPS: You'll need a greased baking tray, shallow plate with cold water, wooden spoon, candy thermometer and a rolling pin (marble works best) for rolling out the sticky candy. Reserve a wooden spoon especially for candy making so that the unwanted flavours of other food are not inadvertently transferred to ruin your batch of candy.

If your jaggery is soft, then it will take a half a cup of water but if the jaggery is harder you may have to add about a quarter cup more. Soft jaggery has more moisture than the hard jaggery. For that reason, it facilitates the candy making process because you don't have to cook it as long and there is less chance of it turning dark or burning.

1 lb	unsalted blanched peanuts
12 ounces	jaggery
¾ cup	water
1 Tablespoon	sunflower oil (for greasing baking tray)

Step 1

Spread the peanuts on a baking tray, use a heavy object to flatten them and separate them into halves. Roast them at 150°F until golden—about 2 hours. Let them cool and set them aside.

Step 2

Boil the jaggery and water until the jaggery melts. Strain the jaggery mixture through a fine sieve. Then, return it to the saucepan and let it cook on medium heat until thick.

TIP: Noorbanu puts the jaggery and water in the microwave and cooks it on high for 1 minute intervals—stopping to stir and break up the jaggery between each cycle. It takes about 8 minutes this way and saves her needing to stir it constantly like the stove-top method.

Step 3

Place a shallow plate of cold water on the stove beside the boiling pot of jaggery.

Step 4

Test the jaggery to see if it is at the "hard crack" stage of candy making by dripping a few drops of the jaggery mixture into the cold water (set this up ahead and keep it beside you). Pick up the jaggery that you dripped into the water between the thumb and forefingers of your hands. If it cracks apart when you try to break it, then it is at the "hard crack stage" and it means it is done. This usually happens

when a candy thermometer reads 300 °F. If it just stretches and bends like sticky toffee or caramel, it is not ready.

TIP: Be careful to keep the heat on medium. It may take a little longer at this temperature but it will prevent the sugar from burning.

Step 5

Add the roasted peanuts and mix well once the jaggery hits the hard crack stage.

Step 6

Quickly spread the mixture onto a greased baking tray.

Step 7

Roll thinly with a marble rolling pin, then cut into desired shapes while still hot.

Step 8

Store in an airtight container (this is especially important if you live in a humid environment as humidity makes the candy sticky).

Nan Khatai

CARDAMOM SHORTBREAD COOKIES

TIME	YIELD	*VEGETARIAN*
60 minutes	20 pieces	

This recipe comes from Noorbanu's daughter Khadija. She also baked the Nan Khatai you see in this photo. They are rich like a shortbread cookie but with a pleasant and unexpected crunchy texture provided by the use of semolina. We love Khadija's Nan Khatai and hope you will too.

1 lb	butter, at room temperature
1½	cups sugar
1	egg, at room temperature
½ teaspoon	vanilla
1 cup	semolina (*sooji*)
3½ cups	flour
4 Tablespoons	Bird's Eye Custard Powder
2¼ teaspoons	baking powder
¾ teaspoon	baking soda
½ teaspoon	ground green cardamom seeds, optional
Ghee (page 43)	
Cherries	

① Preheat the oven to 350°F.

② Put the butter and sugar in the bowl of an electric mixer and beat on high until creamy and fluffy.

③ Add the egg and vanilla and beat well again.

④ Stir in the semolina by hand.

⑤ Mix the flour, custard powder, baking powder, baking soda and cardamom (if using) in a separate bowl until well mixed and then add this to the first bowl—mixing by hand until well incorporated.

⑥ Form golf ball size round balls and place them in rows on baking trays lined with parchment paper.

⑦ Flatten each ball with the tines of a fork, pressing twice at 90-degree angles.

⑧ Cut a cross on the top of each cookie with a knife.

⑨ Bake for about 30 minutes or until pale golden brown.

Variations:

Instead of leaving the cookies plain as above you can decorate them in the following ways:

ORIGINAL YELLOW DOT COOKIES
Flatten the balls slightly and cut a 1-inch long cross on each cookie. Combine a ¼ teaspoon of yellow food colouring with 1 teaspoon of water. Dip a cotton tip applicator in the colouring and then dot the colour in the centre of the cross and bake as noted above.

CHERRIES
Place ⅛ of a maraschino cherry in the centre of each cross and bake as noted above.

PISTACHIO
Place a pistachio in the centre of each cross and bake as noted above.

CHAI MASALA (PAGE 274) WITH NAN KHATAI

Pera

CREAMY SQUARES

TIME	YIELD	GLUTEN-FREE
90 minutes	20 pieces	*& VEGETARIAN*

Khadija made these beautiful little fudge-like cookies in decorative forms for these photos. They're elegant and oh so tasty.

1 cup	whipping cream
1 ½ cups	evaporated milk
1 cup	unsalted butter
1 ½ cups	sugar
½ teaspoon	ground green cardamom seeds
¼ teaspoon	ground nutmeg
1 lb	skim milk powder
1 ounce	slivered pistachios

① Combine the whipping cream, evaporated milk, butter, sugar, cardamom and nutmeg in a saucepan on medium-high heat and bring to a boil.

② Boil for 5 minutes, then turn the heat down to low.

③ Add the powdered milk gradually. Stir constantly to prevent the milk from scalding. After about an hour, the mixture will turn a pale yellow colour indicating it's ready for the next step.

④ Roll 1 Tablespoon of this mixture in the palm of your hand—while still warm—forming it into a yo-yo shape.

TIP: You can find decorative forms for the Pera in the candy making sections of fine kitchenware stores.

⑤ Garnish by pressing a few slivered pistachio nuts on top.

Sev Paak

TIME	YIELD	
20–30 minutes	24 pieces	*GLUTEN-FREE & VEGETARIAN*

You might not be familiar with the Gum Arabic and Sev, which this recipe calls for. Read about them in Chapter One and know that we promise these things are well worth the trip to an Indian Grocer to get them.

1 Tablespoon	Gum Arabic (*gund*)
1 cup	Sunflower oil, for frying
7 ounces	toasted *Sev*
5½ ounces	unsalted butter
2 Tablespoons	desiccated coconut
2 Tablespoons	powdered skim milk
5½ ounces	almond flakes
1	(13½ ounce/370 mL) can condensed milk
½ teaspoon	coarsely ground cardamom
½ teaspoon	nutmeg, freshly ground using a microplane
¼ teaspoon	saffron threads
¼ cup	finely chopped pistachios, as a garnish

Step 1

① Heat the oil in a deep-fryer or wok to medium heat and fry the Gum Arabic ½ Tablespoon at a time until done. When it pops, remove it with a slotted spoon and set it aside on paper towels. Discard any Gum Arabic that did not pop.

② Break the Sev into small pieces.

Step 2

① Melt the butter in a clean saucepan on medium heat.

② Stir in the Sev and cook on low heat for 2 minutes.

③ Stir in the coconut and cook for a further 2 minutes.

④ Stir in the powdered milk and cook for another 2 minutes.

⑤ Stir in the almonds, cardamom, nutmeg, and saffron.

⑥ Stir in the condensed milk and cook on very low heat, stirring the mixture continuously for about 2 minutes—until all of the ingredients are well mixed.

⑦ Stir in the fried Gum Arabic (*gund*) and keep stirring until the mixture leaves the sides of the saucepan.

TIP: If the mixture has not consolidated, add a little more condensed milk. The mixture should be moist.

⑧ Transfer the mixture to a 12 × 8-inch pan and spread it evenly.

⑨ Garnish with pistachios while the mixture is still warm and press them down with the back of a spoon, so they stick.

⑩ Let the Sev Paak cool for 10 minutes and then cut it into squares.

⑪ Allow it to cool completely before removing the squares from the pan.

Thepla

SOFT AND SWEETLY SPICED JAGGERY BISCUITS

TIME	YIELD	*VEGETARIAN*
45–60 minutes	8 biscuits	

These little biscuits were one of Noorbanu's husband's favourites. Food has the power to bring back fond memories of times with those we love like nothing else.

1 cup	all-purpose or whole wheat flour
½ cup	brown sugar
1 Tablespoon	oil
1 Tablespoon	beaten egg
1 Tablespoon	semolina (*sooji*)
1 teaspoon	ground fennel seeds
¼ teaspoon	baking powder
¼ teaspoon	nutmeg
¼ teaspoon	ground green cardamom
½ cup	evaporated milk
Sprinkle	white poppy seeds
1 teaspoon	flour
Water	
8	blanched almonds (optional if allergic)
Sunflower oil for frying	

① Combine the flour, sugar and oil using your hands until the oil is well dispersed.

② Add the egg, semolina, ground fennel seeds, baking powder, nutmeg and cardamom.

③ Stir in the evaporated milk with a wooden spoon until the mixture comes together to make dough.

④ Divide the dough into 8 equal balls and roll each one into ½-inch thick circles.

⑤ Sprinkle the balls with poppy seeds and roll slightly, so the poppy seeds stick on the Thepla biscuits.

⑥ Make a thick paste with the flour and water and dip each almond into the paste and then press one into the centre of each Thepla.

⑦ Heat oil in a wok at 350°F and deep-fry until golden brown.

⑧ Transfer to a paper towel-lined baking tray to drain.

⑨ Enjoy as a snack.

TIP: Use a cookie cutter to make nicely-shaped biscuits.

Thepla 2

JAGGERY BISCUITS

TIME	YIELD	*VEGETARIAN*
45 minutes	30 – 40 biscuits	

2 cups	all-purpose or whole wheat flour
Pinch	salt
4 Tablespoon	oil
½ cup	milk
¼ lb	jaggery*
Sunflower oil for frying	

*Jaggery is the semisolid form of sugar cane. Sometimes it is very hard and difficult to grate. It can be broken into small pieces and it will melt when boiled with milk. If it is too hard, soak it in milk for an hour, and then boil it.

① Sift the flour into a bowl, add the salt and rub in the oil with your hands. Set aside.

② Bring the milk and jaggery to the boiling point in a heavy-bottomed pot on medium-high heat and then strain through a sieve.

③ Make soft dough by combining milk and jaggery mixture with the flour mixture.

④ Divide the dough into 3 equal parts and while still warm, roll each ball into ¼-inch thick circles. If soft biscuits are preferred, roll the dough out thicker.

⑤ Cut the dough into diamond shapes, or cut with your favourite cookie cutter.

⑥ Heat the sunflower oil in a wok or deep-fryer to 350°F. Gently roll each cookie one more time before frying them in small batches until golden brown.

⑦ Enjoy as a snack.

Topra Paak

COCONUT SQUARES

TIME	YIELD	*GLUTEN-FREE*
30 minutes	16 squares	*& VEGETARIAN*

Coconut flavours this delicious recipe.

1 cup	sunflower oil for frying
1 ounce	Gum Arabic, remove tiny stones and debris and chop into peppercorn-size pieces
4 Tablespoons	butter
3 cups	fresh grated coconut OR unsweetened desiccated coconut soaked in a ½ cup of milk
½ teaspoon	ground green cardamom seeds
Pinch	saffron
⅔ cup	sweetened condensed milk
1 ½ teaspoon	finely slivered almonds
1 ½ teaspoon	finely slivered pistachios
½ teaspoon	white poppy seeds

① Heat the oil on medium heat and fry Gum Arabic—a little at a time—until it pops. Remove with a slotted spoon to a bowl and set aside. Discard any Gum Arabic that does not pop.

② Melt the butter in a saucepan on medium heat.

③ Add the coconut and fry until the coconut is golden brown, stirring continuously.

④ Add the cardamom and saffron. Stir well.

⑤ Add the condensed milk and keep stirring for 3 to 4 minutes—until the mixture thickens.

⑥ Add the reserved fried Gum Arabic and mix well.

⑦ Press the coconut mixture into an 8 × 8-inch square baking pan.

⑧ Sprinkle the top with almonds and pistachios and press them into the mixture with the back of a wooden spoon.

⑨ Sprinkle the poppy seeds last and then cut into diamonds or squares.

⑩ Cool before serving.

INDEX

ABOUT THE PHOTOGRAPHER

Pauli-Ann Carriere is a photographer and entrepreneur who lives in Vancouver, B.C. Her work is drawn from the world at large and she's been greatly inspired by annual trips to India with Karen Anderson. Her photographic art captures transitory encounters of people, places, colours, texture and light. Pauli-Ann is a featured artist at *Provide Home* in Vancouver.

 **PAULI-ANN CARRIERE**
(SELFIE)

ABOUT THE AUTHORS

This Taste Canada award-winning book is the fourth installment in Noorbanu Nimji's *A Spicy Touch* cookbook series. An Ismaili Muslim with roots in Gujarat, India, Noorbanu was born and lived in Nairobi, Kenya before moving to Canada in the 1970s. She has cooked for her family for over sixty years, and this book holds their favourite dishes. Both novice and competent Indian cooks will enjoy the clarity of the recipes presented here and most importantly, how mouth-wateringly good the results are. After all this time, Noorbanu still has A Spicy Touch.

Karen Anderson is founder, owner, and operator of Alberta Food Tours, Inc. She is a Taste Canada award-winning author for this book and a World Gourmand award-winning travel writer for *Food Artisans of Alberta*. She leads annual culinary and cultural trips to different regions of India. Since 2006, Karen has worked at Noorbanu Nimji's side testing recipes and teaching Indian cooking classes.

NOORBANU NIMJI AND KAREN ANDERSON,
PHOTOS: JEREMY FOKKENS

FAREWELL SEEDS (MUKWAS)
SEE PAAN MASALA PAGE 33